AF644285

Contemporary Methods of Social Work

Contemporary Methods of Social Work

Edited by

Gracious Thomas

SHIPRA

All rights reserved. No part of this publication may be reproduced, stored in a retrieval system, or transmitted in any form or by any means, electronic, mechanical, photocopying, recording or otherwise, without the prior written permission of the copyright holder.
The views and opinions expressed in this book are author(s) own and the facts reported by him/her have been verified to the extent possible, and the publishers are not in any way liable for the same.

Rs. 995; US$ 49.75

ISBN: 978-81-7541-831-8

First Published in India in 2016

Contemporary Methods of Social Work

© Gracious Thomas

Published by:
SHIPRA PUBLICATIONS
LG 18-19, Pankaj Central Market, I.P. Ext.
Patparganj, Delhi-110092, India
Tel: 91-11-2223 5152, 2223 6152
E-mail: info@shiprapublication.com
www.shiprapublication.com

Preface

In this book 'Contemporary Methods of Social Work', we have examined social work practice in the light of fast changing global scenario and through the lens of a new global definition and twelve methods of social work discipline both traditional and contemporary with the aim of contributing to the knowledge and skill base of the profession. Social work practice includes the range of direct social work intervention with individuals, families, small groups, and communities and policy formulation interventions. The effectiveness of intervention is based on the broad range of social work practice methods and skills. The contemporary methods of social work are expected to bring about a positive change in social work practice by extending/expanding the space/strengths of social work profession.

The six contemporary methods discussed in this book are advocacy, awareness campaign, resource mobilization, public interest litigation, networking, and strength based practice methods. Each of these contemporary methods are meticulously discussed with the intention of facilitating learners, practitioners and academics. This volume is an effort made by social work faculty from some prominent schools of social work in India under the direct supervision and guidance from the Editor. The discussion on advocacy as a method of social work has been presented through three chapters while the other five contemporary methods have been presented through two chapters each. The introductory chapter gives a new global definition of social work along with its objectives and characteristics of social work.

The method of advocacy is very handy for social workers to achieve the goal of social justice and social welfare in the changing global scenario. The basic assumption behind the development of 'advocacy' as a method of social work is the potential role advocacy can play in providing justice to people at large, especially the vulnerable sections who may not be in a position to seek justice or even meet their basic needs. Advocacy actions in social work interventions can take many forms and range depending on the nature of the issues, problems and the helping process. The discussion on advocacy as a contemporary method of social work along with its relationship with other methods are presented in chapters—two, three and four.

Awareness campaign has always been a part of professional social work practice. Social workers deal with multidimensional and complex problems and issues facing individuals, families, groups and communities, which demand responses from social workers in varying degrees. The contemporary method of awareness generation is directed to create and enhance awareness of people about various issues and causes and improved the knowledge and skills of the client to develop their decision making capacity. The method of awareness campaign helps the social workers to educate the people to know about the different mechanisms available to tackle the prevailing issues in the society. Chapters five and six have been devoted for the deliberation on this method.

Social workers are historically linked to orchestrating client's betterment through mobilizing various resources. It is very critical for social workers to mobilize resources from the client system and from the community to enhance the helping process. Contemporary methods of social work will enhance the practice realm of resource mobilization to new phase. Through chapter seven and eight the method of resource mobilisation has been extensively discussed along with its relationship with other methods of social work thus enabling the reader to comprehend the linkage of this method while practicing the profession.

Public Interest Litigation (PIL) is a legal action initiated in a court of law for the enforcement of public interest or general interest in which the public or a class of the community have pecuniary interest or some interest by which their legal rights or liabilities are affected. A social worker needs to know the application of law for addressing the problems of their clients and provide effective social work intervention. As a contemporary method of social work, a social worker can effectively practice PIL to empower the vulnerable and disadvantaged sections to reform social institutions, and to ensure social justice rather than to win or lose cases. While chapter nine explains the what, why and how of PIL, chapter ten discusses the relationship of PIL with other traditional and contemporary methods of social work.

The method of 'Networking' reminds the social work fraternity that success of social work interventions, to a large extent, depends on the quality of relationship and networking involved in the helping process. In social work practice networking implies the establishment of cooperative and collaborative relationship with likeminded people and institutions for mutual development and support for rendering help to the clients. Through a properly planned and well-designed networking, information can be shared with other people and help sought. The method of networking is very effective for enhancing social work interventions to client system as well as in promoting social work profession by sharing of new knowledge and outcomes of research. Chapters eleven and twelve present the method of networking and its linkage with other methods.

The strengths based practice method believes in the strengths, resources and capacities of the clients – individuals, groups, families and communities. Development of strengths based practice as a method of social work has brought about a new phase in social work practice and intervention. Along with focusing on the strengths of the clients it also benefits from the strengths of the worker as well as that of the profession's ethics, values, principles and the lessons learned over a period of over one century of the practice of social work. Chapters thirteen and fourteen of this book have elaborately examined this method and its relationship with other methods of social work.

Social workers pursue social justice by practicing the profession through various methods. The methods of the profession have evolved over a period of time. The western universities continued to teach the traditional six methods namely social case work, group work, community organisation, social welfare administration, social action and social work research. Most of these methods are also taught in Indian universities although the University Grants Commission (UGC) Model Curriculum of Social Work discipline does not gives emphasis on social action. The absence of Social Action method in the UGC curriculum has also influenced the curriculum of several universities in India. The curriculum of social work in the undergraduate and postgraduate programmes of the Indira Gandhi National Open University (IGNOU) has included both the traditional and contemporary methods of social work.

Contents

Preface v

1. **Relevance of Contemporary Methods of Social Work** **1**
Gracious Thomas

Definition/1; Methods of Professional Social Work/3; Contemporary Methods/4; Conclusion/7

2. **Advocacy** **8**
Asutosh Pradhan

Advocacy – Nature and Meaning/8; Evolution and Scope of Advocacy in Social Work/9; 'Advocacy Action' and 'Advocacy Work'/11; Purpose of Advocacy/11; Beneficiaries of Advocacy Work/11; 'Advocacy Work' as a Method of Social Work/12; How 'Advocacy Work' is different from 'Self-advocacy'/12; Role of Advocacy Organisations/12; Why should Advocacy Work be considered as Social Work Method?/13; The Selective Use of Social Work Methods/13; Types of Advocacy/14; Assumptions of 'Advocacy Work'/15; Objectives of Advocacy Work/16; Strategies in Advocacy Work/16; Principles of Advocacy Work/17; Skills in Advocacy Work/20; Challenges in Advocacy Work/20; Conclusion/21

3. **Models and Phases in Advocacy** **23**
Asutosh Pradhan

Models of Advocacy/23; Levels of Advocacy Action/25; Phases in Advocacy Work/27; Conclusion/38

4. **Advocacy and its Relation to other Methods of Social Work** **39**
Asutosh Pradhan

The Selective use of Social Work Methods/39; Social Casework and Advocacy/40; Social Group Work and Advocacy/41; Community Organisation and Advocacy/42; Social Action and Advocacy/43; Social Work Administration and Advocacy/44; Social Work Research and Advocacy/45; Awareness Campaign and Advocacy/46; Strengths-based Method and Advocacy/47; Networking and Advocacy/48; Public Interest Litigation (PIL) and Advocacy/49; Resource Mobilization and Advocacy/50; Conclusion/50

5. Awareness Campaign **52**
Archana Kaushik

Awareness Campaign and Awareness Raising/52; Awareness Campaign as a Method of Social Work in Indian Context/53; Salient Features of Awareness Campaign Method/54; Factors Affecting Awareness Campaign in Social Work/59; Models of Awareness Campaign/62; Principles of Awareness-Campaign/67; Process Involved in Awareness Campaign Method/68; Conclusion/71

6. Awareness Campaign and its Relation to other Methods of Social Work **72**
Archana Kaushik

Social Casework/73; Social Group Work/74; Community Organization/75; Social Action/76; Social Welfare Administration/77; Social Work Research/78; Advocacy/78; Networking/79; Public Interest Litigation (PIL)/80; Resource Mobilization/81; Strengths Based Practice/82; Conclusion/83

7. Resource Mobilization **86**
Sheeba Joseph

Definition/86; Classification of Resources/88; Classification of Resources88; Aspects of Resource Mobilisation/90; Challenges to Resource Mobilization/92; Resource Mobilization Approach/93; Elements to Strengthen Resource Mobilisation/93; Steps Involved in Resource Mobilisation Plan/94; Principles of Resource Mobilization/95; Conclusion/99

8. Resource Mobilization and its Relation with Other Methods of Social Work **101**
Sheeba Joseph

Social Case Work and Resource Mobilization/101; Social Group Work and Resource Mobilization/103; Community Organization and Resource Mobilization/103; Social Welfare Administration and Resource Mobilisation/105; Social Action and Resource Mobilization/105; Social Work Research and Resource Mobilization/106; Networking and Resource Mobilization/108; Awareness Campaign and Resource Mobilization/109; PIL and Resource Mobilization/109; Advocacy and Resource Mobilization/110; Strengths Based Practice Method and Resource Mobilization/111; Conclusion/112

9. Public Interest Litigation (PIL) **114**
P.D. Mathew

PIL and Social Work/114; Meaning of PIL/115; Origin of PIL/116; Nature of PIL/117; Essentials of PIL/117; Constitutional Provisions/118; New Interpretations of 'Locus Standi'/119; Persons Disqualified to File PIL/120; Issues Related to PIL/120; Examples of PIL/121; Procedure to File PIL/124; Steps to be Followed While Filing PIL/125; PIL and Role of Social Worker/125; Conclusion/125

10. Public Interest Litigation and its Relation with Other Methods of Social Work **127**
N. Ramya

Social Case Work/128; Group Work/129; Community Organisation/129; Social Action/130; Social Welfare Administration/131; Social Work Research/131; Resource Mobilization/132; Networking/132; Strengths Based Method/133; Awareness Campaign/133; Advocacy/134; Conclusion/135; References/135

11. Networking **137**
Nita Kumari and *Rafat Aara*

Definition/137; Importance of Networking in Social Work/138; Objectives/138; Essentials of Networking/139; Functions of a Network Method/141; Types of Network/142; Networking as a Method of Social Work in the Indian Context/143; Social Work and Social Networks/144; Approaches and Models of Networking in Social Work/144; Conclusion/146

12. Networking and its Relation with Other Methods of Social Work **148**
Nita Kumari

Social Case Work and Networking/148; Social Group Work and Networking/150; Community Organization and Networking/151; Social Welfare Administration and Networking/152; Social Action and Networking/153; Social Work Research and Networking/154; Advocacy and Networking/155; Awareness Campaigns and Networking/156; Resource Mobilization and Networking/158; Public Interest Litigation (PIL) and Networking/158; Strengths based Practice and Networking/159; Conclusion/159

13. Strengths Based Practice Method **161**
Aneesh Kurian

Development of Strengths Based Method/162; Strengths Based Practice as a Method of Social Work Practice/163; The Principles of Strengths Perspective/164; Features of Strengths Based Practice/165;

Strengths Based Practice and Values of Social Work/167; Implication of Strengths Based Method/169; Conclusion/169

14. Strengths Based Practice and its Relation with Other Methods of Social Work **172**
Aneesh Kurian

Social Case Work/172; Social Group Work/174; Community Organization/174; Social Action/176; Social Welfare Administration/177; Social Work Research/177; Public Interest Litigation (PIL)/179; Resource Mobilization/180; Networking/181; Awareness Campaign/182; Advocacy/183; Conclusion/184

Contributors 185

Index 186

1

Relevance of Contemporary Methods of Social Work

Gracious Thomas

Professional social work education and practice is over a century old on this planet. Just as several other professions evolved in the society, social work also emerged as a profession with convincing definitions, code of ethics, values, principles and methods of practice. Over 2500 institutions across the globe are involved in imparting social work education. Several countries have their own accreditation bodies, associations and councils that provide the much needed guidelines to the professionals so that they are able to practice the profession keeping in view required quality contents of the cultural and environmental situations in each country. Methods, principles, values and code of ethics are evolved over a period of time, and are also reviewed and updated from time to time. In this volume we are presenting a revised definition of social work, along with its characteristics and salient features of the six contemporary *methods of social work for the benefit of the professionals* across the globe. The School of Social Work (SOSW) at Indira Gandhi National Open University (IGNOU) is pioneer in teaching these methods under its undergraduate and post graduate programmes of study as contemporary methods while reflection of these methods are found in the curriculum of several schools of social work all over the world.

Definition

Professionals, national and international bodies release definition of social work from time to time. In the present day context let us re-define social work in the following words: "Social Work on the one hand is a practice profession that works with people across the board to empower and liberate them from socio-economic and cultural inequalities by bringing about change and development at par with national standards, while on the other hand it is equally engaged in mitigating the plight of the disadvantaged and the poorest of the poor, living under neglect and non-conducive environment."

It is undoubtedly clear from the above definition that social work has certain unique characteristics which distinguishes itself from other academic disciplines while focusing on two specific objectives that encompasses every human being across all the nations, communities, groups, families and individuals.

The unique characteristics of professional social work are:

- It is a practice based profession
- It has its own methods and principles
- It has its own code of ethics and specific core values which are drafted and updated regularly in the environmental context
- It is based on a body of knowledge derived from social and behavioural sciences which are updated from time to time
- Its values, principles, code of ethics and methods are culture specific giving utmost importance to human relations and dignity and worth of every individual
- It is a profession consciously chosen by people who have the capacity to deal with the concerns and problems of fellow human beings
- It is a profession adapted to suit cultural and environmental contexts keeping in view the national standards and practices.

Two specific objectives of professional social work that are evident in the above definition are:

(i) To empower and liberate people from social, economic and cultural inequalities by bringing about change and development at par with national development standards.

When people are confronted with problems in their everyday life, they need to be empowered by those who have the expertise, knowledge, wisdom and understanding. Professional social workers are social doctors who have the capacity and the required expertise to empower those in need of empowerment. Empowerment is essential for liberating people from social, economic and cultural inequalities. Professional social workers are change agents. They are professionals with passion to serve the less privileged and the poorest of the poor in environmental contexts. They can empower people for bringing about the much needed change which will pave way for all round development. People need empowerment to face life's environmental situation in every sector under *the sun: health and education* settings, rural, tribal and urban settings, correctional settings, cultural settings, as well as every social and economic situation. These environmental situations are country specific as well as caste and class specific. Every country has its own unique cultural background and diversities, and in a country like India the diversities are notable even in each state and region as well. Therefore social work practices have to be country specific as well as caste and class specific and should aim at national standards of each country rather than imitating the western pattern. One also needs personal or emotional support, no matter under what social status one lives.

(ii) To engage in mitigating the plight of the disadvantaged and the poorest of the poor living under neglect and non-conducive environment.

The history of social work takes us to the era of Mary Richmond and Octavia Hill who responded to the plight of the masses faced with every kind of problems in re-settlement colonies in the latter part of the nineteenth century in the United States of America and United Kingdom respectively. Their engagement with the poorest of the poor and the displaced masses through 'friendly visits' scheme to families, brought about the much required emotional support to cope with the problems in their new environment that emerged as a result of industrialization. Same was the situation in several western countries where some people consciously decided to embark on a mission to mitigate the plight of the masses caused by industrial revolution.

The situation that existed in USA and the UK during the latter part of the 19th century continues to exist in most parts of our planet today-whether it is in sub-saharan Africa, countries in south America, middle east, eastern Europe as well as the South Asian countries. Migrating labour population, millions living in refugee camps, self-exiled masses (such as the Tibetans in India), victims of war, riots, national calamities and those facing separation from kith and kin as a result of partition and separation form a significant percentage of the global population. Along with them, we have the socially and economically disadvantaged sections of societies as a result of caste and class barriers; people faced with life threatening illnesses as a result of communicable diseases such as HIV/AIDS and leprosy and millions who are victims of mental illness and physical disabilities. Every one of the millions in correctional settings and particularly those languishing in jails in one's own home country or jails in foreign countries also form the masses termed under "poorest of the poor" no matter whether they hail from economically well to do families or caught under corruption scandals or political vendetta. Once in prison, they are deprived of their fundamental rights and basic human rights of living with one's own family, which enable one to experience the worth of the individual self.

The intervention that is required of the professional social workers is certainly philanthropic in nature. One cannot expect these 'poorest of the poor' to benefit from change or development. What they need is emotional support to cope with their life threatening environmental situation which money and other material resources cannot provide. For a person who was head of a government or country as well as the Chief Executive Officer (CEO) of a multibillion company, prison life makes him/her 'poorest of the poor" Only a professional social worker can respond to the plight of these masses whom we call "poorest of the poor". Therefore, professional social work has the twin objectives of addressing the problems and challenges of the well to do, as well as the neglected and vulnerable groups living in non-conducive environment.

Methods of Professional Social Work

The history of social work teaches us that the initial work of Mary Richmond and her counterparts in the western world, used social case work extensively in their interventions. Family visits and particularly the concept of 'friendly visitor' was popular among the promoters of social work who worked with utmost commitment, sincerity and objectivity. Subsequently other methods began to find place in the practice of professional social work educators and as a result university curriculum prescribes six methods of social work namely: Social Case Work, Social Group Work, Community Organization, Social Work Research, Social Action and Social Welfare Administration.

Although all these methods are being taught in University designed curriculum across the globe, three methods are highlighted as primary methods of social work namely, case work, group work and community organization. The comparatively less importance given to the three secondary methods have almost weakened the very identity and uniqueness of the profession which made every social worker a 'social doctor' who should be an embodiment of this practice profession.

There is no justification for placing social work research as secondary method since research findings are equally important for the growth of the profession and for imbibing the core value of competence. Similarly, Social Welfare Administration is the nerves system of professional social work as it enables the service providing organization and their functionaries with the required ingredients for performing their role as 'social doctors' using various methods, principles, values and code of ethics. Social action is the most time tested method which has enabled some of the world's largest democracies including India and South Africa get independence from foreign occupation. This method has been given least importance particularly in the curriculum of the Indian Higher Education system. The efforts of Mohandas Karamchand Gandhi and Nelson Mandela in leading India and South Africa respectively, towards freedom and independence through non-violence and social action method have made history. Thus it must be realized that there is no justification for promoting social work research, social welfare administration and social action as secondary methods during our time.

Contemporary Methods

Time has come for the profession to widen its scope and areas of intervention to address people's concerns as enshrined in the two objectives of the profession stated earlier in the beginning of this chapter derived from the definition. It is a fact that social workers and development functionaries have been making meaningful interventions with individuals, families, groups, communities and nations with several other methods other than the six methods that are being taught by social work academics. Six of these methods that I propose for social workers to practice with equal importance are:

(1) Advocacy
(2) Awareness Campaign
(3) Resource Mobilization
(4) Public Interest Litigation
(5) Networking
(6) Strengths Based Practice

Advocacy

The method of advocacy is very handy for social workers to achieve the goal of social justice and social welfare in the changing global scenario. The basic assumption behind the development of 'advocacy' as a method is the potential role advocacy can play in providing justice to people at large, especially the vulnerable sections who may not be in a position to seek justice or even meet their basic needs. Advocacy actions in social work interventions can take many forms and range depending on the nature of the issues/problems and the helping process. Advocacy method is a strong weapon in the hands of professional social workers in the fight against social injustice, social deprivation, social evils and will enable the professionals to advocate on behalf of clients- individuals, groups, families and communities. Advocacy has become a popular method particularly among social workers and social activists across the globe during the third millennium. Politicians, social activists and media continue to use advocacy to drive home contemporary issues that are relevant to masses around the world.

Awareness Campaign

Awareness campaign has always been a part of professional social work practice. Social workers deal with multidimensional and complex problems and issues of individuals, families, groups and communities, which demand the responses of social workers in varying degrees. The contemporary method of awareness generation is directed to create and enhance the awareness of the people on various issues and causes and enhance knowledge and improve decision making capacity of the clients. The method of awareness campaign helps the social workers to educate the people to know about the different resources available to tackle the prevailing issues in the society. This method is very effective to reach the larger population in lesser time. Some of the very recent awareness campaigns that have helped in saving lives of thousands of people living in coastal areas are the results of the metrological department, media and government machineries about the impending tsunami. Similarly awareness campaigns have immensely helped in the prevention and control of deadly diseases like HIV/AIDS and Ebola.

Resource Mobilization

Social workers are historically linked to orchestrating clients betterment through mobilizing various resources. It is very critical for social workers to mobilize the resources from the client system and from the community to enhance the helping process. Contemporary methods of social work will enhance the practice realm of resource mobilization to new phase. Social workers mobilize various resources for the betterment of the clients – individuals, groups, families and communities. Resource mobilization is acquisition of needed services, and it requires the knowledge of service networks and the term encompasses natural, physical, financial, human, community, social and academic resources. Resource mobilization has strong relationship with other methods of social work such as case work, group work, community organization, social action, social welfare administration, social work research, strengths based practice, networking, PIL and advocacy.

Public Interest Litigation (PIL)

Public Interest Litigation means a legal action initiated in a court of law for the enforcement of public interest or general interest in which the public or a class of the community have pecuniary interest or some interest by which their legal rights or liabilities are affected. A social worker needs to know the application of law for addressing the problems of their clients and provide effective social work intervention. In the current global scenario of possessing minimum knowledge of laws of the land is not enough for effective practice of social work. Professionals have to be well versed with the process and procedures of each law and its implication in the practice field. As a contemporary method of social work, a social worker can effectively practice PIL to empower the vulnerable and disadvantaged sections to reform social institutions, and to ensure social justice rather than to win or lose cases. It will help the professionals to make use of the existing legislations in the best interests of the clients/agencies. Some of the well known positive outcomes of PIL pertain to the release of several under trials in Indian jails who were in the prisons for decades together.

Networking

The method of 'Networking' reminds the social work fraternity that success of social work interventions to a large extent depends on the quality of relationship and networking involved in the helping process. In social work practice networking implies the establishment of cooperative and collaborative relationship with likeminded people and institutions for mutual development and support for rendering help to the clients. Through a properly planned and well-designed networking, information can be shared with other people and help sought. Networking helps the professionals to establish contacts with other people and institutions working in the same or related fields within the country and beyond the boundaries. Social workers seek membership in different national and international associations and come in contact with other professional social workers. The method of networking is very effective for enhancing social work interventions to client system as well as in promoting social work profession by sharing new knowledge base, and outcomes of research. Through network a social worker can make connections, and build enduring, mutually beneficial relationships.

Strengths Based Practice

The strengths based practice method believes that clients—individuals, groups, families and communities—have strengths, resources and capacities help one to bounce back from difficult life situations. Development of strengths based practice as a method of social work has brought about a new phase in social work practice and intervention. Strengths based method is being practiced along with other methods of social work according to the needs of the client and the practice context. It depends on the strengths of the clients, the worker and the profession to enhance the effectiveness of social work interventions in the environmental contexts. Along with focusing on the strengths of the clients it also benefits from the strengths of the worker as well as that of the profession's ethics, values, principles and the lessons learned over a period of one century. The Institute of Strengths Based Practice at Brisbane, Australia organizes an international conference every year in one of the developing countries with a specific theme aiming at facilitating professionals to practice this method.

Conclusion

The impact of social work intervention largely depends on the effective use of various methods of social work. Every method has its own merits and relevance depending upon the client and the environmental context in which the practice of the profession is envisaged. Traditionally social work educators and associations across the globe advocated six methods under two categories namely, primary and secondary methods. The profession is over a century old now and the human society has been engaging other methods in the problem solving process. Time has come to compile and promote some of these most relevant methods that are commonly found in various countries such as strengths based practice, public interest litigation, advocacy, networking, awareness campaign and resource mobilization.

REFERENCES

1. Pulla, V. (2006). Strengths Based Strategies, in Pulla, V. & Montgomery, (Eds). Strengths based Strategies, resilience as opposed to deficits: working with strengths, Brisbane Institute of Strengths Based Practice, Australia.
2. Saleebey, D., (Ed.). (1992). *The Strengths Perspective in Social Work Practice.* White Plains, NY: Longman.
3. Peiris, G.L. (1991), 'Public Interest Litigation in the Indian Subcontinent: Current Dimensions,' *International and Comparative Law Quarterly*, January 1991.
4. Pincus, A. and Minahan, A. (1973). *Social Work Practice: Model and Method.* Ithaca, Illinois: Peacock Publishers.
5. Schneider, R. L., and Lester, L. (2001). *Social Work Advocacy: A new framework for action.* Brooks/Cole.
6. Sayers, Richard (2006). Principles of awareness raising for information literacy, a case study. Thailand: Communication Information. UNESCO.
7. Norton, Micheal. (2003). *Getting Started in Communication: A Practical Guide for Activists and Organisations.* UK: Sage Publications.

2

Advocacy

Asutosh Pradhan

History is replete with instances of inhumanity to humans. People have been discriminated and oppressed on the basis of colour, creed, religion, caste, ethnicity, region and gender. Due to mental or physical disabilities, sexual orientation, old age, etc. some others have been persecuted by their near and dear ones possibly because they are a burden on the family or society. Such vulnerable sections of society are not treated in a just manner and their basic rights may be violated which leads to their marginalization. Because of various reasons they may not be in a position to defend themselves against the injustice done to them. Reasons could be social and cultural, illiteracy, lack of awareness, powerlessness, minority and refugee status, age, frailty, lack of understanding of legal provisions, lack of self-belief etc. Faced with marginalization and oppressive social structures and institutions, such clients may need advocacy to seek justice and access to life-sustaining goods and services so that it would lead to an enrichment of their life conditions and a life of dignity and worth. Advocacy actions in conjunction with and on behalf of clients are therefore required to secure the services and resources to which clients are entitled to (Hepworth, 2013).

Advocacy – Nature and Meaning

The word 'Advocacy' means different things to different people. A lawyer would refer to advocacy as the art of speaking in court, representing their client's case and examining witnesses. Social workers also act as advocates for their clients who are disadvantaged in some way or the other. A doctor or nurse may also raise his/her voice against mal-practices that may be followed in hospitals or clinics where a particular treatment process is found to be faulty. Often such interventions by medical care professionals may not be considered as advocacy since the primary job of a medical practitioner is to treat the patient. However, such interventions could effect positive change in the way future patients would receive treatment. A non-governmental organisation (NGO) working in an urban community may fight against the municipal body for the restoration of hygienic conditions in the locality. A village community may be led by an NGO to prevent illegal felling of trees in the nearby forests. Citizen's groups may challenge the authorities for malpractices in the service delivery system in the town. Similarly, social work trainees in the course of their field work practicum may want to facilitate easy access to social security services like old age pension and housing schemes of the government for the poor and less privileged in society. These actions, at times, may not be viewed by activists or professionals representing others' concerns as advocacy even if the process involved means so. It is thus clear that different people will be engaged in different forms of advocacy that could range from quasi-legal, to meeting personal services, issues in welfare administration or to the fulfilment of the rights of specific groups or populations.

Evolution and Scope of Advocacy in Social Work

The early history of the social work profession is rampant with the efforts of activists who viewed themselves as reformers, drawing the attention of the people toward social injustice and seeking to correct these ills that existed in society. However, as social work wanted to establish itself as a profession, it slowly began to reduce its emphasis on its advocacy role believing that such a de-emphasis was a necessary concession for increased professional status. This change of course notwithstanding the role of advocacy was often used by professional social workers when there was an instance of human rights violation or the denial of basic entitlements.

The roots of 'advocacy action' in professional social work can be traced to the historical commitment of the profession to the ideal of improving the human condition through social reform, social justice, and equality (Brueggemann, 2006). Advocacy in social work has its origins in the 'social casework' that is based on an individual model of representing someone's interests. The term comes from the Latin word *advocatus*, which means the function of an advocate is to give evidence by supporting verbally or making arguments for a cause (Woodrow, 1997). This represents how lawyers have been historically advocating for their clients within the judicial system. Though case advocacy operates primarily at an individual level (as in social casework), it also involves representing the wider interests of service user groups (while working for vulnerable populations) in case of policy advocacy or while seeking justice through the courts.

A renowned author, David Brandon, who has contributed to the development of the definition of advocacy in social work has provided some of the important features of this term: "Advocacy involves a person(s), either a vulnerable individual or group or their agreed representative, effectively pressing their case with influential others, about situations which either affect them directly or, and more usually, trying to prevent proposed changes which will leave them worse off. Both the intent and outcome of such advocacy should be to increase the individual's sense of power; help them to feel more confident, to become more assertive and gain increased choices". (Brandon and Brandon, 1995)

There are a number of key elements of advocacy identified in Brandon's definition. That 'advocacy work' can be undertaken at both the individual (i.e., while working with clients in certain contexts of social casework practice) or group level (i.e., while practicing social group work or community work). It also stresses on the idea of advocacy as an empowering practice and one which may bring psychological benefits to the clients involved, giving greater self-confidence and building assertiveness.

Schneider and Lester (2001) also were some of the firsts to have made a definite contribution to the evolution of the term advocacy as it has been used in social work literature. According to them "Social work advocacy is the exclusive and mutual representation of clients or a cause in a forum attempting to systematically influence decision-making in an unjust or unresponsive system."

Interpretations of the term advocacy ranged from "identifying with the client" and "pleading on behalf of the client" to "securing social justice" to "promoting change" to "accessing rights and benefits" to "demonstrating influence and political skills." Advocacy actions can take many forms and a range. It could include actions by an individual or the collective involvement of people who act in a concerted manner to remedy a social ill or injustice faced (Dobelstein, 1990). Professional social works can advocate on behalf of an individual client to counter the various forms of injustice faced, to remedy legislation or change policies that serve to disadvantage specific social groups and populations. The need for collective action arises when individuals or small groups feel that it is beyond their capability and reach to get justice when they act alone and to bring about change (Ezell, 2001). The process require strategies aimed at radical transformation of values, consciousness, and social institutions (Middleton, 1985).

Advocacy actions are an integral part of social workers practice as pointed out by Manthorpe and Bradley (2002) to initiate a process of "social change (that) would be necessary to challenge cycles of deprivation and systems of inequality".

Advocacy thus appears to have multiple meanings and it is worth accepting this fact that the views are and will be different because the client with whom the social worker is involved is different in terms of the nature and degree of the problem or issue faced, his potentials and capabilities, and the situation in which the client is. The profession has not been able to develop it as another core method of social work, even though social workers have been using advocacy very often than not in providing justice to its clients. Many like Litzelfelner and Petr (1997) would unequivocally speak out in favour of client advocacy referring it to be "an ethical responsibility and a primary function of social work practice".

The lack of academic rigour in evolving advocacy as a complete method of social work, the profession has been long neglected to develop it further so as to sharpen practice efficacy in social work. Questions do often crop-up as to how can social workers advocate well and be more effective in bringing people out of trouble and difficulties.

'Advocacy Action' and 'Advocacy Work'

Advocacy work is referred to as a 'social work method', a professional activity, undertaken by trained professional social workers. 'Advocacy Action' on the other hand is referred to as the actions taken by clients either independently or in partnership or with the help of professionals like lawyers, social workers, doctors, therapists, etc. in finding solutions to troubles and hurdles they face in meeting their needs or in the protection of their rights, entitlements or interests.

Purpose of Advocacy

The purpose of advocacy work with client(s) is to:

- prevent human rights violations, promote people's rights and help maintain control over own lives;
- realisation of constitutional safeguards and fundamental rights;
- facilitate the equitable allocation and funding of resourced for welfare, provision of social services and social development;
- protect individuals and groups facing harassment and ill-treatment by effecting structural changes in social and political systems and institutions;
- promote social inclusion and raise awareness of the barriers faced by socially excluded groups and communities;
- support and empower people and groups to speak for themselves, on behalf of other members and groups in their neighbourhood who are unable to speak or fight for their own rights;
- help people to explore the range of options available to fight against oppression and clarifying a particular course of action;
- facilitate the process of establishing new policies to tackle social injustice and protect vulnerable groups and populations, that also includes making changes in existing policies and legislations to rectify flaws and plug loopholes.

Beneficiaries of Advocacy Work

Advocacy is active promotion of a cause or principle. It involves actions that lead to a selected goal for which many possible strategies are used. Advocacy as a social work method may be used either for such clients who may not be in a position to fight for their own rights or participate in the process of redressing their difficulties because they may be lacking the capacity to do so e.g. child labourers, children under abuse, the elderly, terminally ill, mentally ill, mentally retarded, etc. or they may be beyond the reach of the professional like bonded labourers, women facing domestic violence, tribals living in remote areas and minorities facing social exclusion. Those in reach of the professional would be facilitated to participate in the process of advocacy action. The focus of Advocacy is not in providing direct services but in making the client's environment conducive to providing prompt services and establishing a just environment free from discrimination and exploitation. Advocacy does not necessarily involve confrontation or conflict but it may be used selectively depending upon the situation.

'Advocacy Work' as a Method of Social Work

Advocacy Work as a social work method is to be used when the rights of individuals, groups, communities are at stake. People who are facing injustice, exploitation, harassment, neglect or ill-treatment have a right to lead a life of dignity and worth which is the core value in social work. In many cases, age old social and cultural norms and practices hinder individuals and social groups from realizing basic rights and privileges.

Advocacy work would thus involve challenging accepted norms and rules that restrict people's lives. It is used as a social work method when a set of wrongs have to be set right and is at the heart of the helping process.

Advocacy can empower the powerless and give people a voice. Advocacy is caring about injustice. Indeed, advocacy is the reason why many people choose to work in the helping professions. Caring about the way people are treated and feeling that you can do something to help is why most of us decided to take on such jobs. Credible professionals are prepared to raise uncomfortable issues and to highlight where things are wrong.

How 'Advocacy Work' is different from 'Self-advocacy'

There are situations when people can themselves fight for their rights and demand for the fulfilment of their entitlements. This is referred to as self-advocacy which implies that those who are directly affected by the problem – the sufferers of injustice, the clients, the service users – can act on their own and advocate for their own selves. On a few occasions when individuals decide to challenge existing unjust situations they most effectively do so by coming together, act collectively and adopt legal action. Led by potential leaders among the group or those who are more aware of the legal procedures involved, the groups and their members adopted a quasi-structured approach to their advocacy. The growing development of anti-discrimination legislation and the strengthening legal basis of human rights law ensure that collective self-advocacy will remain a recurring feature of activity by marginalised groups of people. But experience suggests that they too may require the help and assistance of professionals as supports.

Role of Advocacy Organisations

Advocacy organisations play crucial roles in preventing and alleviating abuses.

They either act singly or in loosely formed networks and undertake numerous tasks – researching and reporting on violations; drawing attention of the general public and the government in particular to abuses; providing services and advice to threatened individuals, minority or ethnic groups; applying pressure strategies such as sanctions and boycotts; and lobbying national and international governments to implement more forceful measures.

Why should Advocacy Work be considered as Social Work Method?

Successful advocacy work, however, is represented by a set of core assumptions, values, goals and objects, principles, process, strategies and skills that are common to all forms of advocacy, with slight variations, that becomes necessary to address the wide range of problems and issues it caters to. Hence, an attempt is made here to present advocacy as one of the contemporary methods of social work that has a scientific base for achieving successful advocacy action.

Advocacy has to be treated as a full-fledged method of social work because of the unjust social, economic and political environments in which people live. More so, advocates have to face or counter opponents who are in a powerful position and can deny the required services or entitlements of their clients. They happen to be bureaucrats, politicians, officials who handle service provision, heads who represent grassroots social and political institutions and perhaps senior members in the family. Sometimes what is being sought is clear and structured – for example, social security benefits governed by legal rules; at other times it is unstructured and without clear boundaries.

In cases where the problem is of individual nature and relates to access to specific services, the goals to be achieved through advocacy action are quite clear, definite and time bound. However, if issues of access are more systemic in nature and affect larger sections of the population who are discriminated against on grounds of class, caste, creed, race, religious denomination, region, linguistic differences, in such cases the complex nature of the problem or issue calls for a more methodical manner in which advocacy action has to be undertaken. Hence the need for the development of an appropriate methodology of advocacy action, that would be flexible enough to be applicable to various situations and problems. Whatever the type of problem or the level of intervention, advocacy action must be structured if it is to be effective. Hence the effort to establish "advocacy work" as a distinct method of professional social work.

The Selective Use of Social Work Methods

Social work methods are used at various levels – individual, groups, community and larger population groups, especially helping clients meet unfulfilled needs, address difficulties and problems faced and immediate issues and concerns. These methods of social work often come into play when the client or clientele group approaches the social work professional for help or on occasions when social workers initiate *suo motto* action in case of clients who are identified as vulnerable and are not aware of the nature of help and assistance social workers could provide. The focus of intervention with the use of particular social work methods – either singularly or in combination, depends upon the pre-existing social, cultural and political environment of a particular nation or region or nascent client population. The nature of problems as found in the more developed western countries are more psycho-pathological result of individualistic and atomistic living. This requires a focus on the use of social case work and social group work methods. Relatively poor nations which have large sections of poor people and are relatively less developed, with its people having low incomes and scarce resource base are more dependent on state run institutions and state sponsored schemes and programmes for meeting citizens' need and addressing common problems. In such situations where the overall GDP of the country is not conducive to meet the needs of teaming millions, non-state actors come up with interventions that stress more on community-based and community-initiated strategies that call for the use of community organisation or social action as a social work method.

Social action as a method is more appropriate where the issues faced by communities are in a relatively larger scale than that faced by a single community. The development and establishment of social action as a pure form of social work method having a clear domain has been quite fluid. It has dilly-dallied between outcome-based approach to problem resolution at the community level and as an unending or sustaining process-focused method. The later in particular is considered to be an ongoing process with shifting goals and objectives, based on the premise that problems and issues of the community change over time and require constant realignment in strategies and leveraging.

There are other contexts and socio-cultural and political environs where populations are deemed to be in vulnerable situations and the client population facing various forms of human rights violations. Innumerable social workers are active in additional ways, affecting social policy by being active in coalitions, interest groups, and agencies and by acting independently to challenge injustice and to work for social justice.

Types of Advocacy

The levels of social work practice and whether social work practice is direct or indirect will decide the type of advocacy work that has to be undertaken. A list of rudimentary types of advocacy work is given below:

- *Relational Advocacy (Micro-level)* – dealing with family problems like domestic violence, divorce, child abuse, etc.
- *Social Advocacy (Meso level)* – dealing with social work interventions at the levels of community level social institutions like the panchayat, khap panchayat, caste panchayat, religious and caste institutions, social institutions like marriage, education, etc.

- *Service Provision Advocacy (Exo-level)* – dealing with the effective functioning of the administrative and service delivery machinery; consumer protection; police and correctional systems; insurance cover for vulnerable populations like indebted farmers, small farmers, etc.
- *Political Advocacy (Macro-level)* – dealing with the proper functioning of political and legal institutions that are entrusted with the promotion and dispensation of justice – individual and social.
- *Policy Advocacy (Macro-level)* – that deals with the establishment of new policies, laws and programmes, or effecting necessary changes in existing ones.
- *International/Transnational Advocacy (global-level)* – that deals with formation of transnational coalitions for advocacy work to tackle issues and problems of international nature like migration, civil war crimes, human rights violations in prison camps, human trafficking, displacement, climate change, etc.

Assumptions of 'Advocacy Work'

Advocacy work comes to play:

1. When people (clients) are faced with exploitative and oppressive situations and relationships;
2. When the dignity and respect of the individual(s) is violated;
3. When people are unable to resist and fight against oppression they had faced in the past and continue to face in the present;
4. When the client in question has failed to counter forces of exploitation and has been suffering on a sustaining basis;
5. When people lack awareness of legal and statutory entitlements and the provisions in law to counter the injustices meted out to them;
6. When a pattern exists that promotes and sustains a climate of exploitation and human rights violations;
7. When services or practices are dehumanizing, confrontational, or coercive;
8. When discriminatory practices or policies occur because of race, gender, sexual orientation, religion, culture, family form, or other factors;
9. When people lack representation or participation in decisions that affect their lives;
10. When a significant group of people have common needs for which resources are unavailable;
11. When systemic and structural deficiencies are found in the delivery of social services, welfare services and social justice; and
12. When social exclusion is deep-rooted and hinders development of the excluded communities.

Objectives of Advocacy Work

Advocacy work represents a process of affecting or initiating change either with or on behalf of client groups. It is undertaken mostly by professionals, activists and organisations that stand or show concern for the upliftment of the vulnerable, oppressed, exploited sections of society. Most often than not such actions are in the context of legal/policy advocacy action by organisations that involve macro-level practice. As a social work method it endeavours to fulfil the following objectives and ensure desired outcomes:

(i) obtain services or resources that would not otherwise be provided;
(ii) protect vulnerable individuals, social groups and communities from abuse, oppression, and violation of their human rights;
(iii) modify or influence policies or practices that adversely affect groups or communities; and
(iv) promote legislation or policies that will result in the provision of requisite resources or services.

Strategies in Advocacy Work

A strategy is defined as a contingency plan to achieve one or more goals under conditions of uncertainty. The word 'strategy' as per Freedman21 (2013) denotes "a comprehensive way to try to pursue political ends, including the threat or actual use of force, in a dialectic of wills"... in which both adversaries interact. The various strategies and techniques that could be used and have been found essential by activists and advocacy organisations alike are:

a) *Evidence gathering*: data collection and aggregation – to highlight the extent of violations of human rights, plight of destitute and neglected, the harassed and oppressed; filing of RTI.
b) *Filing representations*: speaking, writing, or acting on behalf of another.
c) *Scaling-up reach*: to broaden the support-base; glocalisation (from local to global levels).
d) *Volunteer mobilisation*: mobilising cause lawyers; civic engagements.
e) Leadership building.
f) *Fund mobilisation* for large scale advocacy campaigns.
g) Highlighting issues in the media and electronic advocacy.
h) *Organisation building*: developing network of individuals at the grassroots level.
i) *Networking and coalition formation*: Individual clients, social workers or advocacy NGOs on their own may turn out to be weak players while working against the relatively powerful opponents. However, as part of advocacy work by linking with other more powerful actors like national and transnational NGOs, political representatives, famed social activists, etc. advocacy networks can gain greater influence or

leverage for change. By linking causes to things that people value (like money, trade or prestige) advocacy networks can create material leverage for their cause. Advocacy networks also exercise moral leverage. When governments realise that they risk public shaming because of their actions (for instance, torturing prisoners), they may think twice before tarnishing their reputation on the international stage. In democratic countries, politicians depend on votes and the threat of a damaged reputation can put the politician's job in jeopardy.

j) *Legal awareness and seeking legal redress*: filing of cases in appropriate courts, public interest litigation (PIL).
k) Demonstration, agitation, sit-ins, rallies etc.
l) *Using various forums to highlight issues*: A forum is any assembly designated to discuss issues, regulations, rules, public matters, laws, or differing opinions, or to settle disputes. Examples are public hearings, legislative committees, agency board meetings, and supervisory sessions. Two features are usually present: (i) a set of specific procedures to guide the conduct of the participants, and (ii) a decision-making mechanism (Kutchins and Kutchins, 1987).
m) *Policy advocacy*: advocating for policy changes; establishing new policies; lobbying for the enactment of new legislations or making changes in existing ones.
n) Balanced resource allocation that is open and fair.

Principles of Advocacy Work

The principles in social work act as guidelines that help professionals to fulfil their roles and responsibilities towards the profession and clients in particular.

(a) *Need-based*: Prioritisation of action is imminent in case the client(s) is (are) facing impending danger of exploitation or threat to survival. A proper assessment of the client(s) vulnerability has to be done to especially focus on meeting the emergency needs like protection in the case of children and abused children in particular; individuals facing physical and sexual violence and torture within the family or in establishments; people living in war zones or facing civil war; refugees; displaced people; minority and ethnic population facing violence and ethnic cleansing; people faced with starvation and destitution to name a few.

(b) *Client Directed*: Professional social workers should work on behalf of the client. If need be, social workers may advise clients regarding the various options of intervention available, and the pros and cons of each alternative. The client(s), however, may have to be facilitated to make an informed choice i.e., in choosing the best from among the options presented in view of the past experiences and future difficulties the client(s) may face.

(c) *Conflict Avoidance*: Though examples of conflict in advocacy action may be on the higher side, it is generally held that confrontational strategies should be avoided, unless all forms of non-confrontational modes or strategies fail. Confrontationist strategies is often a drain on energy and time; it may lead to either party to challenge each other and may prevent the progress of the change process. However, confrontation as a strategy, could be the only option when the client is faced with serious life threatening situations or when there is a consensus that things would not change for the better unless systems – social, structural and political – are challenged.

(d) *Cultural Sensitivity*: Professional social workers must take into consideration the social and cultural context in which the client(s) live. Linguistic and communication aspects needs to be understood so that materials designed for campaigns are developed keeping in view the local language. The help of linguists and experts having grounding in local language/dialect and literature may have to be taken to design messages that have appropriate content which are emotionally tinged and generate wide interest and acceptability among the clientele population.

(e) *Duty of Care*: It is the bounden duty of the professional to avoid such actions that are illegal or may cause impending and significant harm to the clients. It is often witnessed that in a confrontational mode of protest and campaigning, especially when large scale movements are initiated to create pressure on the government or the social or political systems being opposed, some from among the campaign participants may resort to acts like stone throwing, destroying public property, physically challenging officials and opponents. These may be in violation of existing laws of the land, and should be avoided. Professionals have the duty to monitor every action of members or groups involved in campaigns so that any untoward incident could be avoided that may have the potential to nullify or negate whatever achievements have been made in the course of the advocacy process.

(f) *Avoiding Conflict of Interest*: The professional because of the position he/she enjoys as one of the frontline leaders in advocacy work or campaigns, may be in an enviable position to appropriate or apportion some of the benefits that may accrue to the clients. Violating this basic principle may lead to disastrous consequences in terms of a premature termination of the advocacy process. A visible conflict of interest may create doubts in the minds of the clientele population, and may lead to some clients dropping-out and others may challenge or oppose the leadership, development of fissure and factions within the group.

(g) *Critical Thinking*: Social injustice is often located in social and political structures. Hence a 'critical' thinking in terms of structures is essential to locate and identify the forces at work that sustain an oppressive and exploitative system. Critical analysis focuses more on socio-economic outcomes and collective injustices. Here structures are forces that shape social policy, which underpin prominent social oppressions, injustices and inequalities. As Young (2000) suggests 'a person's social location in structures differentiated by class, gender, age, ability, race, or caste often implies predictable status in law, educational levels, occupation, access to resources, political power and prestige ... one reason to call these structural is that they are relatively permanent'. Hence, locating the forces of oppression that are deep-rooted within the socio-political systems have to be identified and challenged to bring about lasting changes in the client(s) situation and for removing them from injustice. Welfare states may be more or less successful in tackling structural injustices. But when the state fails in its duty to protect the rights and entitlements of its citizens 'advocacy work' has to come to play its challenging role.

(h) *Empowerment as Sustainable Change*: Clients' capacity and opportunity to change and to address their own needs will get a boost if the advocacy work undertaken adopts a participatory approach so that the client(s) as actors in advocacy work gain confidence in themselves by learning the process and steps involved in advocacy. Of course this strategy may not fit to cases where the client referred to is not in a position – physically, mentally, economically – to participate in the process of advocacy work.

(i) *Identifying and Challenging Systemic Flaws and Institutional Barriers*: It is necessary to identify and challenge systematic flaws and institutional barriers that promote and sustain exploitation and oppression. This should be a prime principle on the basis of which social workers approach the issues of injustice and oppression faced by clients and clientele population.

(j) *Limited Use*: Frequent use of advocacy to solve all types of problems of clients especially when it is in the domain of personal or quasi-personal relationships like marriage, family, neighbourhood, closely knit communities etc. may cause more harm than provide relief to the client. Though this may provoke feminists and activists alike as representing a paternalistic view, which should be shunned, a judicious decision for staggered use of other methods of social work that precede advocacy action is called for.

(k) *Establishment of Social Justice*: Valuing advocacy for social justice involves a deep sensitivity to the needs of all people, but most especially, to the needs of the poor, oppressed and disenfranchised. It embraces a global perspective, believing that an injustice to one is an injustice to all. A vital aspect of the social worker's training is his immersion in the values of social justice, equality and empowerment. For this purpose advocacy work involves promoting policies that safeguard the rights of, and confirm equity and social justice, for all people. Flaws in existing policies have to be identified through an exercise called "policy analysis" and a plan of action for advocating change in existing policies will have to be initiated.

(l) *Networking and Collaborative Initiatives*: Large scale issues and problems or issues; or for that matter even micro-level problems where the opponent is politically strong and powerful, there may be a need to build networks and partnerships to make concerted efforts so that the challenges are minimal. Network of individuals, groups, communities, general public, and advocacy organisations is therefore essential to draw energy from one another and become a force to rekon.

Skills in Advocacy Work

Advocacy work involves particular actions such are representation, influencing and the use of a forum to bring about specific change. Specific skills for advocacy work required either singly or in combinations include policy analysis, group facilitation, public mobilisation, communication, competency in negotiation and the analysis of multidimensional and systematic information. In the process of advocacy work, a state is reached when the clients realise the extent and manner in which they have been befooled, exploited, their human rights violated and face deprivation from basic entitlements. This causes a lot of dissension and anger in the minds of the client(s). This restlessness unless restrained may lead to coercion and violence. Therefore, anger management and conflict resolution skills would be required by the social worker to manage the situation. Any premature and erroneous action may lead to undesired or embarrassing consequences.

At the micro level, social workers have to understand the social and cultural forces that are the cause of oppression Social workers must understand the major social, political and economic forces that have shaped the development of social policy.

To expand the support base of the clients needing advocacy the social worker has to posses networking skills for building coalitions of individuals, groups, communities and organisations so that the network and coalition can become a force unto itself. The sheer numbers in the coalition and the backing of experienced organisations in the field of advocacy would create a systematic intervention plan for advocacy actions.

Challenges in Advocacy Work

The Code of Ethics of social work obligates all professionals to commit to and practice advocacy. However, social workers are faced with numerous barriers to practice advocacy. Some of this may be due to lack of appropriate attitudes which often inhibit professionals from using advocacy work as a method of social work intervention.

Advocacy work is too demanding on time, energy, and finances (Ezell, 2001; Hoefer, 2006; Schneider and Lester, 2001). When social workers want to change local, state, or national policies and laws, they often do it in their free time, using personal leave, and pay for travel and other out-of-pocket costs themselves. A misconception among social workers, that advocacy often adopts a 'confrontationist approach', also prevents them from using it more often than not (Sheafor and Horejsi, 2003). It is also perceived as risking important and necessary collaborative relationships; lack of employer's support when the state or the powerful elites start to adopt arm-twisting techniques and hence the risk of losing one's job; or advocacy work and advocacy actions heavily depend on working with multiple stakeholders and coalition partners. Though an expansive network has strength in terms of numbers, it however faces challenges in equal measure. As opposed to a closed, consensual process in smaller and local networks, policy issues in a larger national level and transnational networks may often face contestation between multiple competing groups (Golden, 1998; Sabatier 1991). Moreover, it turns out to be a very tedious exercise with innumerable preconditions for its sustenance and success. These are in terms of building consensus and trust among members and partners; previous experience of working together; issues of logistics when the coalition becomes too large and it becomes taxing to organise meetings, communicate about upcoming activities and report results; difficulty in equitable distribution and sharing of responsibility and expenses; dominance of a few members/partner agencies; agreeing on rule of the game; and working out strategies as to how resources could be leveraged for the advocacy campaign.

Advocacy is an activity requiring patience, tenacity, compromise, long-term commitment, energy, broad bases of support, research, political skills, knowledge of government, and capacity to analyze (Schneider and Lester, 2001). This is a challenge posed before individual social workers, volunteers, collaborating agencies, including client(s) who would like to have a quick-fix solution to their problems.

In the context of clinical social work practice, it is often seen that clinical social workers do not prioritize the interrelationship of clients' needs and laws. Effective and lasting interventions often depend upon advocacy at the individual and systemic levels. However, social work agencies and their staff often devote most of their energies to direct service programmes (O'Connell, 1978) even if they have been instructed to include advocacy whenever required. Social workers have often been found to limit themselves to service delivery, and stay away from, advocacy action. Moreover, social service agencies have been found not providing sufficient resources to promote or engage in advocacy practice (Ezell, 2001). It is also a sad traversity of the evolution and current practice in social work education and training that sufficient opportunities are not provided to students to show as to how advocacy can be actually practiced in such situations. Hence, the need to evolve and promote 'advocacy work' as a key method in professional social work.

Conclusion

Advocacy as a contemporary method of social work will bring a new dimension to social work practice especially in developing countries. The basic assumption behind the development of 'advocacy work' as a method is the need to emphasise the role advocacy can play in providing justice to people at large, especially the vulnerable sections who may not be in a position to seek justice or even meet their basic needs, because of debilitating conditions in which they may be living or due to a lack of awareness of the human, legal and constitutional rights they are supposed to enjoy or because of powerlessness and oppression.

REFERENCES

1. Hepworth, D. H. (2013). *Direct Social Work Practice: Theory and Skills*. Australia: Brooks/Cole, Cengage Learning.
2. Brueggemann, W. G. (2006). *The Practice of Macro Social Work*. Thomson-Brooks/Cole.
3. Woodrow, P. (January 01, 1997). Nurse Advocacy: is it in the patient's best interests?. *British Journal of Nursing (mark Allen Publishing)*, 6, 4, 27.
4. Brandon, D., Brandon, A., and Brandon, T. (1995). *Advocacy: Power to People with Disabilities*. Birmingham: Venture.
5. Schneider, R. L., and Lester, L. (2001). *Social Work Advocacy. A New Framework for Action*. Brooks/Cole.
6. Dobelstein, A. (1990). *Social Welfare Policy and Analysis*. Chicago: Nelson-Hall.
7. Ezell, M. (2001). *Advocacy in the Human Services*. Australia: Brooks/Cole Thomas Learning.
8. Middleton, E. J. (1985). *A View from the Field*. Ann Arbor, MI: School of Social Work, University of Michigan.
9. Manthorpe, J. and Bradely, G. (2002). Managing Finances, in Adams, R., Dominelli, L., and Payne, M. (2002). *Critical practice in Social Work*. Basingstoke: Palgrave.
10. Litzelfelner, P., and Petr, C. G. (1997). Case advocacy in child welfare. *Social Work*, 42, 392-402.
11. Bateman, N. (2000). *Advocacy Skills for Health and Social Care Professionals*. London: Jessica Kingsley Publishers.
12. Freedman, L. (2013). *Strategy: A History*. Oxford, NY: Oxford University Press.
13. Young, I. M. (2000). *Inclusion and Democracy*. Oxford: Oxford University Press
14. Ezell, M. (2001). *Advocacy in the Human Services*. Belmont, CA: Wadsworth/ Thomson Learning.
15. Hoefer, R. (2006). *Advocacy Practice for Social Justice*. Chicago: Lyceum Books.
16. Shaefer, B. W., and Horejsi, C. R. (2003). *Techniques and Guidelines for Social Work Practice* (6th ed.). Boston: Allyn and Bacon.
17. Golden, M. M. 1998. Interest groups in the rule-making process: Who participates? Whose voices get heard? *Journal of Public Administration Research and Theory: J-PART* 8 (2): 245–70.
18. Sabatier, P. 1988. An advocacy coalition framework of policy change and the role of policy-oriented learning therein. *Policy Sciences* 21:129–68.
19. O'Connell, B. (1978). From service to advocacy to empowerment. *Social Casework*, 59(4), 195-202.

3

Models and Phases in Advocacy

Asutosh Pradhan

Advocacy originates from advocare, 'call to one's aid' or to speak out on behalf of someone, as a legal counsellor. Advocacy is the deliberate process, based on demonstrated evidence, to directly and indirectly influence decision makers, stakeholders and relevant audiences to support and implement actions that contribute to the fulfilment of children's and women's rights (UNICEF, 2010). Advocacy is a core process for addressing inequality and disparities. As a powerful method of social work, 'advocacy' has certain models of practice, and a strong theoretical base. Theoretical knowledge and understanding of models and phases of advocacy, will enable the social workers to link the contemporary method of 'advocacy' with the other methods of social work, and enhance social work interventions with diverse issues among widely differing groups.

Models of Advocacy

There are several models or forms of advocacy. Some of the important models of advocacy are:

1. Moral Approach

A dominant theoretical perspective holds that individuals and organisations advocating for their clients should be seen primarily as "principled" entities working to help "victims" of atrocities. As per this view, victims spark nation-wide or transnational activism either directly, by appealing for support directly or indirectly, and activists moved by their suffering, take action to support them. The results are networks that grow organically, from the "bottom up," selflessly serving the needs of the abused (Bob, 2010). This view gives undue importance to the contribution of advocacy and human rights organisations, and more recent, critical perspectives challenge this 'moral theory' view.

2. Collective Action Approach

The limitation of individuals to achieve on their own, due entitlements, services and facilities for growth and development is well known. This is more critical an issue, when we are concerned with vulnerable people. Hence, a network of individuals at the community level, organised around a common need or an issue, and facilitated to work jointly by an NGO or other grassroots organisation, will help in gaining confidence in order to make concerted efforts for a solution.

However, the collective action approach has its own problems that limit its impact as a productive venture. The collective action approach for advocacy action depends heavily on the continued voluntary participation of individuals outside of a formal organization. This is problematic because in the case of campaigns which require action in long-term, sustaining volunteer participation, and even client(s) active involvement, may be difficult since the initiative may enter into a period of lull and may 'cool-off', if results are not visible.

This inherent limitation of collective action has led to the emergence and structure of advocacy organizations as entrepreneurial undertakings. Consequently, it is important to remember that advocacy organizations represent solutions to the collective action problem rather than manifestations of it. When a group is established, it reflects an effort to consolidate resources and reduce the challenges of voluntary coordinated political participation.

3. Advocacy-Coalition Framework Model/Approach

This model provides an understanding of the processes involved in implementing policy-level social change. Policy advocacy actors make attempts to include various policy participants from all levels of government, multiple interest groups, NGOs and Civil Society Organisations, research institutions, and the media. This model, however, requires sustained efforts in the longrun, ranging from at least five to ten years, an understanding of subsystems, the involvement of multiple levels of government, and an understanding that belief systems can change priorities and policies.

The Advocacy Coalition Framework (ACF) was propounded by Sabatier (1988) who pleaded for policy advocacy as a mechanism for bringing about planned change and preventing negative change or mal-development. Sabatier has strong faith in the power of coalitions and networking to effect changes in social policy that would ultimately improve the service delivery systems and justice delivery mechanism. However, he goes on to caution that effecting policy changes is a lengthy process and time consuming and often takes "a decade or more" to fructify; involves focused work and intervention involving 'policy subsystems' which refer to 'the interaction of actors from different institutions interested in a policy area'; and that it involves the conceptualization of policies and programmes "in the same manner as belief systems, i.e. as sets of value priorities and causal assumptions about how to realize them." Weiss (1977) too was of the opinion that a focus on short-term decision-making would underestimate the influence of policy analysis, and trivialise the exercise. Policy research has the difficult task to alter the perceptions and conceptual apparatus of policy-makers over time taking into consideration the administrative and political inertia that often prevails such institutions. The literature on policy implementation also points to the need for utilizing timeframes of a decade or more, both in order to complete at least one formulation/implementation/reformulation cycle and to obtain a reasonably accurate assessment of the success and failure of the policy and programmes under implementation (Mazmanian and Sabatier, 1983).

4. Social-Cognitive Model/Approach

The role of training in advocacy has been considered as an important strategy to involve and mobilize people in more numbers to participate in 'advocacy action' and become a force or a pressure group to bring about policy or legislative changes. Winkleby, Feighery, Altman, Kole, and Tencati (2001) used the social cognitive theory to empirically establish that direct interventions such as advocacy trainings could influence self-efficacy and affect individuals' motivation to engage in the political process. Training helps in creating awareness in people both clients and advocacy actors regarding the nature and degree of violation of rights and entitlements, oppression and subjugation and discrimination and harassment. It also increases the capabilities of participants by way of developing leadership qualities, risk taking, problem analysis, strategizing, networking and coalition building. The researchers concluded that as a result of specific training, individuals can be motivated to effectively impact public policy.

5. Empowerment Model/Approach

One of the major objectives of social work is to empower individuals, groups and communities to tackle their problems on their own, and take decisions and steps to address issues that have impact on them. The process of social work help and providing assistance should integrate aspects of action and intervention that will increase the capabilities of client(s) to manage their own affairs without seeking assistance in future, however utopian this may sound. The aim of empowerment is to assist client(s) to understand that they have various rights and entitlements as humans and citizens; belief that they possess the means and resources individually and as groups to find solutions to their own problems; a belief in themselves as having skills and strengths; the ability to associate with peers and enter into partnerships at the community and broader level to make concerted efforts to find solutions and strive for change; the ability to understand power structures and its complex nature and identify openings available for influencing them so that their problems are addressed and solved.

Levels of Advocacy Action

The levels of practice in social work are an important determinant of the nature of social work intervention. Help provided to the client(s) through advocacy as a method of social work could be at the micro or individual client level; or at the mezzo or the group or community level; or at the macro or the policy and legislative level. Advocacy action also depends on the nature of the problem, the target population, the desired scale of change or impact, etc. Working at each of these levels and meeting the needs of clients, addressing the issues or difficulties faced by clients would require different sets of procedures of action and intervention. The same has, therefore, been dealt with separately.

1. Micro-Level Advocacy Work

Direct social work practice done with individuals has been referred to as micro-level social work practice. Some of the services provided to individuals as part of direct social work practice are counselling, psychosocial therapy, access to services, basic needs fulfilment, etc. Social casework, though connotes working with individuals in a face-to-face situation, there are occasions when the caseworker too has to involve himself/herself in Indirect Social Work Practice. Advocacy actions in conjunction with and on behalf of clients are sometimes required to secure the services and resources to which clients are entitled. This is especially true when the client's problems relate to non-receipt of social services or welfare services from government agencies which are mandated by law to provide these services. Examples of such services are old age or disability pension, reservation in jobs, physical aids for people with disabilities, housing subsidy, food stamp, and access to health facilities by people living with HIV/AIDS. Welfare agencies and government service delivery systems may not be functioning efficiently and effectively because of lax agency personnel or corrupt practices. A direct social work practitioner may be working at a time with a number of individual clients and may come to know of systemic failure of the delivery systems. This would prompt the social work practitioner to use 'advocacy work' and adopt a variety of advocacy strategies to provide relief and justice to his/her clients that include but is not limited to legal recourse, lobbying, filing complaints with higher authorities, publicising such concerns and issues in the media, and the like with the intent to reach out to large sections of the deprived category of clients.

One of the important services provided by social caseworkers to individual clients is counselling. In the interest of clients and also for their own professional existence counsellors and state and national counsellor organisations in the US frequently employ lobbyists to promote legislation that give counselling a professional status. In this context, Solomon way back in 1982 had aptly written:

Counsellors and other human service providers are in a pivotal position to effectively communicate the concerns of people they serve to policy makers at local, state and national levels of government. They are in an even better position to shape legislative initiatives, bills and laws to more appropriately address counselling issues that directly impact the counselling profession as well as the people they serve. Most of the political successes that affect the counselling profession will depend largely on counsellors themselves (Solomon, 1982).

2. Mezzo-Level Advocacy Work

Mezzo-level social work practices goes beyond the intimate personal relationships that exist in the family and the context of troubles and problems as faced by individuals. It refers to interpersonal relationships that individuals have with different parts of their social environment – be it in self-help or therapy groups, peer groups at school or in the workplace, etc. Mezzo-level practice is also in the context of relationships that clients have with various service providers like the nearest hospital or clinic, the local, block or district administration that provides services under various schemes of government, various agencies mandated under law to provide protection and legal services to vulnerable people. In this context, advocacy actions in conjunction with, and on behalf of, clients may be required to gain access to the services and resources that is due to the client(s) or are part of their entitlement.

3. Macro-Level Advocacy Work

Macro-level advocacy action typically involves policy advocacy initiatives, influencing the manner in which programmes and policies are implemented and pressing for institutional and structural changes. More often than not, the target of intervention is the government or agencies of the government at the national and/or state level. Because of the scale and complexities involved in such initiatives, it has been found that the lead role, in advocating for change, is played by organisations belonging to the non-governmental sector. Interventions at the policy level are meant to effecting changes in existing laws, removing flaws in legislations or policies and making laws and policies more stringent.

Phases in Advocacy Work

It is evident from the above text that advocacy has various dimensions, levels of intervention, and forms of intervention. It is therefore imperative to understand that a single template or framework for advocacy work and advocacy actions is difficult to suggest. A brief outline is suggested as to how advocacy work could be undertaken.

Phase-1: Research and Assessment Phase

(i) Identifying the problems and the policy issues

- *From where do we start?* Essential to the development of social work practice is a precise formulation of clients' needs or a problem definition whether it is in the field of mental health, disability, school social work, human rights, poverty alleviation, sustainable livelihoods, rural and tribal development, child protection and care of dependent individuals.

- *Identifying concerns that affect individuals, groups and community rights and entitlements*: Identifying issues is a difficult task that requires quite a bit of research and soul searching – by advocating professional social work, the agency which takes up the issue for advocacy, and the client(s) also to a large extent. We have found that the best method for locating issues is to be fully aware of the entire array of legal rights and entitlements that pertain to clients' lives.
- *Developing awareness on human rights transgressions/violations and unfulfilled entitlements*: Time and again it has been seen that human rights violations have taken place because of the lack of information and awareness among people as regards the legal entitlements they have. This may also be as a result of the inability on the part of the clients to handle and circumambulate the complex and intricate formal procedures relating to seeking redress from formal institutions – administrative and legislative. The professional has to develop modalities as to how the clients could be.
- *Research specific to Advocacy Campaigns*: In the case of advocacy campaigns targeted for policy changes or addressing systemic flaws in governance systems, the social worker has to undertake research on issues or problems faced by specific population categories and groups facing oppression, exploitation and exclusion. The preliminary task is to collect primary data and information and/or issues highlighted by the media or as reflected in existing research.
  Advocacy organisations which are part of campaign coalitions may identify good practices in operation elsewhere, and may adopt it as a benchmark for the activities of their organisation. Is there a policy dimension to the problems faced by clients? A thorough analysis of existing policy in relation to the issues at hand, will also help in identifying flaws and loopholes because of which recipients of social and welfare services may not be receiving their entitlements. Can changes in current policies lead to an improvement in the condition of the clients and the fulfilment of their rights?
- *Providing client adequate space to voice their concerns*: Whether it is working with individuals, groups or larger populations in need of advocacy, advocacy work entails the strategic representation of client'(s) concerns and issues in her/his or their own words. Wroe (2012) feels that it is critical to adopt a narrative approach to presenting the case of clients, since it puts across the message that '... the agency lies with the subject of oppression or domination and that it is their desire that drive social change work, rather than the desires of a humanitarian organisation or campaigner'. This will help the campaign gain visibility and momentum. Moreover, this gives the clients(s) a platform to tell their stories and make their demands.

Through a process of critical story-telling individuals in distress and minority groups are empowered to take up their own struggles where they are often merely represented by someone. If this does not happen, Rainbird (2011) says that support organisations often have inadvertently demonstrated to perpetuate the social exclusion... by acting as gatekeepers in their representation. Professional social workers using advocacy work as a method need to be conscious of this professional requirement of practice.

(ii) Deciding on advocacy goals and objectives

The second stage is to define and decide upon the shared goals of social work intervention and advocacy work. Clarity should be there as regards the ultimate outcome of the advocacy initiative.

Participants should envision how the concerns of the individual client or the policy environment in the context of macro-level social work practice will be changed as a result of their advocacy efforts. Unless workable solutions and tangible benefits accrue, clients may not be motivated to work in its achievement. Will it improve access to information and the desired social services or entitlements? Will it promote dialogue between the parties concerned, and strengthen voice and influence of clients?

Examples of advocacy goals could be varied – it may be the permanent removal of hurdles in the social services delivery systems; access to information, resources and entitlements; relief from exploitation and harassment; empowerment of the client and confidence-building; policy changes and/or formulation of new policy or legislation, etc.

(iii) Analysing the policy environment: Identifying relevant policies, laws and regulations

After deciding on advocacy goals as part of preliminary work, the next stage of advocacy work involves closer analysis of the policy environment. Policy advocacy is initiated with an audit of the relevant policies and political institutions. What are the policies in operation at the local, state and national level? How are these reflected, or not, in the form of laws, rules and regulations, programmes and modes of implementation? Relevant international treaty obligations, laws and standards needs to be studied, so that gaps in international treaties in relation to human rights obligations are identified and pointed out to the government.

(iv) Mapping relations of power, influence and decision making

The next step in policy advocacy is critical to bringing about policy changes. One has to identify the people, departments, ministries and other agencies like regulatory bodies who are responsible for and have influence in the decision-making process. Interest groups within the political parties, state legislatures and parliament will have to be identified and influenced upon so as to garner support and represent the case in appropriate forums. Mobilising support and lobbying with various stakeholders cutting across party lines would be a very effective way to counter inter-party opposition that a particular policy may face in the absence of consensus.

(v) Considering the options for policy change

Time and again it has been seen that effecting policy and legislative changes always does not lead to bringing about social change. The failure of legislations in India relating to corruption, dowry, juvenile crime, domestic violence against women, etc. are glaring examples of the failure in establishing social justice. Alternative approaches may have to be innovated to make the translation of policy into effective practice. A dialogue between the general public, clientele population, network partners etc. would help in assessing the amount of support that a particular course of action and strategies could garner.

Phase-2: Planning Stage - Developing an Action System for Intervention

(i) Relationship-building and Forging Coalitions

Individual social workers, advocacy organisations and to an extent, local networks may not be capable of achieving advocacy goals single-handedly. Hence, in the initial phase, advocacy work needs to focus on building networks with various partners at different levels. Advocacy action, especially those that address socio-structural and political issues, would depend largely on the networks that professional social worker or an organisation builds with other organisations, working in the same field, with shared visions and objects, and the clientele population at large. Intellectual capital and expertise available with coalition partners could be strategically utilised to maximise effectiveness and impact. This is especially important when national and international policies are to be established or changed. Leading international and national organisations could be consulted in order to plan advocacy actions, strategising for optimising effectiveness and mobilise resources.

Keck and Sikkink (1998) have very succinctly elaborated on the importance and relevance of transnational advocacy networks, and the need for local NGOs to align with them. Transnational advocacy networks also help in highlighting and internationalising local issues by associating relevant actors – who are bound together by shared values, a common discourse, and close exchange of information and services, to work internationally on (such) issues and drawing visibility and international support.

Further, strong and effective advocacy networks are dependent on (a) strong and efficient relationships which ensure the easy and efficient flow and diffusion of information throughout the network; (b) reliable and quality information flows to all members and member organisations. Reliability is not simply a matter of being able to get information when it is needed; (c) associating experts and specialised organisations from diverse fields; (d) broadening the network by inviting and admitting new organizations which agree to the network's mission and goals; (e) regular meetings of partner organisations to respond to current events and strategising for the future; and (e) appointing spokespersons who can represent the network to the media.

(ii) Credibility Building

Though credibility of a professional social worker, an organisation, a partnership or coalition is built in the eyes of the public, over a period of time, it however precedes any advocacy initiative. Moreover, it is likely to be a deciding factor for the success of advocacy action, since clients would also participate in equal measure, when they are sure of the achievements of their goals and redressal of their problems and concerns. Credible organisations also at times are mandated by the government to represent certain sections of society and speak on behalf of those who normally do not have the ability to represent their cases. To appear credible, organisations associate experts and experienced people who are respected in the development sector. Networks often approach leading activists to support their cause. Examples are many, in present day India like Medha Patkar, Aruna Roy, Anna Hzare and Swami Agnivesh. with whom grassroots networks would like to associate.

(iii) Developing the strategy for achievement of goals and objectives

Finalising the goals and objectives of advocacy action in more specific and realistic terms is an imperative to leapfrog to the next level of making concrete steps in establishing change and social justice. A framework that deals with various operational issues in the implementation of advocacy activities, sharing of responsibilities among network partners, including the client(s), has to be chalked out. It is also necessary to develop a roadmap and time-frame to achieve the goals and sub-goals. This has to be a joint exercise between all network and coalition partners so that there are no major differences later on that may impede progress.

(iv) Identifying the target audiences

In professional social work language, the client that is to be served or the target system for change has to be properly identified – be it the voluntary clients, involuntary clients, tangential clients, or the collaterals and significant others. This is all the more important in a country like India where there are hardly any agencies specifically involved in case work, group work and referral services. It is useful to distinguish between primary targets that refers to institutions, and the individuals within them, who are in positions of power, whether in social or political institutions, and have authority to make/take decisions; or secondary targets who could influence the decision makers.

The difficult part is to identify the secondary targets that are to be mobilised for supporting the cause for which the advocacy campaign had been initiated. These may include politicians, local leaders, public servants, the media, development agencies, influential NGOs and so on.

(v) Mobilising support

The most critical phase in advocacy action is the mobilisation of large number of people, other stakeholders, and non-governmental organisations to draw support. Organisations working in similar field, and sharing the same goals for their clients, should be contacted and a loose or strong network be established to ensure support. Volunteer recruitment is another key step in this exercise of mobilisation, since this will help in the sharing of tasks that involve advocacy work and campaigns.

People with the right skills and convictions only should be associated with the campaign. For this, selection of volunteers and other associates should take place, based on the principles of organising, which involves identification of various tasks and roles in different phases in the advocacy action process. This will ensure focus in action and proper coordination among all actors participating in the campaign.

Effective mobilisation depends on how well we try and know our audience and assess what would motivate them to be part of the campaign. Messages that will inspire people to get involved have to be painstakingly developed. Reasons as to why they should get involved have to be made clear. One has to support this with appropriate data and statistics regarding the concerns and conditions of the client(s) in order to justify one's actions.

(vi) Selecting the advocacy approach

The most crucial part in advocacy work is to decide upon advocacy strategies. These have to be carefully chalked out keeping in view the fluid situations in which such campaigns and advocacy initiatives are taken up. What strategies would work – is it through dialogue and negotiation or creating public pressure, awareness generation and rights education to promote self-advocacy or fighting on behalf of the client(s). There can be innumerable such permutations and combinations depending on the challenges faced in the course of advocacy work and when in different phases. A thorough 'risk analysis' before-hand will help in countering forces of resistance or potential failures.

(vii) Designing the content and message

In every advocacy campaign, communication strategies are important to inform, and enhance knowledge among the general public and all other stakeholders who would benefit out of such campaigns. An advocacy campaign benefits greatly from a well-run media outreach programme. Advocacy campaigns undertaken in the context of a larger audience has to share appropriate, strategy-specific information with multiple-stakeholders, including clientele population, network and coalition partners, other advocacy organizations, policy makers, the media, and grassroots citizens. Such information sharing can range from the dissemination of research undertaken, to the announcement of a rally in front of a Minister's residence or at such other location that will attract maximum visibility.

Development of key messages in simple and understandable form is important so that the concerns and issues relating to the client(s) concerned are well spread out. Messages should have emotional appeal; persuasive; present bare facts; and the subtle nature of exploitation, oppression, and discrimination.

The message is the heart and soul of any advocacy campaign. It should be as specific as possible, and it should be delivered in the clearest possible language. To be effective different messages need to be developed for different audiences such as the public in general, coalition partners, the media and the social media. Campaign tools may consist of leaflets and fact sheets, a letter to an elected official, posters and banners, petitions – written or email, letter and postcard writing to decision-makers, street theatre, SMS/text messages, photographs, campaign specific merchandise like T-shirts, badges, wristbands, hats and DVDs or CDs outlining client(s) issues. Experts and professional hands at developing these messages have to hired or could be done by volunteers who have specialised skills.

Phase-3: Planning, Budgeting and Resource Mobilisation

(i) Listing the broad and specific activities

Effective advocacy requires good activity and organisational planning. At this stage it is important to be systematic in mapping out the actions to be taken to achieve results. Measurable progress indicators have to be identified in the form of milestones and timelines. Preparing a plan of action covers the range of specific activities that are to be carried out (a) as part of providing advocacy services in case of individual clients or (b) as part of an advocacy campaign. In the former case, specific tasks may include – writing a representation or complaint; accompanying the client to present a verbal representation and seek clarifications from concerned officials who are responsible for providing a particular type of service; filing an RTI (under the Right to Information Act) seeking information regarding status of delivery welfare or development services; filing a case in the courts or a complaint with a particular commission like the Women's Commission, The Human Rights Commission, District Consumer Forum, so on and so forth; pressuring the police authorities to file an FIR if it is refused in the first instance; seeking the assistance of police in case of harassment and exploitation; preparing a case for the 'cause lawyer' who would fight the case in a court; facilitating the receipt of legal aid services; protection of children, the mentally disabled, and infirm elders who may be vulnerable within the family or the institution where they might have been placed for rehabilitation; offenders within prisons and juvenile homes who are faced with exploitation or inadequate facilities; and many more. The range of activities would depend on the nature of the issue, injustice or vulnerability faced.

In the case of the latter, for initiating advocacy campaigns, activities include media outreach, public talks, meetings with politicians, building networks and coalitions, public rallies, exhibitions, petitions and many other creative ways of getting the message out. Rather than undertaking isolated actions that are unlikely to have much impact, the planned activities should build on each other for greater effectiveness. Focusing first on highlighting the issue being advocated in the media or other platforms, for example, may convince decision makers to have a discussion with the concerned authorities.

One of the central things that a professional social work agency needs to undertake is in the field of grassroots advocacy that seeks justice through the legislature, the judiciary or other statutory bodies. This is possible when one is able to understand the nature of advocacy actions that must be initiated much beyond the period immediately before and during the legislative session or much before the case is filed in the court of law. Thinking of one's tasks in the context of the advocacy cycle helps ensure communication, engagement, and action on the issue through the year, and helps expand and strengthen the work as it proceeds to the next phase.

The action plan for advocacy campaigns should spell out the goals, target audience, partners and the distribution of responsibilities among the staff, volunteers, and network partners who would execute their roles under independent teams and under designated team leaders, to be completed within a given time frame. However, the plan should be flexible enough to allow for changes in the plan in a changing environment or in case planned actions are faced with hurdles during implementation.

Timelines and benchmarks are then prepared on paper or using the help of Gantt Chart. This would help in monitoring the progress of work. The involvement of such people who would help legitimise the planned course of action also has to be ensured.

(ii) Budgeting and Resource Mobilisation

In case of direct social work practice where the individual seeks advocacy services the agency may charge for the services provided which may be factored in into the fees charged. A rough estimate could be made based on previous experience as regards the costs involved. Detailed break-up of the cost of services offered should be clearly provided for the information of the client.

In case of advocacy campaigns, however, it may not be possible to recover the cost of services provided because the clients served are at large and the social worker or advocacy organisation may not be approached by the client. In such a case, resources have to mobilised from various sources like national and international funding agencies who have similar or shared goals and objectives in relation to specific social issues and concerns. The various heads of expenditure have to be listed out.

Decisions taken with regard to a particular approach to be adopted in advocacy campaigns is dependent on the funds available and potential funds that could be mobilised. In case of policy review and policy related dialogues, the funds required could be very less, because such work requires limited staff and most of it could be handled by volunteers. However, if the media is used for the campaign, this may incur substantial costs by way of publicity. Poster and print-based campaign materials too require a substantial amount of funds. Advocacy networks will have to frequently harness and use new age ICT like email, text messaging, Web 2.0 technologies, twitter and other social media campaigns in their advocacy work for coalition building and mobilisation.

Hence, an inventory of available resources is prepared – lists of equipments, potential volunteers, vehicles, etc., which are in possession with the organisaiton, the community at large and the potential sources that could be also mobilised in future as per requirement.

(iii) Risk assessment

Risk analysis involves assessing the impact of potential risks involved in advocacy work and the likelihood of it happening. Advocacy work has the potential to achieve major changes but it also entails significant risks. For example, an aggressive media campaign would expose the advocacy organisation's analysis of a cause or issue for all to see if it is flawed or biased. This would hamper their reputations since their objectives, methods and some of the strategies adopted in campaigns may be perceived as being 'too political' or may challenge the stakes of another group. In case the spokespersons of the campaign lack the guile and skill in giving appropriate logic and ability to properly defend some of the campaigns actions and strategies, even then there would be a loss of face in the eyes of the public. Subsequently, this may lead to loss of support, reduced funding or withdrawl of a particular strategy.

In case the advocacy work becomes successful, the clients may immediately or at a later stage face a backlash from those whose power or vested interests are being challenged. In case of issues faced by individuals and groups, advocacy work may change the dynamics of inter-personal relationships and the affected person may seek revenge. In the field of domestic violence especially, the victims often face further persecution and a heightened degree of violence after the professional relationship is terminated.

In case of broader campaigns, advocates and affected communities may suffer intimidation, violence or even death. If the campaign is against the government there are chances of the core leaders being rounded up and put in jail. This may affect the organisational ability of the campaign in the absence of key leaders. In such instances, network partners often fill in the void created. These security risks are real and cannot be ignored. Though management of risks is essential, people involved in advocacy work often admit that safeguards are often ad hoc and may not be successful. At times advocacy work may be truncated or scaled-down mid-course and hence may fail to exploit opportunities to make change happen.

(iv) Capacity building and human resource development

Orientation and training is another important aspect of advocacy work – especially because people from diverse walks of life are involved in the campaign. Developing a shared vision and goal is important for the smooth functioning of the various activities charted out. This is possible only through a rigorous process of orientation and training.

Progressively higher levels of training opportunities have to be provided based on evaluation of earlier actions and after assessing future requirements.

Leadership development, both at the level of volunteers and among the clientele population at large, has to be given priority so that the philosophy and goal of empowerment, through advocacy, is achieved.

Phase-4: Implementation

(i) Getting the message across

In the case of small or large-scale campaigns, good communications is at the core of effective advocacy. This requires attention to the content of the message, the type of audience and the modes of delivery. The message needs to be clear; people should be able to easily understand what is being said, why the campaign is needed, and what difference it would make in the lives of the people for whom the campaign or movement has been initiated. It also needs to be compelling; it should be crafted to the interests and knowledge of the audience. One has to choose from among various means of delivery of message to reach out to various people. It could be a mix of many methods i.e., a written or face-to-face representation, a public demonstration or participation in media discussions. It is rare that a single advocacy message or a single means of dissemination of the message can reach out to all the different types of stake holders. Further, the message needs to reinforced, by repetition and through the influence of secondary audiences.

(ii) Using the media in the case of advocacy work at the macro-level

Not all advocacy work requires the use of media. This is so in the case of micro-level social work practice, wherein social workers have to deal with the needs and issues of individual clients. The media – traditional radio, community radio, television, newspapers and online or social media – have a particular role to play in public advocacy initiatives, especially campaign-based approaches. The media can bring a mass audience, potentially increasing profile and credibility, but they can also bring bad publicity and may contribute to mobilising opposition as well as support. Using the media requires specialised skills, including building media contacts, knowing the media audience, writing press releases, placing stories in the newspapers, being interviewed, providing visual imagery and organising public discussion forums.

(iii) Employing tactics and negotiation

Advocacy work has to be a two way process in which one has to interact and negotiate with, the perceived opponents, the policy makers and decision makers. Adopting a dialogical approach is essential to making small achievements in phases. One has to address and tackle the counter arguments that might be posed by the opposite party. Those who may stand to lose if the campaign succeeds may launch counter campaigns to build pressure on the policy makers to refrain from changing the status quo. Mid-course corrections may have to be made in order to adopt a win-some and lose-some approach. However, the campaign leaders have to be very clear about the non-negotiable well in advance so as to have a stand.

(iv) Assessing progress

Every plan of action and implementation should have an inbuilt mechanism to assess progress made. This has to be an ongoing process and should fit into the next phase of implementation for necessary changes or course-corrections. Achievement of advocacy tasks and sub-goals have to be monitored, the satisfaction of individual clients has collected in case of micro-level practice; or the impact of media coverage and expressions of public support or dissatisfaction gauged in case of macro-level advocacy work. Baseline data and data indicating progress of work and achievements made have to be maintained. This has to be an on-going process so that changes in strategies and advocacy actions could be made to make the process more effective. In case of policy advocacy practice, it has often been experienced that the situation can change for social, political or economic reasons. The ability to respond quickly and flexibly, to spot windows of opportunity, and to anticipate new challenges requires a constant review of the policy context and of broader trends.

Phase-5: Termination and Evaluation

On achievement of the advocacy goals and desired outcomes the advocacy work reaches a point that has to be terminated and preparations to work with other clients or client populations has to be initiated. But before winding up, necessary evaluation of the services provided to client(s) or the campaign undertaken has to be evaluated. Feedback from all stakeholders and participants in the advocacy campaign has to be collected. Questions that could be posed to oneself are:

- What did the advocacy effort or advocacy campaign accomplish?
- Were the right targets chosen for effecting change?
- What were the unexpected hurdles in the change process and in accomplishing the goals? How can these hurdles be removed in future?
- What were the unexpected successes? How can one learn from these surprises?

Other activities that could be included as part of the termination process are:

- Thank all partners, volunteers, policy makers, and others who contributed to the change effort.
- Recognizing success and the contribution of particular volunteers or agencies.
- Explore one's own efforts and that of the organisation one represents.
- Media publicity to highlight the achievements of advocacy campaign.
- Reporting of the findings and achievements for record purpose and also for to submit the same to various partners in the coalition and related ministry/department if required, and
- Reviewing one's accomplishments within the organisation and

following it up to carry forward changes in implementation in the next cycle of advocacy work in case of another client(s).

Conclusion

Advocacy as a contemporary method of social work, has great potentiality in strengthening social work interventions. Advocacy has various dimensions, phases, models, levels and forms of intervention. Conceptually, advocacy fits into a range of activities that include organizing, lobbying and campaigning for social welfare and justice, the ultimate goal of social work. The method of advocacy will enable social workers in their action for the most disadvantaged, marginalised, downtrodden and weaker sections in claiming their rights.

REFERENCES

1. Bob, C. (2010). The market for human rights. In Prakash, A., and Gugerty, M. K. (2010). *Advocacy Organizations and Collective Action*. Cambridge: Cambridge University Press.
2. Sabatier, Paul (1988). An advocacy coalition framework of policy change and the role of policy-oriented learning therein. *Policy Sciences* 21:129—168 (1988). Dordrecht: Kluwer Academic Publishers.
3. Mazmanian, Daniel and Sabatier, Paul (1983). *Implementation and Public Policy*. Chicago: Scott Foresman.
4. Winkleby, M., Feighery, E., Altman, D., Kole, S., and Tencati, E. (2001). Engaging ethnically diverse teens in a substance use prevention advocacy programme. *American Journal of Health Promotion*, 15 (6), 433 ± 436.
5. Solomon, C. (1982). Special issue on political action: Introduction. *Personnel and Guidance Journal*, 60(10), 580.
6. Wroe, L. (2012). *A Study of Refugee Advocacy: Paradoxes of Helping in a Climate of Hostility.* Unpublished PhD thesis, University of Manchester. In Mayo, M., Mendiwelso-Bendek, Z., and Packham, C. (2013). *Community research for community development*. Hampshire: Palgrave Macmillan.
7. Rainbird, S. (2012) Asylum Seeker 'Vulnerability': The Official Explanation of Service Providers and the Emotive Responses of Asylum Seekers. *Community Development Journal* 47, 3.
8. Keck, Margaret, and Kathryn Sikkink. 1998. *Activists Beyond Borders – Advocacy Networks in International Politics*. Ithaca and London: Cornell University Press.

4

Advocacy and its Relation to Other Methods of Social Work

Asutosh Pradhan

Generalist social work practice calls for an integration of various methods and approaches of social work. It is believed that whatever be the nature of the problem the various social work methods either singly or in combination can be used simultaneously or as and when the situation demands during various phases of the social work process. Developing a basic understanding among social work trainees and practitioners in the application of various methods at appropriate stages of the social work process is critical to the effectiveness of the social work profession.

This chapter makes an attempt to draw a relationship between Advocacy Work and the various other methods including the contemporary methods propounded in this volume. Advocacy work as a social work method is to be used when the rights of individuals, families, groups and communities are at stake. People who are facing injustice, exploitation, harassment, neglect or ill-treatment have a right to lead a life of dignity or worth which is the core vale in social work. In many cases, age old social and cultural norms and practices hinder individuals and social groups to be deprived of basic rights and privileges. Advocacy work in combination with other methods is believed to empower the powerless and give people a voice.

The Selective use of Social Work Methods

Social work methods are used at various levels and with different categories of clients – individuals, families, groups, community and larger population groups, especially helping them meet unfulfilled needs and address difficulties and problems faced in day to day life. These methods of social work often gain momentum when the client or clientele group approaches any social work professional for help or on occasions, when social workers initiate *suo motto* action in the case of clients who are identified as vulnerable and are not aware of the nature of help and assistance social workers could provide. The focus of intervention with the use of particular social work method – either singly or in combination, depends upon the pre-existing social, cultural and political environment of a particular nation or region or nascent client population. The nature of problems as found in the more developed western countries is more psycho-pathological and as a result of individualistic and atomistic living; this requires a focus on the use of Social Case Work and Social Group Work methods. Relatively poorer nations which have large sections of poor people and are relatively less developed, with its people having low incomes and scarce resource base are more dependent on state run institutions and state sponsored schemes and programmes for meeting citizens' need and addressing common problems. In such situations where the overall GDP of the country is not conducive to meet the needs of teaming millions, non-state actors come up with interventions that stress more on community-based and community-initiated strategies that call for the use of Community Organisation or Social Action as a social work method.

Social Casework and Advocacy

Social casework is a method of helping an individual or individuals through a one-to-one relationship. When individuals are faced with problems in social functioning and are not able to solve their own problem, may need the assistance of a professional social worker. Case Work comprises of activities in a wide variety of settings, aimed at assisting individuals, couples, or families to cope more effectively with problems that impair social functioning. Clients among whom social case work as a method is used are the ones who may have unmet needs; lack confidence and self-belief; be of tender age or children in difficult circumstances or suffer from various handicaps, and may lack the capability to overcome their handicap; suffer from social stigma, trauma and Post-Traumatic Stress Disorder (PTSD) be faced with exploitation and harassment; be in conflict with law; and lack access to basic services and entitlements.

The focus of social case work during the 20th century was limited to psycho-therapeutic interventions with the purpose of changing the individual and not structural issues that were the causes for the persistence of these problems and issues faced by the clients. Advocacy work while working with individuals and families (in the casework context) from a rights perspective is increasingly being used to claim the entitlements of the individual/client or protect the client from oppression, harassment and subjugation. In the new millennium, professional caseworkers have expanded their role as advocates for social justice and locating problems of clients from an eco-systems perspective in the structural inequities existing in society. Traditionally speaking, caseworkers have been working as counselors in varying problem contexts. Jacobs, Batchetler and Sauceda (2008) suggest that there is a need for a philosophical shift and role reconciliation in caseworkers to bridge the gulf between the-counselor-as-healer-scientist and the counselor-as-social-change-agent ideologies. Hence, the focus has increasingly shifted from changing the individual to changing the larger systems and institutional arrangements that are the main reasons for the occurrence of the problems and their persistence.

The clinical social worker is well versed in "structural inequities inherent in a capitalist society and the role of culture and belief systems in perpetuating inequality" (Cornell, 2006, p. 54). Clinical work focuses on the environment and "educating clients and empowering them to change the structure that contribute to their oppression rather than helping them to adapt to the *status quo*" (Cornell, 2006, p.64).

Social Group Work and Advocacy

Social Group Work is a method of social work that attempts to solve the problems faced by individual clients through groups. The underlying assumption is that the group provides a forum to each individual member to interact, share, understand oneself in relation to others more closely, assess personal strengths and weaknesses, develop belief in the strength in mutual help, develop close bonding, plan and act together for achieving shared goals and much more. The social worker is responsible to facilitate this process of group formation and making the group act to achieve the shared goals; guides their interaction in programme activities and help the group as a whole experience growth opportunity in accordance with their needs. In this process social group work helps each individual in the group enhance their social functioning through purposeful group experience and cope more effectively with their problems. The power of the group to influence individual minds has been aptly said by Tocqueville (1982) – "...human mind is developed only by the reciprocal influence of men (and women) one upon another". Meeting the need to belong and using mutual aid for empowerment are still the raisons d'être for the use of groups in social work practice.

As part of social group work one of the types of groups that social workers are expected to form and work with are advocacy groups. Advocacy groups in the context of advocacy work are such groups that are formed of individuals who might have been the target of human rights violations, discrimination, stigma and exclusion – be it by the state, state agencies, social institutions, social groups or families. Advocacy work with such groups focuses on building awareness of rights and entitlements, legal recourses available and the processes involved in seeking justice, representing before appropriate authorities seeking redressal of their grievances, etc. The purpose of advocacy work through group work is to orient the group to recognise injustices, violations of human rights, and barriers to seeking justice. It thus engages the group in the practice of human rights and social justice to promote social well-being among people faced with similar distressful life situations. Advocacy work with groups focus on the systemic and ecological aspects related to the problems they face and those that work against the client's (group members) interests. This requires skills such as coalition building to enlarge the popular support-base, positioning, lobbying, testifying etc.

A distinction needs to be made as regards the possibility of contrasting advocacy groups that could be formed for undertaking advocacy work, which are referred to here as 'client advocacy group' and 'non-client advocacy group'. 'Client advocacy group' are formed of those members who have a common need or problem; while 'non-client advocacy group' comprises of such individuals who have an interest on a particular social issue or concern and come together with the aim to promote social justice and human rights of vulnerable sections of society. 'Advocacy work' needs to reach out to, or promote these two forms of advocacy groups. Advocacy work in fact need to focus also in bridging the link between the client and non-client advocacy groups so that the expertise often available with 'non-client advocacy groups' could be utilised to give direction and teeth to the campaigns undertaken by the 'client advocacy groups'. The 'non-client advocacy groups' in-turn get an opportunity to ground and contextualise their work at the grassroots and help benefit local people and communities in a more realistic manner. The professional social worker in such a case would be that of playing a 'system-linkage role'.

'Client advocacy groups' and organisations also exist to work for their membership. They will often intervene to help their members cope with uncooperative systems. Organizational pressures of this type depend on the existence and availability of such supportive associations. Examples of work of 'non-client advocacy groups' are often found in the form of 'environmental advocacy groups' that have a critical role to play in shaping public perceptions of different potential approaches for solving environmental problems.

Community Organisation and Advocacy

Murray G. Ross (1955) in the classic titled "Community Organization. Theory and Principles" laid emphasis on the need for the community as a whole and its individual members to be united in spirit, possessing cooperative and collaborative attitudes, identification with the community. If all take interest and participate in the affairs of the community, share common values and goals, develop responsibility for the condition and status of the community etc. The focus of community organisation as a method proposed by Ross was more on organizing the members of the community, planning for change, acting together to solve the common problems faced by the community as a whole and achieve the shared goals.

Contrary to the view of Ross, Rinku Sen (2003) argues that "community organizing should now move into practices that support the emergence of new social movements with the potential to win large-scale progressive change". This is where the essence of 'advocacy work' lies, in the context of working with communities. The earliest view of community organisation as a primary method in social work focussed more on how the community could solve its common problems within the community itself, by involving members of the community in cooperative and collaborative work.

'Advocacy work' with communities and their common needs, issues and problems, changes the focus and target of social work intervention from within the community to outside the community. The centre of focus needs to shift now from within the community to without. Since modern societies have empowered the state in the governance of the citizens, the hold of the state has become more pronounced. This is where issues of governance and ineffective implementation or administration of policies, legislations, programmes and services have been adversely affecting the common man. It is therefore imperative that the focus of community work too, should be the integration of 'advocacy work' during social work intervention process, so that factors that are external to the community and influence the social development of the community could be managed and effectively redressed. 'Advocacy work' related to development of any community, whether rural, tribal or urban, involves representing before the concerned authorities regarding the unmet needs of the community, non-implementation of development programmes or flaws therein, etc. Corrupt practices that affect the quality of services provided, or quality of infrastructure created like the Integrated Child Development Services (ICDS) and mid-day meal programme in schools in India, health services provided by the hospital or Primary Health Centers (PHC), educational services and school infrastructure, roads, water supply, electricity etc. could be dealt with more effectively if the community is organized by the professional social worker to fight against corrupt or insensitive measures. This is how 'advocacy work' helps the community to claim its due share of entitlements and fulfill community needs etc. especially in Indian rural settings. The Right to Information Act (RTI) in India has been a boon to the general public to seek information from the government and public agencies; plan and strategize their 'advocacy work' so that governance systems become more accountable to the general public.

Social Action and Advocacy

The initial focus of social work profession till the 1930s and 1940s was the therapeutic paradigm. Margot Breton (2006) is of the view that "the therapeutic paradigm was designed to address personal problems (relationship or mental health problems, for example) not social justice problems". However, the 1950s saw the emergence of a new paradigm in social work practice that was committed to establishing social justice through social action. This resulted in the evolution of all other traditional social work methods that emphasize client advocacy perspective.

History is witness to a number of social movements, small and large-scale that were initiated by people and groups who were directly affected by issues and forces that were oppressive, discriminatory, exploitative etc. However, not always do people who are faced with such problems and issues can fight for their rights and seek justice. Such category of clients are child labourers; bonded labourers; trafficked girls and women; sexually abused children, girls and women; prisoners and offenders facing trial and living in deplorable conditions; refugees; mentally ill and mentally challenged; the poor; tribals; victims of involuntary displacement; and the like. Many of these problems are a result of structural inequalities and disparities existing in society, or the prevalence of exclusionary forces that persist in society. Advocacy work – as a method of social work – in dealing with such issues, focuses on advocating policy changes or the formulation of new policy, legislations and programmes. Professional social workers using advocacy work can effect changes in governance of welfare institutions and delivery systems. However, as is the experience of advocacy groups, it is very difficult to organize disempowered and fragmented groups.

Social Action as a method is more appropriate where the issues faced by communities are on a relatively larger scale than that faced by a single community. The development and establishment of Social Action as a pure new form of social work method, having a clear domain has been quite fluid. It has dilly-dallied between outcome-based approach to problem resolution at the community level, and as an unending or sustaining process-focused method. The later in particular, is considered to be an ongoing process with shifting goals and objectives, based on the premise that problems and issues of the community change over time, and require constant realignment in strategies and leveraging.

There are other contexts and socio-cultural and political environs where populations are deemed to be in vulnerable situations, and the client population are facing human rights violations. Innumerable social workers are active in additional ways, affecting social policy by being active in coalitions, interest groups, and agencies, and by acting independently to challenge injustice and to work for social justice. In such cases, social action as a method of social work is used to mobilize masses in order to bring about structural changes in the social system or to prevent adverse changes.

Several movements were started at the behest of advocacy groups referred to as 'external agents of change'. Members of such advocacy groups who would fight for the cause of others are often represented by the elite and intellectual class, lawyers, political leaders, etc. Advocacy done by external agents has the inherent danger to muffle the voices of the actual clients. It has been seen in several cases that the advocates retain the power to decide those issues and perspectives that are legitimate and those that are not. The clients may tend to be used as mere local "informants" and not equal "participants". Care needs to be taken to include those who are directly impacted by the issues that the group is fighting to change. A core aspect of organizing is providing opportunities for people affected by injustice and inequality to acquire the skills to fight for themselves and to build their own power.

Social Work Administration and Advocacy

Social Work Administration typically refers to the conceiving, planning, developing, mobilizing, organizing, coordinating, and delivering of human services. Social work administration is different from public administration or other forms of delivery of social services in the sense that while conceiving or delivering these services to the people who need them, it uses the basic values and principles of the social work profession; the specific principles of social casework, social group work, community organisation, and social action; and the ethical codes of professional social work. The delivery of services – whether universal services or targeted services – are aimed at building the capacities of the people. It also involves the application of rational problem-solving techniques and evidence-based methodologies to conceiving, developing, coordinating, and delivering human services. Social planning is a process used to involve people at the grassroots levels, in the identification of needs and voicing the concerns that affect them, and including these in the projects and programmes to be developed. This at times is promoted or advocated by the non-governmental organisations working in the locality, or at the state/national level. Planning can be carried out locally, regionally, nationally, or internationally, and addresses such problems as poverty, child and family welfare, aging, housing, crime, delinquency, mental health, and so forth. At the village level in particular, social work administration needs to be concerned with activating the Gram Sabha and ensuring the active involvement of people in discussion of issues and concerns that impact them and make the government machinery function in a more effective and accountable manner, in meeting the needs of the village and individual recipients of services.

Advocacy work as a social work method in relation to social work administration would therefore be concerned with making potential services users aware of their rights to basic and quality service, training them in making a proper assessment of the services provided by the government machinery; building their ability to monitor the implementation of various government programmes; raising issues of quality and ineffective service delivery with the concerned authorities; highlight the specific needs and concerns of vulnerable social groups and populations like the dalits, tribals, handicapped, homeless, slum populations in urban areas, concerns of children, the elderly and offenders living in welfare and care institutions; raising issues of regional imbalances in development at the macro or national level and much more. In the domain of International or Transnational Social Work practice, "Advocacy Work" when inter-twined with social work administration would refer to working for the fulfillment of the rights of such clients who are refugees, migrants, persons trafficked for the sex trade or for forced labour, people displaced or effected by civil war etc.

Social Work Research and Advocacy

Social work research in the context of 'Advocacy Work' is to challenge the obvious, that is, making the world and the 'client' or 'clientele group' see beyond what has been kept or remained hidden from society. Much of advocacy work depends on finding out the real life situations of clients and client populations and the oppressive factors or agencies – individuals, groups, social and political institutions, policies and programmes etc, that are responsible for the problem situation in which the clients are. With commitment to social change, longitudinal research and cohort studies in particular, can help understand how change is, or not, taking place in spite of the implementation of various developmental programmes that seek to transform the conditions of life of large sections of people. Social work research would help in identifying the structural and functional deficiencies within social and public institutions, service delivery systems, justice dispensation mechanisms, and the like that deprive people of their rights and entitlements, especially of the vulnerable and oppressed.

An understanding of social work practice can be systematically explored by reflections on experiences, and the constant testing, challenging and reinterpretation of assumptions put in practice. On the other hand, the large data-sets like those compiled by the Census of India, National Sample Survey Organisation (NSSO), National Crime Records Bureau (NCRB), National Family Health Survey (NFHS) on demographic matters and specific concerns like health, crime, domestic violence, etc. need to be analysed and understood from a macro perspective. This will help in locating forces and issues of systemic injustice and deprivations that may be hidden from the dominant development discourse and identify the nature of advocacy work to be undertaken. Qualitative research methods, case studies and narratives of the plight of individual clients who have faced long-term oppression, exploitation and deprivations would help in developing awareness and sensitivity among human service professionals to fight for justices among such clientele populations.

Research that focuses on peoples movements at the grassroots, advocacy work undertaken by individuals and citizen groups can add to the knowledge-base of social work and repertoire of 'advocacy work' as a method. Action research on 'advocacy work' undertaken can help in recording the successful processes involved in 'advocacy work' and in developing evidence-based practice solutions for replication in settings or problem situations that have similar concerns.

Awareness Campaign and Advocacy

The success of advocacy work depends, to a large extent, on the creation of public opinion in society on issues of injustice, oppression, deprivation, exploitation, harassment, corruption and the like. A few campaigns that have benefitted the public in general, and specific populations in particular, are worth mentioning. Awareness campaigns about the plight and ill-treatment of HIV patients has advocated for dealing with discrimination and stigma in hospital and institutional settings. Awareness campaigns regarding the ill-effects of smoking and *gutka* (processed tobacco) chewing have led to policy changes banning smoking in public places and the production and sale of *gutkka*. The scourge of domestic violence was highlighted by a spirited national and international campaign by feminist movements, human rights activists, non-governmental organisations, the media and others and set in motion the political and policy discourses in India that led to the enactment of the Protection of Women against Domestic Violence Act in 2005.

Media-oriented advocacy awareness campaigns involve multiple areas of work and strategies that include – preparing news releases and placing stories, commissioning photographs or a video, designing posters and other campaign materials; using email, text messaging and Web 2.0 technologies to assist in data gathering, coalition building and mobilization.

Strengths-based Method and Advocacy

A review of literature related to strengths-based social work practice reveals the fact that till the 1980's, social work education and practice had an overdose of psychosocial approaches based on individual, family, and community pathology, deficits, problems, abnormality, victimization, and disorder. Critics of psychosocial approaches in social work assessment and intervention contributed to the evolution of a more strengths-based view of social work practice. Dennis Saleebey (1996) a strong votary of the strengths-perspective is of the view that the 'problem-centred approach' in social work though is important, it has failed to build upon the possible strengths that lie inherent in people and their institutions. Trying to maintain a balance between the two he very succinctly goes on to say that "it is as wrong to deny the possible (a belief that things can change) as it is to deny the problem (a state of possible despair and hopelessness)". Strengths-based method in social work should thus use peoples' personal strengths to aid in recovery and empowerment; it is about reframing personal perception to search for hope even in the worst situations. Saleebey (2010) goes further to say that the professional social worker facilitates the client in the discovery and embellishment, exploration, and use of his/her/their strengths and resources in the process of helping them achieve their goals and realize their dreams. Rapp (2006) is of the belief that clients are most successful at achieving their goals when they identify and utilize their strengths, abilities, and assets. Pointing out strengths and conveying respect is the concern of professional social workers. The strengths-based method of social work equips clients in countering common presumptions that clients who were faced with persistent challenges, multi-stressed, economically distressed, vulnerable and at-risk, etc. Black (2003) says that while working with clients, "almost anything can be considered a strength under certain circumstances," such as personal qualities and traits (e.g., sense of humour, ability to write, and compassion) and lessons they have learned from the journey of life. The strengths-based method affirms and builds on resources and potential available at the disposal of the client and the client system, as also in the environment, to overcome barriers and thrive in the face of adversity and multi-systemic failures. It is to reiterate that such resources could be available at various levels – micro, mezzo and macro.

While relating "advocacy work" and "strengths-based method" the focus of intervention is more in the mobilisation of resources for the vulnerable and the needy. The strength in social networks, also referred to as social capital, could be used to build pressure on service delivery systems in providing timely and quality services to the clients. Making people realise the strength in 'social networks' and preparing the client(s) for 'self-advocacy' is at the heart of 'advocacy work' as a method of social work. Being with the client through the process of advocacy work to continually boost the confidence and morale of client(s), facilitating the shared goals, strategising and lobbying for the fulfilment of entitlements and protection of human rights is at the core of advocacy work that seeks to capitalise on the strengths of clients. Strengthening the resolve of individuals, groups and communities to fight for their rights so as to make government and welfare systems more transparent, responsible and accountable is the combined or integrated approach of both 'strengths-based' and 'advocacy work'. The end result would be the development of resilience in clients and the ability to recover or adapt successfully in adversity, and in the dismantling of barriers to needs fulfilment and seeking opportunities in one's environment that would promote success.

Networking and Advocacy

To make advocacy work effective and achieve the avowed goals and objectives, professional social workers have to work at various levels to network with individuals, groups, communities and masses. It would be worthwhile to introduce Woolcock's (1998; 2001) distinction of the various types of networks – bonding, bridging and linking networks. Social work practitioners are expected to be involved in networking of individuals at the community or local level, since this facilitates the development of strong bonds among the members of the network which further facilitates the sharing of ideas, goals and resources and helps in strategizing for effective action as a group against forces of oppression. Bonding is a social adhesive that promotes solidarity, trust and confidence. Bridging, creates the social adhesive that promotes inter-group connectedness and expanded configurations of trust. Bridging networks are essential in the case of issues and problems that cut across communities and diverse social groups. The targets of intervention often are corrupt and malfunctioning state agencies or adversaries which are stronger and distant. Linking is a yet broader concept of relationships based on institutional arrangements that promote the exchange of power, wealth and status among different social groups. Advocacy work, while working with different forms of networks, and at various levels involves informing network members about their rights and entitlements, making members conscious about the strengths and weakness of the adversaries; legal awareness; filing representations; developing strategies for joint action that may range from organizing rallies, *bandhs* or strikes, *gheraos*, sloganeering, picketing, etc.

Another classification indicates types of networks as horizontal and vertical networks. Horizontal networks comprise of individuals and groups at the local level who are living in a contiguous area and in similar living conditions and situations. In 'social capital' parlance these forms of networks are called 'bonding social capital' – in which a strong bond exists among members. To make advocacy work successful, development of strong bonds in people's networks is critical to challenge forces of oppression and exploitation. Existence of a strong bond in the network will help to sustain advocacy work, undertaken against a common adversary who would always be looking for ways and means to break the unity among the group. Such horizontal networks and 'bonding social capital' are essential to act as pressure groups at the local level, to avail of adequate and quality services provisioned by the state, particularly in the context of delivery of social and welfare services through various government programmes. 'Bridging social capital', as the metaphor suggests, is essentially horizontal, that is, connecting people with more or less equal social standing. The purpose is to utilize the strength embedded in larger number of people, creating a mass base which in turn gives legitimacy to the movement. 'Linking social capital' is more vertical – referring to 'vertical networks', that connects people to key political resources, social activists, NGOs working in the field of advocacy, transnational organisations, etc. Such advocacy networks are key to influence policy and legislative issues that influence large sections of society and socially excluded groups. Professional social workers' ability to use modern communication tools like the internet, print and visual media, and social media among others would help in setting agenda and giving visibility to issues on a larger scale.

Public Interest Litigation (PIL) and Advocacy

A major channel or method of providing help and direct justice to groups, communities and society as a whole facing economic exploitation (labourers not being paid minimum wages); torture and harassment of scheduled castes, scheduled tribes, and economically backward classes; atrocities on women and children; illegal confinement; or problems like environmental pollution, degradation of natural wealth; food adulteration etc. is the filing of PIL against the culprits who have committed the offence. It is often found that vulnerable people have been the target of various forms of exploitation. When such social ills are found to be wide-spread, it is the responsibility of the general public and literate or conscious people in general, to advocate for the protection of rights of such vulnerable sections. PIL is a legal tool that could be used in such situations. PIL is an ideal form of 'Indirect Social Work Practice' that could provide justice to clients in large measure. PIL is a method for seeking justice and providing relief to clients through the courts. Though PIL does not involve much of 'direct social work practice', the professional however has to meet and understand the conditions in which the oppressed people are, investigate the nature of problems faced. Regarding the human rights violations, they can collect evidence, prepare cases and clients who would testify in the court, run a signature campaign to mobilize support for the cause, participate in debates and discussions in the media to highlight such issues to ensure public support and generate public opinion, consult law professionals particularly those who are in the business of 'cause advocacy'. PIL as a form of advocacy work would help benefit people at large. It may even point out flaws in the justice dispensation system or the administrative mechanisms that are mandated to provide services to people.

Resource Mobilization and Advocacy

Resource mobilization is an essential method in social work that brings to life a whole range of intervention initiatives and programmes. A key function of social work is to make provision for social services and social welfare services to people in general, and specific sections in particular. Social work professionals often work in and through agencies which design programmes for intervention and change, keeping in view the needs and desires of the clientele population served – individual, families, groups, or communities. Resources needed for different sets of clients, or in the context of a particular problem, may be either tangible or intangible. Tangible resources could be in the form of cash or kind, while example of intangible resources could be counselling, physical assistance, care and attention as well as giving time. When resources are scarce and the client population to be served are in large number, 'advocacy work' would involve advocating for, and representing the cases and conditions of resource-starved clients before such agencies, both government run and NGOs, at the local, district, state, national and international levels. Designing of projects and programmes with intent to provide for various types of needs and services to the clientele population to be served and for which funding could be mobilized from national and international funding agencies is a critical area of cause-advocacy work. This would also help supplement the intervention efforts of the government.

Conclusion

Advocacy is fundamentally linked to all other methods of social work as it is a powerful method to intervene when the rights of individuals, families, groups and communities are at stake. The incorporation and knowledge of advocacy method will provide a new dimension to the practice of social work in the present day context where the rights and justice of thousands are neglected and deprived due to various issues and concerns. Advocacy helps the professional social workers in their intervention for human rights and social justice and to promote social well-being and welfare among the clients with distressful life situations.

REFERENCES

1. Jacobs S.C., Batchetler, A. and Sauceda, E. (2008). Community-Based Action Research in Leong, F. T. L. (2008). *Encyclopedia of Counseling*. Los Angeles, Calif: SAGE Publications.

2. Ross, M. G. (1955). *Community Organization. Theory and Principles*. Harper & Bros: New York.
3. Sen, R. (2003). *Stir it up: Lessons in community organizing and advocacy*. San Francisco: Jossey-Bass.
4. Breton, M. (2006). Path Dependence and the Place of Social Action in Social Work Practice. *Social Work with Groups, 29,* 4, 25-44.
5. Saleebey, D. (January 01, 1996). The strengths perspective in social work practice: extensions and cautions. *Social Work, 41,* 3, 296-305.
6. Rapp, R. C. (2006). Strengths-based case management: Enhancing treatment for persons with substance abuse problems. In D. Saleebey (Ed.), *The Strengths Perspective in Social Work Practice* (4th ed., pp. 128-147). Boston: Pearson Education, Inc.
7. Black, C. J. (2003). Translating principles into practice: Implementing the feminist and strengths perspectives in work with battered women. *AFFILIA*, 18 (3), 332–349.
8. Woolcock, M. (1998). Social Capital and Economic Development, Towards a Theoretical Synthesis and Policy Framework. *Theory and Society,* 27:151- 208.
9. Woolcock, M. (2001). The Place of Social Capital in Understanding Social and Economic Outcomes. *Canadian Journal of Policy Research,* 2 (1): 66-88.

5

Awareness Campaign

Archana Kaushik

Awareness-raising is a process that provides opportunities for information gathering in order to improve understanding and develop competencies and skills necessary to enable changes in social attitude and behaviour of people in a given community or society. Awareness campaign is being extensively used as a method of social work by several practitioners over a period of time. Sayers (2006) maintain that to raise awareness of something – good, bad or indifferent – is to promote its visibility and credibility within a community or society. It is also to inform and educate people about a topic or issue with the intention of influencing their attitudes, behaviours and beliefs towards the achievement of a defined purpose or goal. It is a constructive and catalytic force intending to bring positive change in the behaviour and actions of the target people. The target people can be individuals, families, groups, organisations, and communities.

Awareness Campaign and Awareness Raising

While awareness-raising is increasing the level of knowledge or information among the target people on a particular issue, awareness campaign is a method that is directed to create/enhance awareness among comparatively larger audience. It is promoting an idea/attitude/behaviour/action for a social cause by social workers and social activists. Awareness campaigns are often the first step to introduce the audience to new services, programmes, facilities or actions. It is aimed at building familiarity to a desirable behaviour, say, promoting immunization or improving public health. Thus, the purpose of awareness-raising is to inform a community's attitudes, behaviours and beliefs with the intention of influencing them positively in the achievement of a defined purpose or goal (Sayers, 2006).

Raising awareness is not the same as telling the public what to do – it is explaining issues and disseminating knowledge to people so that they can make their own decisions. However, providing information and creating awareness about an issue does not automatically lead to behavioural change. Attitudinal and behavioural changes are highly complex and complicated process, which requires understanding of human behaviour and then meticulously chalking out steps to bring about the desired change in the behaviour of the people. For this, people must be encouraged to move through successive stages to reach the point where new behaviour can be adapted and maintained. Social work professionals have been involved in this process by addressing crucial issues for several decades now.

There are different ways to raise public awareness. Awareness campaigns can be manifested through specific planned events, poster campaigns, websites, documentaries, newspaper articles, face book, twitter, audio-visual advertisements, radio and TV programmes. Strategies of awareness campaigns are carefully chosen keeping in view the socio-demographic profile of the target group and cultural and political context of the area by the social workers. Mass media has a crucial role in promoting awareness campaigns. While, traditionally information passed on in one to one setting was limited or restricted (say, doctor to patient), with the advent of mass media the reach and scope of awareness campaigns have expanded many folds. Even the 'limited reach' of print media such as brochures, pamphlets, posters and newspapers have given way to electronic media driven strategies such as television, video-conferencing, web conferencing, you-tube, blog-spots, web-circulation and SMS. In fact, due to these awareness-campaigns, media have become a vehicle for awareness campaign aimed at advocacy for social, political and legislative changes in society. The movements we are witnessing with regard to the 'Narmada Bachao Andolan' of Medha Patkar as well as 'Lokpal Act' spearheaded by Anna Hazare are examples of the impact that advancement in media technology has on such initiatives.

Awareness Campaign as a Method of Social Work in Indian Context

We may have witnessed many awareness-campaigns in the recent years including Polio eradication - a dreaded disease, which was recently eliminated from India, thanks to the concerted and rigorous efforts of the government through launching of campaign strategies like 'Do-Boond-Zindagi-key', polio-ravivar (Sunday). In 1999, the super-cyclone in Odisha caused death of more than ten-thousand people. In 2013, the Phailin cyclone in the same area with almost the same intensity could not claim much lives, and the credit goes to awareness-campaign. "A fully aware, well informed and properly trained population is the best guarantee of safety and of successful response to any disaster." If one could reach out to communities before disasters and inform them of what to do 'just in case', impacts could be reduced dramatically. Whether, it is disaster management or public-health [universalizing immunization, reducing IMR, MMR], education [enrollment drive, girl-child education] or electoral reforms, awareness-campaigns have provided critical first-step in influencing behaviour and affecting lasting social change. Several social work professionals working with the government as well as with NGOs were instrumental in reaching out to the masses through awareness campaign method of addressing such issues. There is a strong, rather inseparable link between social work and awareness-campaign.

Salient Features of Awareness Campaign Method

Goal-similarity: Awareness-raising is one of the pillars on which public participation can be built. Moreover it is the basis for taking the right choices and the appropriate decisions. The goal of public awareness, by disseminating information and education, is to develop knowledge, understanding and skills to behave and act for the protection of natural and cultural environments and promote sustainable development. Access to and effective use of essential information plays a significant role in reducing the inequities within and among countries and societies. Public awareness is viewed by many policy-makers and educators as critical to the creation of an equitable global 'Information Society' in which both developed and developing nations can share in social and economic development (Sayers, 2006). Social work profession also aims to ensure complete health, wellbeing and empowerment of all sections of society, thereby working for an egalitarian and just society. This reflects common goals of awareness-campaigns and social work. In fact, awareness-campaign is a means to achieve the aims and objectives of social work interventions. Awareness campaign initiatives by professional social workers gain special momentum because social workers follow certain ethics, values, and principles which uphold human dignity.

The purpose of the awareness campaign should be clearly spelt out and that should guide and inform the content of the message. It is important to ensure that the central message is not side tracked or compromised while paying more attention to other aspects like presentation style or channels of communication. While initiating any plan of action using any of the methods of social work including awareness campaign, one should have clarity regarding the goal and the issues being addressed.

Scope: The scope of social work is omnipresent and in that of awareness-campaign. Social work interventions are at – preventive, curative, ameliorative, rehabilitative, promotive and management levels. And awareness-campaigns, too, are directed for preventing certain harmful behaviours, promoting healthy practices, curbing negative acts and managing activities for harm-reduction. Social work interventions and awareness campaigns are commonly witnessed in the areas of health and hygiene, education and skill-development, safety and security, disaster-management, dealing with abuse, inequality, exploitation and marginalization. Both, social work and awareness-campaigns aim at bringing desirable and positive change in the attitudes and behaviours of the targeted individuals, groups and communities. Awareness campaigns by social workers are expected to yield better results since a social worker is expected to be a friend, philosopher and guide to the client.

Systematic and Scientific: Social work methods including awareness-campaign have well-defined stages, steps and systematic manner of carrying out the tasks and functions. They rely on designing need-based and target-specific, culturally sensitive interventions that begin with fact-finding, problem-diagnosis or situational analysis in a scientific manner. Planning, execution, monitoring and evaluation/feedback are the components of awareness-campaigns and other methods of social work. Every method of social work follows certain prescribed steps, principles and modalities of operation. Awareness campaigns when initiated by the professionals follow similar strategies which promote positive outcome.

Theoretical Base: All the social work methods including awareness-campaign are guided by a set of specific theoretical frameworks from the behavioural sciences. Health belief model, theory of reasoned action, social cognitive theory, social learning theory, diffusion of innovation, theory of gender and power, empowerment and ecological framework are some of the theoretical underpinnings that direct awareness-campaigns. They are widely and frequently used by social work professionals while getting involved in awareness campaign.

Skill Base: Observation, analysis, problem-identification, planning, organizing, networking, coordinating, motivating, training, resource-mobilizing, communicating, team-building, leading, persuading, research and documentation and budgeting, are some of the many skills that professionals social workers exhibit in awareness-campaign. While learning and practicing various methods of social work, one is facilitated to acquire these skills and imbibe the much needed social work values.

Values and Principles: Equality and social justice are the value-base of social work and awareness campaigns. Social work methods adhere to 'client's self-determination' after providing choices and alternatives to the target-audience. Professional social work and its methods are guided by same sets of values and principles. Thus, it may be inferred that awareness-campaign is one of the methods of social work well-ingrained into the social work profession, which needs to be recognized. Awareness campaign method also takes into account the values of social work such as hard work, teacher ship, cultural sensitivity, integrity, importance of human relationship, dignity and worth of the person as well as loyalty to the profession.

Positive Influence: It is strongly intended that awareness-campaigns in social work are meant to influence the target community in a positive manner guided by the perspective of equality, social justice and empowerment of weaker sections of the society. Every effort of a professional is focused on positive outcome which is the mission of social work.

Equitable and Sustainable Change: Awareness campaigns aim to bring about developmental change. They do not merely provide information; rather aspire to achieve lasting attitudinal and behavioural changes. With theoretical understanding of human behaviour and approaches to awareness-raising, it is possible to create positive, equitable and sustainable change. The very object of social work intervention is for change and the professional is a change agent. Sustainable change towards better living conditions for human beings is the focus of social work.

Policy-change: One of the crucial objectives of awareness-campaign is to bring about positive change in the policy initiatives pertaining to the issues being addressed. It is a vehicle of legislative and policy change, which, in turn, result in the desired behavioural change among the public. Social workers are social doctors who are capable of prescribing required perspectives for change in social policies based on the changing social scenario, cultural sensitivity of the people and level of understanding and preparedness for change by the target community.

Cultural Sensitivity: Cultural contours are often overlooked in awareness-campaigns, yet they are of vital importance. Appraising cultural-context helps the professional in learning about the target-group's social hierarchy, life-style, preferences, economic-issues and in understanding the reasons for the choices they make. It aids in gaining insight into reaching out to them and motivating them into action, thereby, making the message more effective. Cultural sensitivity is one of the values of social work. For the success of every intervention by a professional with individuals, groups, and communities, cultural sensitivity has a unique role and a social worker is trained to be aware of it. Against this backdrop, following sub-points are important:

a) *Age*: Differential communication skills and awareness-campaign strategies are required for various age groups such as children, adolescents, youth, women, differently abled and adults. We have seen that children, as target-groups, have later become the change-agents and carried forward the cause, be it hygiene and sanitation or prevention of child-sexual abuse. Likewise, adult teaching-learning principles are very different in terms of complexity of messages, formality, openness, rigidity and the like. In this contest principles of social work are also of great importance.
b) *Sex*: Sex is a crucial variable that influences the communication channels, strategies and presentation of information. Research studies have shown the differences in communication patterns and understanding of meanings by males and females.
c) *Group-identity*: Certain cultural norms adhere to strong group-conformity while others are more individualistic. Awareness-campaigns need to identify group-identity, if any, among the target-group so as to customize and make the message effective. Therefore the linkage between social group work and awareness campaign is of great importance.
d) *Religion, caste-class dynamics*: Socio-demographic variables like religion, caste and class, can impact the way an individual perceives message content. In addition, these factors could also have bearing on the images that are used in campaign such as photographs and other audio- visual materials. A professional social worker has the

expertise to sensibly and selectively use media tools keeping in view the target audience.

e) *Language*: Attention needs to be given to language used within and among communities and differences found in dialect and regional tone. Even the very carefully planned campaign can go in vein if it fails to address the lingual-cultural dynamics of the target community. One of the challenges that the professional social workers confront in India is the draught of print, audio, and video materials on social work in vernacular language while indigenously developed materials are scarce. Most students in India pursue their social work studies either in English or Hindi. Even the materials in Hindi are not adequate. The school of social work at IGNOU has developed materials in English and Hindi for both BSW and MSW. Similarly some video programmes are also made available in both English and Hindi. However, there is hardly any material available on social work in officially recognized 22 languages of India (as per the eighth schedule of the Constitution of India). This is certainly a challenge to professionals working at grassroots to learn as well as make interventions in vernacular. Most social workers in India can interact at least in two Indian languages while several also have the expertise in three or more languages. In an awareness campaign knowledge of local language and dialect is essential.

Special Audience: While planning awareness-raising campaigns, it is of great impotence that audiences with special needs are not overlooked. For instance, awareness-raising strategies while communicating a message to visually impaired people might include audio channel, so that the message can be heard rather than read. Alternatively, printed materials can be reproduced in Braille or recorded onto tapes or compact discs for later playback. Use of advanced technology in communication network is essential for social workers.

Migration: It is important to note the migration pattern in the region as well as the country, so as to gain adequate insight into the actual target audience and message content. For instance, the Gujarat State AIDS Control Society in collaboration with Orissa State AIDS Control Society developed communication material in Oriya language for Oriya-migrants working in cloth mills of Gujarat in north India. Professional social workers also require continuing education so that they are aware of the latest and fast changing social scenario in the country and act accordingly.

Credibility: The credibility of any campaign is vital to its success. Research shows that, higher the level of credibility, greater is the degree of positive influence and behavioural change. The speaker's credibility is highly significant in ensuring the success of the campaign. The professional social workers spearheading or guiding an awareness campaign should have credibility in terms of knowledge, acceptance, social work training etc. to name a few.

Need-base: To be effective, the awareness-campaign must meet the needs and interests of the target-group. One of the very important aspects of awareness campaign is the extent of dissatisfaction among the target group on the issue being addressed. If the target audience does not perceive the issues as a matter of concern and priority, then the support from the audience would be limited which will not provide positive results. This will in turn hamper all types of social work intervention by the same worker as well as the agency.

Multiple Approaches and Techniques: Though approaches and strategies are chosen on the basis of socio-demographic profile and cultural context of the target-audience, an effective awareness-raising campaign uses a mix of communication approaches and techniques (strategies) to ensure that their central messages are received and understood by diverse target audiences. However, the choice of approaches is guided by various considerations like the reach and coverage of awareness-raising campaign, simplicity or complexity of messages, availability of communication infrastructure and community preferences, to mention a few. The professional must be competent enough to use the various techniques and intervention strategies.

Resource-availability: One of the salient guiding principles of awareness-campaigns is the availability of resources – financial, material and human. Here the importance of the linkage to the method of resource mobilization and awareness campaign needs to be considered.

Recognize and Respect local Traditions: Awareness-campaigns that take into account traditional dance, song, theatre, puppetry, local innovations and utilize these in imagery or presentation, easily get credibility and success. At times, community does not trust or does not have access to new technology, such as blogspot. In such situation, relying on local channels of communication would be a judicious decision. The importance of value of cultural sensitivity needs to be noted.

Impact: It is usually more effective to design a coordinated, long-term awareness-campaign than creating large, short-term campaign. It is advisable to communicate a little at a time and aim for quality over quantity. For positive impact, a professional needs to plan and design a set of intervention beginning with addressing issues that have immediate and direct impact on the client system (individuals, group or community). This is essential to win over the confidence of the target audience and for the long term committed support.

Feedback: It is always useful to get a realistic feedback of the awareness-campaign. For this the worker must have continuous evaluation strategies so that corrective measures can be taken as and when required.

Communication Barriers: Communication barriers can be physical or environmental (for instance, hot/cold weather, noisy, congested-open space), cultural/language related or psychological ones but play crucial role in success or failure of the awareness-campaign. The professional must use the method of networking in order to have strong communication strategies in place. The worker's availability does not lie in personally getting down to doing things. The client system have the necessary strengths. Therefore the professional must depend on related methods including advocacy, networking, strengths based practice and resource mobilization.

Public Involvement: Every awareness-raising campaign requires adequate public involvement to be effective. Deciding how much of involvement and influence of the public is desirable or acceptable is a critical decision making point for campaign planners. For example, the cooperation of an influential community leader may be necessary to ensure the successful communication of message to a specific target-group. One of the methods that would help in assessing the extent of public involvement is social work research. A well planned research within the community will help in knowing the extent of public support the professional can expect from the target group. This will also ensure the extent of resource mobilization needed. Therefore linkage of awareness campaign method with other methods social work is of vital importance.

Information-overload: Due to data smog, multitude of messages is observed each day. It poses the difficulty in deciding which messages one should pay attention to, and what information is to be believed. Awareness-campaigns, thus, must aim to overcome public cynicism while competing with a range of other messages in order to be noticed. Part of the solution, is to develop a well-researched communication strategy that acknowledges the need and interests of the target-group and incorporates a mix of approaches and techniques. Social work research would be of great help in prioritizing the messages depending upon their relevance to the target audience.

Factors Affecting Awareness Campaign in Social Work

Let us examine some of the factors affecting awareness-campaigns in social work. These may be grouped into five broad categories.

1. *Personal Communication*: Though, seemingly a simple process of sending and receiving message (information), communication is highly complex and dynamic phenomenon of social life. The critical challenge is the cognitive dimension of communication that is related to interpreting the embedded message. Experiential learning, that is, learning by doing is the best way, but not practically possible in all awareness-campaigns. Therefore, while designing an awareness-campaign, it is essential to keep these communication dynamics in mind. One of the important tools of intervention by a social worker in using any of the twelve methods of social work being described in the book is the effective use of communication.

Personal communication is often the most effective means of selling a good idea, particularly if the sender of the message has recognized credibility.

Personal communication helps in making the audience feel more connected with the message of the campaign and understand the significance of that message in relation to their life. Examples of personal communication include:

- *Word of mouth*: A family visits is one of the most important activities that a social worker uses to convey by word of mouth. The friendly visitor concept of earlier social workers is relevant even today.
- *Community and stakeholder meetings*: Extension workers convincing the farmers about innovative techniques in agriculture or holding meetings with the parents and community leaders to convince them about the importance of educating a girl child are example.
- *Public forums, presentations and workshops*: Health and hygiene workshops conducted for community by NGOs and social workers are examples.
- *Social events*: Many NGOs and professional social workers working on HIV/AIDS awareness and prevention organize walkathon/ marathon on special occasions.
- *Folk media*: In certain societies, where oral traditions dominate, role-plays, story-telling, songs, dances, plays and poems on specific issues are presented in group-situations. For example, college students use street plays and theatre as media to create awareness about the need of elderly care at home.

2. *Mass-Media Communication*: Though personal communication is considered most effective means of raising awareness on issues in smaller groups and communities, it is not always the most efficient strategy for communicating a message to a wider community or target audience. For wide dissemination of information, mass-communication using mass-media is apt. This approach is manifested in awareness creation using printed materials [like billboards, brochures, cartoons, comics, pamphlets, posters, resource books, newspapers, magazines, etc.], audiovisual resources[such as pre-recorded cassettes, videos, CDs and DVDs], and electronic media[say, radio, television are popular media in creating awareness on social issues]. The Internet is the recent, the most powerful, and cost effective medium of creating awareness, say, through websites, email-discussions, web-logs (blogs) and RSS news feeds [or Really Simple Syndication is a method of summarizing the latest news and information from a website in a lightweight form that can be easily read online using news reader or news aggregator software. The aim of RSS is to give users the ability to quickly obtain the latest news and updates from a website in a headline or news digest format]. These are some of the relatively recent innovations but have the potential to greatly assist awareness-raising campaigns in regions and communities where the Internet is available. Also, mobiles are a ubiquitous media technology of the present age. SMS messages to mobile telephones and personal digital assistants (PDAs) have been gaining popularity as effective tools for spreading message including social issues. Participation of professionals in refresher programmes and

continuous education would help them to update themselves with such technological advancements and their usage.

3. *Education*: The UNESCO (2006) states, "Education plays a crucial role in raising awareness". In formal education, children at schools are taught topics like environment conservation, public health, disaster management, and the like as children are, reportedly, better capacitated to apply the knowledge they have learnt at school and inculcating awareness and sensitivity at young tender age is much easier than bringing changes in the crystallized personality of adults.

It may be reiterated that raising awareness on an issue, social cause does not necessarily bring lasting changes in attitudes/beliefs and behaviours. To achieve long-term benefits, awareness-campaigns should be designed in such a way so as to provide audiences with the skills and incentives to change their habits/behaviours. Education is an important factor in awareness-raising and can be quite effective if it addresses necessary changes in attitudes and corresponding behaviour. Two types of education are relevant to awareness-raising campaign namely, (1) formal education in which content and skills that are included in school curricula and taught in the context of local needs and issues, and (2) informal education through workshops, presentations and other co-curricular activities designed primarily to impart information and skills to adults.

Education is a means for creating awareness in situations such as training of trainers (ToTs), workshops, formal and informal educational programmes presented in local schools, colleges, adult learning centres and libraries, static and travelling exhibitions and displays. Social workers need to use education as one of the means for creating awareness depending upon the type of target audience.

4. *Public Relations* (PR): Public Relations or 'PR' is broadly related to the activities designed to establish and maintain the credibility as well as success of awareness-campaigns. The Chartered Institute of Public Relations in Britain describes PR as "the planned and sustained effort to establish and maintain goodwill and mutual understanding between an organization [involving in awareness-raising campaign] and its publics [audience and stakeholders]. Likewise, Bernays has defined PR as "the attempt by information, persuasion and adjustment to engineer public support for an activity, cause, movement or institution". It is managing flow of information between the organisation and the public. It ensures benefits to the public, who are the end users of services. The PR includes analysis of public perception, modifying/designing organisation's policy/programmes in consonance with public interest and then executing the programmes for communication with the public. PR is a factor which can greatly influence awareness campaign. In fact several agencies employ professional social workers as Public Relation Officers (PROs). The training and education of social workers makes them efficient PROs.

5. *Advocacy*: Advocacy and lobbying efforts are sometimes overlooked when planning awareness-campaigns but can be vital in ensuring ongoing support from governments and civil society organisations. Advocacy may be done at various levels – personal level (raising issues concerning daily life), family level (gender discrimination, age related issues like child abuse, elderly abuse; etc.), community level (any section of community not getting equitable share and discriminated against on account of ethnicity, religions, caste etc.), nation (influencing policy intervention, human rights, etc.) and International (issues related to world trade treaties, international loan, global warming, etc.).

Mainly three types of advocacy have been identified – Legislative, Bureaucracy and Judiciary advocacy. Legislative advocacy aims to influence the legislative process and recommend new legislations, amend legislations or raise voice against proposed and accepted ordinance or record dissent against implementation of legislations. Awareness-campaigns with bureaucracy-advocacy approach would target fighting against negative aspects of bureaucratic system and ensuring transparency and accountability such as creating awareness about using Right to Information Act. Judicial advocacy mainly aims at enforcing constitutional and legal rights and bringing desired change in the existing legations. Awareness about filing Public interest litigation (PIL) is an example. Awareness campaign has linkage with other methods of social work including advocacy, networking, resource mobilization, PIL as well as strengths based practice.

Models of Awareness Campaign

It is pertinent to examine three main models of awareness-campaign namely, Awareness-Raising, Behavioural Change communication and Social Marketing.

(i) Awareness-Raising

In this model, the central message of a campaign is communicated to a selected target audience using different approaches and techniques. A communication mix is necessary to ensure better receptivity of the message. There are four key components of an effective awareness raising campaign: Message (M); Audience (A); Strategy (S) and Timing (T).

During the early part of 1990s, the world was witnessing unabated spread of a deadly virus called HIV/AIDS which was perceived as a threat to humanity. Medical scientists were working round the clock to find preventive and curative medicine. Social activists, NGOs and world bodies like WHO as well as governments all over the world did not leave any stone unturned to address the issue. In fact no other disease received the kind of attention that HIV/AIDS received in human history. Even to this day awareness and education are seen as the only way to ensure prevention and control of HIV/AIDS while some kind of preventive medicine and counseling services are in place. In this contest several organizations, donor agencies and positive people's networks have been established all over the world.

The clear-cut message for all the agencies were one, namely, "Awareness and Education for prevention and control of HIV/AIDS". People from every walk of life affected- infants, children, youth and men and women of all age categories. In several countries, there were huge financial losses leading to breakdown of the economy. No one was spared because of one's educational or socio-economic status, profession, religion, sex, nationality, caste and class.

Therefore the audience was "the entire humanity spread across this planet called earth." Concerted efforts were made to educate and create awareness among every one using all types of strategies and sources available. World bodies such as the UNAIDS and National AIDS Control Organizations (NACO) and state AIDS control societies were setup. Separate budgetary allocations were made. Educational materials were prepared in every language and dialects, audio and video programmes were made, documentaries and films were made, scores of philanthropic organizations contributed in major ways towards the cause, every religious groups, educational establishments and social organizations joined the campaign along with print and audio-visual media. The strategy was loud and clear "to reach the unreached across the globe" through every known means of communication.

The first HIV/AIDS cases were detected in 1981 in the US and in India in 1986. By the early 1990s, it became an epidemic affecting particularly the poorest of the poor such as the sex workers and migratory population who kept visiting urban cities in search of jobs for their livelihood. Attention of the world community and the people who mattered namely, the planners, decision makers including the policy makers, policy implementers, the judiciary and the medical and social welfare agencies all came together to implement timely action. The timely intervention was the peak period of the spread of HIV/AIDS namely, the decade 1990s, and continues the same to this day.

Professional social workers and social work institutions across the globe came forward to do everything they could to prevent and control the spread of the HIV/AIDS. The efforts of the School of Social Work at IGNOU through various programmes of study from certificate to doctoral programmes and courses, seminars, conferences and a massive awareness campaigns through "HIV/AIDS prevention guide" within India and abroad, is very well known and recognized.

(ii) Behaviour Change Communication

Behaviour change communication (BCC) is bringing about desired change in the behaviour of people by using effective communication strategies. It is the strategic use of communication to bring positive changes in the health and living conditions of people. Neill McKee offers a comprehensive definition of BCC: "It is a research-based, consultative process of addressing knowledge, attitudes, and practices through identifying, analysing, and segmenting audiences and participants in programmes and by providing them with relevant information and motivation through well-defined strategies, using an appropriate mix of interpersonal, group and mass-media channels, including participatory methods".

Before the conception of BCC, Information Education Communication (IEC) was a popular strategy of development communication popularly used in awareness programmes including the strategies for prevention and control of HIV/AIDS. Let us differentiate the two terms. IEC is the development and application of communication strategies to promote positive behaviours among individuals and communities. On the other hand, BCC is more about identifying the barriers to behaviour change and overcoming the same. It is about understanding the communities, contexts, and environments in which behaviours occur which is one of the core aspects of professional social work. Evidences show that merely informing people which behaviour is appropriate and should be adopted, is not enough to bring about behaviour change. Therefore the sustained intervention by trained social workers is of great importance.

The trans-theoretical model of behaviour change proposed by James Prochaska is quite popular. According to Prochaska, individuals tend to follow a common linear process from initially not being conscious of their risk behaviours. From this, they can be influenced to change their behaviour as we have seen in the efforts which are on for the prevention and control of HIV/AIDS.

Stages of behaviour change, according to this model are:

- *Pre-contemplation*: It is the pre-awareness stage. Individuals are not often aware that their particular behaviours that are risky or unhealthy as in the case of HIV/AIDS.
- *Contemplation*: It is the stage of awareness that comes when information is provided and awareness is generated.
- *Preparation*: In this stage, individuals 'mentally' prepare themselves for behaviour change. Persuasion, negotiation, trial and encouragement are the specific tactics that are followed to mentally prepare the clients and make them 'try' the desired positive behaviour. In the case of HIV/AIDS many changes have been brought about in the behaviours of people whether those involved in the abuse of drugs, sex workers, men having sex with men as well as health care workers.
- *Action*: Discussing benefits of the adoption of new bahaviour provides reinforcement and encouragement and increasing the frequency of occurrence of such behaviours.
- *Maintenance*: Supporting and praising in addition to targeting the required changes in the environment, help maintaining the changed behaviour. This is being done through continuous education and awareness campaigns.

(iii) Social Marketing

Social Marketing (SM) needs to be considered as one of the models for awareness campaign. Social marketing is the planning and implementation of programmes designed to bring about social change using concepts and principles of commercial marketing. Across the world, SM principles are being widely used to improve community health. Kotler (1975) defines social marketing as, "the design, implementation, and control of programmes seeking to increase the acceptability of a social idea or practice in a target group(s)". It utilizes concepts of market segmentation, consumer research, idea configuration, communication, facilitation, incentives, and exchange theory to maximize target group response. According to Andreasen (1995), "Social Marketing is the application of commercial marketing technologies to the analysis, planning, execution, and evaluation of programmes designed to influence the voluntary behaviour of target audiences in order to improve their personal welfare and that of their society".

Further, Smith observes, "SM is a process of influencing human behaviour on a large scale, using marketing principles for the purpose of societal benefit rather than commercial profit". It stresses that behaviour change is meant for societal benefit and not for personal gains.

It may be noted that SM is not social advertising; it is much more than mere publicity or promotion or media outreach. It is a multidimensional and dynamic approach meant for enhancement of positive behaviour and well-being in the society. Therefore it goes very well with awareness campaign as one of its models. 'Exchange' is the key factor in SM, where benefits of adopting desired behaviour/product are highlighted and barriers are de-emphasized. It is based on the fact that before adopting any new behaviour or product, human mind calculates or weighs the pros and cons in terms of exchange. People go through 'cost-benefit' analysis when they have to make a choice in buying/adopting a new product/behaviour. When perceived benefits overweigh the perceived cost, clients adopt the 'desired behaviour/product'.

SM involves knowing the reasons why target audiences adhere to their old or traditional practices or behaviour and how the new desired behaviour can be brought about through awareness. The desired behaviour should be made more attractive and less costly [cost is not monetary only; it is inclusive of psychological and social cost]. For this programme modification is done since social work professionals are social doctors who are interested in promoting the social wellbeing of the people. When people are confronted with problems and issues which could be addressed through education and awareness campaign, social work professionals could play a great role as they are educated, trained and have the required experience and expertise.

Components of Social Marketing

Basic components in social marketing which can be discussed under five Ps are as under:

(i) *Product*: The product is what is offered and its benefits. Unlike commercial marketing where product is a tangible item, here, in SM, product is the behaviour or idea that the social work campaign planners would like the target audience to adopt. The product can be an action (e.g., immunizing children) or material item (like, tonic for hair growth). It is the behaviour/service/product that is exchanged with the audience for a price and benefit.

(ii) *Price*: Price includes the costs associated with 'buying' the product, which is sum total of economic cost as well as psychological cost (for example, embarrassment for women in a conservative society to buy liquor) and social cost (say, possibility of losing face). Among the non-financial costs, time, effort, life style, and psychological cost, that must be calculated to get the net cost of the product. A social worker who has the social work value of cultural sensitivity would be the most ideal professional to project the price of the product to the audience.

(iii) *Place*: Place in the context of awareness campaign comprises of the distribution channels used to make the product available to target audiences. When the product is a physical item, it must be easily obtainable by consumers (for instance, availability of beer in general stores). In the case of product being an idea, it must be socially available and find supported within the consumers' social sphere. Ideas like 'where and when' people might think about the problem/ issue and where/when they could be in right frame of mind (for example, nutrition can be thought of in restaurants, grocery shops, etc.) should be looked into. A professional social worker who has adequate communication skills over the local language would be the most ideal person to reach the unreached.

(iv) *Promotion*: Promotion includes the efforts taken to ensure that the target audience is aware of the campaign. These publicity efforts should be designed to cultivate positive attitudes and intentions regarding the product that pave the way for behaviour change. It is for communicating to the audience about the product, price and place variables using strategies like advertising, media relations, counselling, etc. A professional social worker has the expertise to effectively promote the idea and work towards a successful awareness campaign.

(v) *Positioning*: Positioning means that the product must be positioned in such a way as to maximize benefits and minimize costs. Positioning is a psychological construct that involves the location of the product relative to other products and activities with which it competes. For instance, using mineral water would bring peace of mind plus freedom from water born diseases while using ordinary unfiltered water would lead to many health related consequences with social and psychological underpinnings. A health care professional with training background in social work would know to successfully position the product namely, the topic to the target audience.

Principles of Awareness-Campaign

Social work methods including awareness-campaign are based on certain principles. Some of the principles governing awareness-campaign are as follows:

Principle of Imbibing Social Work Values

Social work values such as service, social justice, importance of human relationship, dignity and worth of the person, integrity, loyalty to profession, hard work, cultural sensitivity, teacher-ship, patriotism and responsibility and commitment form the foundation of awareness-campaigns.

Principle of Addressing the Community and Client Needs

Awareness-campaigns are based on the needs (rather felt needs) of the community. This is important for the acceptability and success of any awareness campaign.

Principle of Giving Importance to Cultural Sensitivity

Social workers need to understand the socio-cultural setting of the community as it greatly influences the service acceptance and in fact, success or failure of any awareness campaign.

Principle of Client-centric Approach

The entire design of awareness-campaign revolves around the client or target-audience. Knowledge about the socio-cultural and psychological aspects of the clients, their attitudes and belief systems on the issue at hand are essential pre-requisites to design the awareness campaign programme.

Principle of Goal Clarity

The success or failure of any awareness campaign depends on the clarity of goals defined. The acceptability by the target audience of the issue and its goals should be specifically and vividly defined.

The Principle of Planning and Reviewing

As a technical component, the process of continuous planning and reviewing periodically is fundamental to the development of meaningful awareness campaign programme. In the context of social-work, planning should be participatory, as far as possible, involving the service users. Mid-term planning and evaluation on completion of each programme is of utmost importance.

Principle of Message Specificity

Message development is of utmost importance. It should bring about the desired change or outcome and be understandable and appealing to the target audience.

Principle of Participation

People's active participation forms the crux of awareness-campaigns. They should not be perceived as passive receptors of information.

Principle of Communication

Culturally-sensitive, and two-way communication is essential to effective awareness-campaigns. Every method and means appropriate to the situation must be used for awareness campaign.

Principle of Sustainable and Positive Change

'Guided social change in the positive direction' is the aim of awareness campaign. The campaigns designed should lead to holistic and positive change among all the sections of the society and should not be on ad-hoc basis or should not be confined to betterment of select few.

Principle of Cost-effectiveness

Based on the socio-cultural context and resource-availability, media channels should be carefully chosen keeping in view their efficiency and cost-effectiveness. Campaigns using multiple delivery channels are more successful.

Principle of Feedback

Creating systems for continuous monitoring and feedback are essential to gain insight regarding successful awareness campaign.

Process Involved in Awareness Campaign Method

The process of designing an awareness-campaign requires certain phases or steps, which are as follows:

Planning Phase

The first step, in this phase, is 'situation-analysis', which is done through baseline data collection. Knowing the 'target-audience' is vital for designing an effective campaign. Social problems are often multidimensional – for instance, there are multiple reasons for child-marriage and varied consequences. Concentrating on a single factor of cause-effect would give misleading results. Using ecological approach, all the factors are studied for holistic analysis of the situation. Background studies are carried out so as to gather relevant and realistic information, covering dimensions like political scenario, policies, legislations and programmes, financial and other resources at hand, socio-cultural milieu, geographical locale, lack of or presence of adequate infrastructure and sophisticated technology. The method of social work research must be used for gathering right information.

The next step is 'analysis of the information/problem' on the theme of awareness-campaign. Various tools may be applied for this. For example, SWOC analysis [is a framework for analysis in which different internal and external factors are examined as Strengths, Weaknesses, Opportunities and Challenges in relation to their impact/role in the viability of the intervention being planned], problem matrix [in which different domains, say causal factors, intensity of the problem, etc., are plotted in rows and columns in the form of a matrix or grid and then analysis is done], problem tree [cause-effect relationship of the problem at hand is seen in the form of a tree where roots are taken as the basic cause and branches signify varied effects of the problem] and mind mapping [is an innovative and creative way of collating information for planning; usually initiating around a single word or text, placed at the centre, related ideas and concepts are added to it using symbols or otherwise] methods are all applicable.

The important tools in planning-analysis are stakeholder-analysis (a process of identifying the individuals or groups that are likely to affect or be affected by, a proposed action, and sorting them according to their favourable/unfavourable/neutral role/impact on the planned-intervention), resource-assessment (identification of resources and capacities within a community) and opportunity analysis (includes identification of the possibilities and potential synergies with other completed, ongoing or future programmes/interventions).

Designing Phase

Based on the information gathered and analysis done in the planning phase, concrete, measurable objectives of the awareness-campaign are chalked out. It should be clearly spelled out whether awareness-campaign would confine itself to disseminating information only or behaviour change is also aimed at. The objectives, thus set, would decide the approach and model of the awareness campaign. In view of the detailed profiling of the community done in the baseline data collection stage, covering dimensions like their age-group, educational level, occupational status, etc., the target-group(s)/audience should be vividly enlisted.

After setting the objectives and demarcating the target-audience, it is essential to structure key messages. Appropriate messages are defined based on socio-demographic profile of each target group, socio-cultural milieu, the issues that are to be addressed and the behaviours/habits to be changed, major obstacles in adopting 'healthy-behaviour' and the available human and financial resources.

Identifying and communicating the correct messages are crucial to the success of awareness-campaign. Generally, a campaign has either one central message or a group of closely related subsidiary messages that are linked to a common theme, say, family planning and mother and child health. Often messages with slogans or short phrases (with less than 10 words) are planned so that target audience can 'retain' easily. Also, messages should be concise and give minimal scope for misunderstanding. Moreover, they should not raise false expectations. In order to make the audience 'feel included', the messages should have some personalisation. More often than not, message should have positive tone. Sayers and Richard (2006) have identified two types of messages – awareness messages [give information that can be used to reinforce importance of informed action and behavioural change] and action messages [describe in detail the actions that should be taken to adopt particular behaviours].

Selection of Communication Channels (Phase)

The third step is selecting channels for communicating the message. Depending upon the resources available, profile of the target audience, targeted reach and coverage of awareness-campaign, etc., the channels are decided. Some of the common strategies and tools that are used in awareness-campaigns are described below:

- *Mass-media*: Television, radio, newspapers and the other periodicals are easily available. Now-a-days, many programmes and documentaries, featured articles and media discussions are available to awareness-campaigners. Community radio is a recent innovation that is being used for creating awareness on community-specific issues.
- *Audio-visual media*: Newsletters, books and pamphlets, brochures, posters, charts, flip-charts, web conferencing, interactive T.V. and radio programmes, CDs, VCDs, DVDs, etc., are commonly used in awareness-campaigns. They are cost effective but have limited reach.
- *Exhibitions, rallies, mobile libraries, cycle-theatre, community-meetings*: These are used to create awareness on one-to-one basis. They are highly effective strategies but have limited coverage.
- *Merchandising*: Merchandising as calendars, agendas, printed clothing, bags and badges, are now-a-days used as PR material as well as effective strategies for awareness-campaigns.

Monitoring Phase

Monitoring is a crucial and fourth step in the design of awareness campaign. Though it begins after the campaign is launched but indicators of monitoring and evaluation are chalked out at the planning stage itself. Based on the objectives, indicators of success or positive impact of campaign are enlisted. Sometimes, before and after the campaign, awareness levels of the target-group on the issue at hand are measured and compared. Often qualitative and quantitative data collection techniques are used in evaluation of awareness-campaigns.

Conclusion

In the developing countries the issues and problems being addressed by professional social workers are diverse and multifaceted. It demands new approaches and methods in social work practice. The method of awareness campaign is directed to create and enhance the awareness of the people on various issues and causes and enhance their power to change for better future. The method of awareness campaign helps the social workers to educate the people to know about the different resources available to tackle the prevailing issues in the society. The extent of awareness raised will determine the effectiveness of social work intervention.

REFERENCES

1. Clift E. (2001) *Information, Education and Communication: Lessons from the Past; Perspectives for the Future.* Geneva: World Health Organization.
2. Development Communications Network. (2001), *Mass Media Communication Strategies for Reproductive Health Promotion in Nigeria.* Lagos: Development Communications Network.
3. Donovan, R.J. and Carter, OBJ (2003). Evidence for Behaviour Change from Media Based Public Education Campaigns. Curtin university: CBRCC Report 031106
4. Kaushik, Archana (2013). *Administration of Welfare and Development Services in India.* New Delhi: Global Vision.
5. Kincaid DL, Jara JR, Coleman PL, Segura F.(1988). Getting the Message: The Communication for Young People Special Project. *Special Study No. 56.* Washington, DC: U.S. Agency for International Development.
6. Sayers, Richard (2006). Principles of awareness raising for information literacy, a case study. Thailand: Communication Information. UNESCO.

6

Awareness Campaign and its Relation to Other Methods of Social Work

Archana Kaushik

'Information is power' is the mantra of contemporary globalized world. Social work profession believes that 'information is the pre-requisite of empowerment'. Creating awareness is the primary task of social workers, in almost all the social work interventions. Awareness campaigns have a wide scope and strong interrelation with traditional and contemporary methods of social work practice. Awareness campaigns as a method of social work contributes significantly to other methods of social work.

Awareness campaign is the method that is extensively used to bring about desired positive change in the attitudes, perceptions and behaviours of target groups and communities by providing information. There are newer approaches and modalities such as advocacy, public relations, social marketing, behaviour change communication, resource raising, and several such others. Usage of folk media, organizing social events, community and stakeholder meetings, mass media communications, are some of the strategies widely employed in awareness campaigns.

Scope of awareness campaigns is very vast and includes issues like promoting family planning, anti-tobacco, drug de-addiction, road safety, disaster management, HIV/AIDS, cancer, leprosy, preventing child sexual abuse, stop child labour, education of girl child, against female foeticide, voting rights, women's health and rights, and so on. Awareness campaigns can cover all the practice arena of social work profession ranging from individual to community and can be at preventive, curative, ameliorative, rehabilitative, promotive and management levels. Awareness campaigns encompass all the social work methods in its extensive practice framework. This chapter aims to examine the linkage of awareness campaign method with other traditional (social case work, group work, community organization, social work research, social action, social welfare administration) and the 'contemporary' methods (advocacy, networking, resource mobilization, public interest litigation, strength based practice), as advocated by Gracious Thomas.

It may be noted that all these twelve methods of social work practice are rooted in the same values (like social justice and empowerment) and principles (such as client self-determination, moving at client's pace), and have common skill base (for instance, problem identification, communication, training, organizing, motivation). These methods share various theoretical frameworks such as health belief model, theory of reasoned action, social learning theory, theory of gender and empowerment and systems theory, to mention some. All the methods of social work rest on similar assumptions namely, the inherent dignity and worth of human beings, the client possessing the intrinsic capability for growth and development and their ability to choose wisely for the management of their own affairs. Let us examine linkage of awareness campaign with other methods of social work.

Social Casework

Social casework is one of the primary methods of social work and involves dealing with problems of individuals. It aims to enhance social functioning of individuals. Hollis (1954) defined social case work as the method employed by social workers to help individuals find solution to problems of social adjustment which they are unable to handle in a satisfactory way by their own efforts. At times, due to certain external or internal factors, a client may have difficulties in adjusting to his/her social environment and/or availing civic and developmental services and opportunities. In such situations, caseworker helps the client to adjust to the situation or bring about desired changes in the social system. Perlman (1957) has discussed the dynamic components, which make up the casework situation namely, the person, problem, place, worker/professional and process. It means a person with a problem comes to a place where the professional social worker helps him/her through the systematic process of social case work.

Awareness campaigns have used case work methods extensively, in HIV setting, while working with high risk groups such as Men having Sex with Men (MS, female sex workers and injecting drug users. In fact, National Aids Control Programmes (NACP) of India has initiated Behaviour Change Communication (BCC), which is one of the significant models of awareness campaigns. Principles of Social Marketing (SM), another model of awareness campaign, have been widely used in NACP especially for promoting condom usage as a strategy for prevention of HIV. Social workers, in varied case work settings, make use of awareness campaigns. Some of the salient manifestations are – a client of drug abuse is enabled to 'change behaviour', after creating awareness; a woman is made aware of family planning methods and encouraged to adopt one; a parent of new born is informed about immunization services; an indigent migrant is encouraged to make use of social security schemes; a bonded labourer is informed about his/her rights under the Constitution of India and social legislation on abolition of labour bondage; and a victim of domestic violence is told about provisions under Prevention of Domestic Violence Act.

Creating awareness and providing information is invariably the driver to empowering. In awareness campaigns, information is customized and tailor-made to suit the requirement of the client and appraising and removing the bottlenecks in effective usage of information. In fact, in almost all casework situations, bringing desired positive changes in attitudes and behaviours of the clients is of critical importance for which usage of BCC and awareness raising strategies becomes imperative for social workers. Accessing and availing developmental services is another crucial task of caseworker. For raising awareness about these services and motivating clients to make use of them, social workers usually rely on awareness campaign method of social work.

Social Group Work

Social group work is a method of social work through which individuals in group settings are helped by a social worker to enhance their social functioning through purposeful group experience and to cope more effectively with their problems. Group work involves social work interventions at group level and through group interactions. Groups can be therapeutic or for meaningful creative pursuits. They can be formed to solve problems at hand, or to provide counselling to members undergoing similar negative experience. There are advocacy-groups, support groups, pressure groups, self-help groups, and many more.

Awareness campaign as a method of social work forms an integral part of group work. Social workers carry out many interventions with amalgamation of these two methods. In urban slums and rural communities, youth groups are formed to create awareness on diverse topics like sanitation and public health, income generating programmes and prevention of HIV/AIDS, communal harmony and disaster management. Mahila mandals (women's groups) in Himachal Pradesh (North India) have had a long history of awareness generation and providing support to womenfolk. Self Help Groups are yet another fine example of disseminating information and accomplishing tasks in and through group setting. Helpage India has initiated a pilot project 'Vridha Sangh' (Elderly Group) in Madhya Pradesh, where information about rights of, and services, for senior citizens was disseminated to group members first, and then these groups helped their needy and destitute fellow beings through awareness campaigns. Peer education work groups of MSM, sex workers, and other vulnerable social groups and make use of strategies and approaches of awareness campaign under NACP. In many slums of Delhi, National Commission of Women has established Mahila Panchayats (local governance at community level) to create legal awareness in the community against gender based violence. There are many support groups of care-givers of patients of Alzheimer's disease, terminally ill cancer patients, people infected with HIV, people with disabilities, persons suffering from Schizophrenia, and such others.

Various approaches and models of awareness campaign method are widely used in diverse group settings, as mentioned above. It has been found that awareness creation is best in a group situation, when an individual becomes much more receptive seeing other group members adopting the information gained. Street plays, theatre demonstrations, drama, and such other strategies of awareness campaign method become handy in group work.

Community Organization

Community organization is one of the core methods of social work practice. According to Kramer and Specht (1975) Community organization refers to various methods of intervention whereby a professional change agent helps a community action system composed of individuals, groups or organizations to engage in planned collective action in order to deal with special problems within the democratic system of values (Kramer and Specht, 1975). Community organization aims to address the problems at the community level, by involving members of the community in the process. Community organization ensures people's participation. A community can be a village, an urban locale, a hilly or a tribal setting. Now-a-days, even virtual communities connected through World Wide Web are also being addressed for social work interventions. The process of community organization, intends to utilize the latent potentialities of the community, to optimize the use of its indigenous resources, to develop its capacity to manage its own life and affairs and to enhance its ability to function as an integrated unit.

Awareness campaigns and community organization go hand in hand. In both of these methods of social work practice, attention is focused on impact of socio-cultural variables like caste and religious affiliations, gender, power-relations, etc., that form part of identity of people of the community, and influence their attitudes and perceptions towards various social services and opportunities. For instance, propagation of family planning in rural Muslim community would have different set of constraints than creating awareness about it in other middle class urban community. Awareness campaigns have been extensively used in organizing community in disaster preparedness and/ or management. Model villages have been developed by many NGOs like People's Vigilance Committee on Human Rights in rural Varanasi (North India) using approaches and strategies of community organization and awareness campaigns. Rural women were empowered through their increased participation in Panchayati Raj system through awareness creation about their roles and responsibilities as elected members. These women panchs, then organized their village communities for resolving challenges like provisions of drinking water facilities, increased accessibility to maternal and child health services, and so on. Many villages in Rajasthan, facing crisis in water availability, now have surplus water. This was done by Tarun Bharat Sangh, an NGO headed by Dr. Rajendra Singh, Magsaysay award winner, using awareness campaigns and organizing communities to do water harvesting and conservation.

Social Action

Social action is one of the auxiliary methods of social work practice. The term Social Action is being used to depict a spectrum of voluntary action or initiatives that aim to address relevant social, political, economic, ecological and ethical issues in the country. In the last few decades, the term has become increasingly ambivalent and ambiguous with interplay of varying meanings and contexts. A wide range of activities like charity, relief work, service delivery, public policy initiatives, advocacy campaigns, social movements, socio-political mobilization, networking for desired social change have been clubbed under the gamut of the term – social action. In a layman's understanding, social action would cover whole rubric of activities directed towards desired social change for the benefit of masses. Varying meanings emerging out of different types and contexts of problems and their interventions makes social action a complex and yet dynamic concept.

Mary Richmond, for the first time, in 1922, made use of the term social action in social work. She has defined social action as "mass betterment through propaganda and social legislation". This definition stresses on improving the condition of huge section of population as an aim of social action with propaganda and social legislations as main strategies. Indeed, use of awareness campaigns becomes an inherent part of mobilization and social action. Wickendon (1956) applied the term social action to that aspect of organized social welfare actively directed towards shaping, modifying or maintaining the social institution and policies that collectively constitute the social environment. Desirable change in social structure is the key element in this definition. Such a change can be achieved only after creating awareness at mass level about the implications of problems at hand and desirable solutions.

Social action addressed the structural inequalities of the socio-cultural environment. Many NGOs in India have been working for ensuring rights of marginalized and oppressed sections of the society, such as Dalits, Scheduled Tribes, poor Muslims and other religious minorities, transgender, and many others. Utilizing strategies and modalities of awareness generation, they conscientize and mobilize the downtrodden to raise their voice against the upper caste, elite, rich and powerful oppressors. Conscientization of the masses is the backbone of mobilization of masses. Conscientization is the by product of awareness campaigns.

Awareness campaigns are used at many stages of social action. In the initial stages, awareness is created to awaken the deprived community, demonstrate how their rights are being violated, and make the marginalized people reflect on their situation. This is done to prepare the oppressed group to take action. For action against the oppressive practices, awareness campaigns play crucial role in demonstration of discontent in front of the authorities, sit-ins, protests, which are the strategies used in social action. Slogans, street plays, singing songs, catch-lines, phrases, to express and emote are extensively used in both the methods of social work practice.

Social Welfare Administration

Social welfare administration as a method of social work, translates social welfare policies, programmes and social legislation into social work practice. Harleigh Tracker interprets social welfare administration as a process of working with people in ways that release and relate their energies so that they use all available resources to accomplish the purpose of providing needed community services and programmes (Harleigh Tracker, 1971). Awareness campaigns and social welfare administration are strongly inter-related.

Awareness campaigns apply all the principles of administration – POSDCoRB [Planning, Organization, Staffing, Directing, Coordinating, Reporting and Budgeting]. Monitoring and evaluation also are core-activities of both, awareness campaigns and administration. All activities related to designing of awareness campaigns begin with planning. First of all, research or base line survey is planned. Based on the information gathered, planning of awareness campaign is done. The planned activities are then organized. Recruitment and training of the staff to plan and execute awareness campaigns is a significant component. All activities, beginning from research to evaluation, are well coordinated to achieve the desired goals. The entire campaign, at each stage, is supervised and loopholes, if any, are removed. Reporting the whole process of awareness campaign is essential for its monitoring and evaluation. Efficient budgeting of awareness campaigns is done, whether it is a small one at a school level, or a huge one, say, at national level.

On the flipside, awareness campaigns play vital role in administration of welfare and developmental services. For instance, awareness campaigns have been widely launched with the beginning of Mahatma Gandhi National Rural Development Guarantee Act (MGNREGA) in India so that the prospective beneficiaries are able to avail the provisions of the Act. Likewise, awareness campaigns have been initiated to popularize flagship programmes like National Rural Health Mission, Sarva Shiksha Abhiyan, and such others. Now-a-days, awareness campaigns first create the 'demand' for the programme in the target area and then demonstrate the features of the programme as 'supply' to fulfill the needs and demands.

Further, cultural context has strong bearing on administration of services and awareness campaigns. For instance, in rural Uttar Pradesh, many upper caste Auxiliary Nurse Midwife (ANMs) were found discriminating the *Dalits* by not touching their infants for immunization. Similarly, awareness campaigns should be designed sensitively keeping the cultural milieu in view. In the HIV care setting, migrants are considered vulnerable group. Large number of people from Ganjam district of Odisha migrate to cloth mills of Surat in Gujarat. Awareness campaigns in Gujarat were not able to sensitize Oriya migrants due to language barriers. State AIDS Control Societies of Odisha and Gujarat coordinated and developed awareness campaigns in Oriya language meeting the needs of Oriya migrants in Gujarat.

Social Work Research

Social work research aims at analyzing social problems and providing suggestions for interventions. Social work research is a systematic and professional investigation into social issues and fields of social work practice to enhance the quality of social work practice. The findings of social work research may help the social worker, the agency/organization and the policy makers to plan effective programmes based on the needs of a particular community".

Social work research helps in knowing the root cause of the social problem at hand. Many times apparent problems on the face value may not be the real ones and unless the real problems are targeted, all interventions based on tackling the apparent problems are bound to fail. Real causes of manifested problems are found through social work research. For instance, awareness campaigns were designed to prevent HIV spread among truckers, without systematically studying their life style challenges. In those campaigns, knowledge on HIV infection was provided to truckers and condoms were supplied. Still rate of HIV infection among truck drivers did not decline. Social work research found out that due to paucity of time to deliver perishable goods from one place to another, the truck drivers have to drive tirelessly throughout the night as well as day time. To keep themselves awake they abuse drugs. And under the influence of drugs they do not remember to use condoms. Then awareness campaigns were re-designed based on the real challenges which brought about success.

When the Government of India found through research that males play critical role in deciding about family planning or men are the perpetrators of domestic violence, making women folk aware and motivated to use family planning methods or say 'no' to violence, it changed its awareness campaigns to 'men make a difference'. In this altered awareness campaigns, males were conscientized to be sensitive and responsible. These campaigns have been quite effective. Thus, we see that social work research forms the first step of knowing the 'felt needs' or 'real problems' of the clientele and then other methods including awareness campaigns become effective instruments to bring about desired change in the social fabric.

In awareness campaign method, fact finding is the first step, whether one uses social marketing or behaviour change communication, awareness raising or education. As a matter of fact, even most creatively designed and ambitiously executed awareness campaigns, may fail in their objectives, if not based on well researched facts. On the other hand, a simple campaign with minimal resources, founded on meticulously designed research, succeeds in achieving its goals.

Advocacy

Advocacy is the process of raising the voice on behalf of the marginalized population groups, who lack socio-political power and economic resources. Advocacy is one of the important methods used by social workers that promote equality, social justice and social inclusion of the deprived groups in a society. Advocacy is a principled activity that encompasses three broad principles of independence, empowerment and inclusion (Dunning, 2010). According to Cohen (2001), advocacy is the pursuit of influencing outcomes-including public-policy and resources allocation decisions within political, economic, and social systems and institutions – that directly affect people's current lives. Social work advocacy is the exclusive and mutual representation of clients or a cause in a forum attempting to systematically influence decision making in an unjust or unresponsive system (Schneider and Lester, 2001). Advocacy leads to empowerment and social workers, making use of advocacy, address issues of rights and social justice and to support people to obtain services and resources for the community.

Awareness campaign is strongly linked to advocacy. In any advocacy initiative, awareness is created first and target/deprived group is mobilized to raise their voice. At times, awareness campaign itself becomes advocacy project. For instance, the NGO 'Breakthrough' launched 'ring the doorbell (bell bajao)' awareness campaign against domestic violence asking the responsive citizens to intervene if any case of violence is observed in their neighbourhood by ringing the doorbell. Similarly, to stop stigma and discrimination against HIV positive people, awareness campaigns became the advocacy programme.

In the same way, advocacy initiatives also create awareness on the project in hand. Demonstrations, protests, sit-ins, rallies, of advocacy groups of sexual minority across several cities of the world created awareness about LGBT (Lesbian Gay Bisexual and Transgender) issues among the general public. Bollywood celebrity Aamir Khan's show *Satyamev Jayate* has been a fine amalgamation of awareness campaign and advocacy methods of social work practice, through which social workers in India created awareness and advocated for the rights of marginalized and deprived groups in the society. On the issue of child sexual abuse (CSA), the show created awareness among parents and guardians and it also advocated for stronger and specific laws against CSA. Likewise, the show made people aware of the plight of rape victims, and advocated for 'one stop crisis centre' and against victimizing and stigmatizing females as a result of rape. Thus, awareness campaigns and advocacy interventions serve dual purpose and are often complementing each other.

Networking

Networking is vital to social work interventions. As a method of social work, networking is the creation of strategic relations of like-minded individuals, social groups and institutions. Through these networks information is exchanged, advocacy efforts are strengthened and resources are mobilized. A network refers to an association of individuals, groups and community that come together to share resources, information, knowledge and skills. Networking is a method of creating useful linkages, both within and among social work profession, communities, organizations, and societies, in order to mobilize resources, maintain good will and achieve various goals. It is a process of developing and activating social workers' relationships to enhance their knowledge and expand service sphere to the client, by efficiently utilizing the available resources.

No social work intervention can be carried out in isolation. In awareness campaigns too, networking forms crucial component. Awareness campaigns require specific inputs in baseline research; designing message keeping in view the cultural requirements; placement of campaigns require particular strategies; and promotion of campaign needs explicit tasks and tactics. For each of these stages and elements of awareness campaign, one needs different set of skills and dexterity :– knowledge of sophisticated statistical package for analyzing data after baseline research; specialization in devising communication materials like brochures, pamphlets, posters, flip charts, banners, boards, hoardings, etc,; tapping different settings for focusing the campaigns such as hospitals, community spaces, bus stands; contacting electronic (television, radio), print media (newspapers, magazines) etc. A social worker cannot accomplish all these tasks alone. He/she has to network with different individuals, organizations, agencies, groups and associations for the same. Thus, networking is an integral part of designing and executing an awareness campaign.

The internet, including many social networking sites, is being used extensively for creating awareness. Now-a-days, Facebook, Twitter, BlogSpot's, emails and SMS, have been among the most efficient and cost effective strategies employed for awareness campaigns and networking. Many times, awareness campaigns lead to collaboration and networking for furtherance of social action. For instance, awareness campaigns to eliminate stigma and discrimination against HIV infected persons resulted in Networks of HIV Positive People. Anti-smoking campaigns gave rise to students' networks and associations to make their university 'No smoking zones'. On the other hand, many networks also design awareness campaigns to voice their concerns. Associations and networks of elderly in urban neighbourhoods launch awareness programmes on healthy and productive ageing or on curbing elder-abuse.

Public Interest Litigation (PIL)

Public interest litigation (PIL) is a type of litigation where the interest of the general public is given priority over all other interests with an aim to ensure social and collective justice. Advanced Law Lexicon (2013) has defined 'Public Interest Litigation' as under:

> "The expression 'PIL' means a legal action initiated in a Court of law for the enforcement of public interest or general interest in which the public or a class of the community has pecuniary interest or some interest by which their legal rights or liabilities are affected. (http://www.Legal blog.in/2011/02/public-interest-litigatiodefinition.html #sthash.gyVLLfUN.dpuf)

In the present context, when the conscience of general public is raised on their citizenry rights and there are myriad of manifestations of violations of these rights, PIL becomes an important instrument and method of social work practice for seeking justice. There are many civil society organizations fighting for the rights of *Dalits* and downtrodden and using PIL against the upper caste perpetrators or State's apathetic behaviour, which are hampering rights of the *Dalits*. Many social workers and environmentalists have filed PIL against indiscriminate deforestation, displacement of tribals, for clearing spaces for business ventures, building dams and other infrastructure development at the cost of displacement and even at the cost or risk of lives of the marginalized and deprived communities. PIL becomes a necessity when protection of the affected under law is unavailable to the public or a segment of it due to ignorance, poverty, fear or lack of organised endeavour. It has come as strength in the hands of social workers. It is one of the methods of social work intervention through policy advocacy or legal intervention.

The linkage between PIL and awareness campaign method of social work is well established. Awareness campaigns can form the basis of social action and PIL for advocating a social cause. For instance, campaigns creating awareness about health hazards of smoking or tobacco intake led to filing PIL against advertisements promoting brands of cigarettes and tobacco pouches and its depiction in media in India. This resulted in ban on electronic and print media to show advertisements promoting these harmful products.

Similarly, PILs also aid in awareness campaigns. After filing PILs, it became obligatory for the government to ensure awareness campaigns, against use of alcohol and tobacco products for stipulated time, before and during screening of movies in cinema halls. All the paan-walas (retail outlets of tobacco product) have to put board in bold letters that cigarette and other tobacco products would not be sold to children (below 18 years). Parallel to this is making it mandatory for all hospitals, health centres, and pathological labs to put boards that 'determination of sex of the unborn child is illegal'. This was done after a PIL against indiscriminate practice of finding the sex of the foetus by healthcare functionaries leading to rampant female foeticide cases in India.

Resource Mobilization

Resource mobilization is a process of raising different types of resources and support services for the client. These resources can be manpower, money, material, various forms of expertise or any other thing which can potentially assist in the process of rendering help offered to the client. Resource Mobilization is a process, which identifies the resources essential for the development, implementation and continuation of works for achieving the organization's mission. Resource mobilization means expansion of relations with the resource providers, the skills, knowledge and capacity for proper use of resources. These resources could be internal (material, space, money, manpower etc.) and external (funding, advice from the experts, other technical assistance etc.). It also means seeking new sources of resource mobilization and optimum utilization of the available resources.

Here again, one may find a strong interrelation between awareness campaigns and resource mobilization. Often, they are intertwined and complement each other. Helpage India, through its awareness campaigns mobilizes resources. Under its Student Action for Value Education (SAVE) project, school children are facilitated to participate in their awareness campaigns on enhancing intergenerational bonding. School children, further mobilize resources through activities like selling festival cards, organizing carnivals, or through collecting donations for the cause of the elderly. Also, in their resource mobilization through selling of Helpage cards (made by children), items like Diya, Candles, etc., Helpage, tactfully, creates awareness on rights of the elderly and works for their integration in the society. In the same way, organizations like Child Rights and You, amalgamate resource mobilization and awareness in their campaigns, thus, achieving the dual purpose.

Currently, numerous NGOs have started adopting resource raising campaigns as alternative to government funding or relying on foreign funding. This move is valuable in many aspects. Donor agencies set their own norms of using funds and NGOs are unable to work on the felt needs of the community. Resource raising through public helps in intervening on demands of the target groups and building credibility. The creative ideas and indigenous initiatives can be practiced if resources are mobilised through local sources.

There are several benefits of combining the awareness campaigns with resource mobilization. It promotes public relations and ensures credibility to the social work agency. It also makes certain community's participation in the programmes, thereby guaranteeing sustainability. Awareness on the social cause is created and resources are gathered for action. It also encourages cost effectiveness and time saving.

Strengths Based Practice

Every human is endowed with certain strengths and resources that facilitate in his/her empowerment. Strengths based practices (SBPs) is a group of modalities and strategies that focus on the inherent strengths of individuals, families, groups and organizations deploying peoples' personal strengths to aid their recovery and empowerment. SBPs are empowering alternatives to traditional methods with individuals, group and organizational work. SBPs refrain from allowing crippling, labeling and stigmatized language. Descriptions and pathology owned by individuals, groups and organizations that suggest acceptance of their condition as hopeless or helpless to change are constructively challenged through SBPs (Pulla V., 2012). SBP is being recognized as a method of social work in the contemporary society by professionals. Strengths based method in brief refers to policies, practice methods, and strategies that identify and draw upon the strengths of individuals, families, groups and communities.

The strengths based method is something that truly guides and influences a social worker to practice as a professional. It is associated and practiced along with other social work methods to bring the optimum outcome to the clients. Literally speaking strengths based method adds 'strengths' to the practice of social work with individuals, groups, families and communities. The incorporation of strengths based method in the practice of other methods help the social work professionals to locate strengths even in the most marginalized, deprived, downtrodden and oppressed clients and to enhance the process of help by building upon the strengths.

The strengths based method enables the social workers to practice the method of awareness campaign upholding the values of cultural sensitivity and dignity and worth of individual. Strengths based method and awareness campaigns are complementary to each other. In Delhi, while commuting with Metro train, one finds Delhi Metro Rail Corporation's awareness campaigns where through big hoardings, messages are highlighted as – "More than 99.5 percent commuters return their tokens at the exit gates"…. "More than 98 percent commuters give their seats to their needy co-commuters". It is innovative and creative manner of awareness campaigns, based on strengths based practices that instills positive aspects and encouraging civic sense to enhance civic responsibility. Likewise, awareness campaigns on blood donation make use of strengths based practices, which is depicted in their slogans like, "Strong guys donate blood"…. "Smart girls donate blood".

In the contemporary world, social marketing strategies and behaviour change communication, that are approaches of awareness campaigns, focus on positive messages emphasizing on the strengths and innate worth of human beings/target population. Such awareness campaigns are effectively accomplishing their desired goals.

Conclusion

Awareness-campaigns are intrinsically related to all other eleven methods of social work. Behaviour change communication (BCC), which is a model of awareness campaign, is widely practiced in casework and group work situations. Community organization extensively uses Information Communication Education (IEC) and Education approaches. Creating awareness in a community frequently adopts strategies of social marketing (SM). Lobbying and legislative advocacy and other approaches of awareness-campaign, are employed by social action for policy level changes. Baseline data collection and evaluation research form part of social work research. Like social welfare administration, awareness-campaigns make use of POSDCoRB [planning, organizing, staffing, directing, coordinating, reporting and budgeting] principles. In current practices, resource mobilisation and awareness on social cause go hand in hand. PIL and advocacy have been complementing and supplementing awareness campaigns. Focus on strengths and capabilities of the target audience have been the popular element of awareness campaigns. All the methods of social work including awareness-campaigns, rest on the values, ethics and principles of social work and aim at creating a better, just and egalitarian society.

REFERENCES

1. Clift E. (2001) *Information, Education and Communication: Lessons from the Past; Perspectives for the Future*. Geneva: World Health Organization.
2. Cohen, D., De La Vega, R., Watson, G. (2001). *Advocacy for Social Justice*. Bloomfield, CT: Kumarian Press Inc.
3. Development Communications Network. (2001), *Mass Media Communication Strategies for Reproductive Health Promotion in Nigeria*. Lagos: Development Communications Network.
4. Donovan, R.J. and Carter, OBJ (2003). Evidence for Behaviour Change from Media Based Public Education Campaigns. Curtin university: CBRCC Report 031106
5. Dunning, A. (2010). A Scoping Study of Advocacy with Older People in Wales for the Older People's Commissioner for Wales. Older People's Commissioner for Wales, Cardiff.
6. Dunning, A. (2005). Information, Advice and Advocacy for Older People: Defining and Developing Services. York: Joseph Rowntree Foundation.
7. Friedlander, W.A. (1958). *Concepts and Methods of Social work*. New Delhi: Prentice Hall.
8. Friedlander, W.A. (1977). *Introduction to Social Welfare*. New Delhi: Prentice Hall.
9. Hollis, F. (1954). *Case Work Diagnosis – What and Why*. Smith College Studies in *Social Work*, (24), 3, 1-8
10. Kaushik, Archana (2013). *Administration of Welfare and Development Services in India*. New Delhi: Global Vision.
11. Kramer, R.M. & Specht, H. (1975). *Readings in Community Organization Practice*. Englewood Cliffs, NJ: Prentice-Hall
12. Kincaid DL, Jara JR, Coleman PL, Segura F. (1988). Getting the Message: The Communication for Young People Special Project. Special Study No. 56.Washington, DC: U.S. Agency for International Development.
13. Mathew, P.D. (2010). Public Interest Litigation. In G. Thomas (Ed.), *Social Work Intervention with Individuals and Groups*. New Delhi, IGNOU.
14. Nanavati, M.C., (1965). Social Action and the Professional Social Work. *Social Work Forum*, III (2), 26-29.

15. Pulla, V. (2012). What are Strengths Based Practices all About? In Venkat Pulla, Leseley Chenoweth, Abraham Francis and Stefan Bakaj (Eds.), *Papers in Strengths Based Practice*. Allied Publishers Pvt. Ltd.
16. Richmond, Marry (1922). *What is Social Casework?* New York: Russel Sage Foundation.
17. Ross, M. G. (1955). *Community Organization: Theory and Principles*. New York: Harper and Brothers.
18. Saleebey, D. (1996). The Strengths Perspective in Social Work Practice: Extensions and Cautions. *Social Work*, 41, 296-305.
19. Saleebey, D., (Ed.). (1992). *The Strengths Perspective in Social Work Practice*. White Plains, NY: Longman.
20. Sayers, Richard (2006). Principles of awareness raising for information literacy, a case study. Thailand: Communication Information. UNESCO.
21. Schaap, W. and Steenbergen F. Van (2001). Ideas for Water Awareness Campaigns. Stockholm, Sweden: The Global Water Partnership. Retrieved from http://etameta.nl/wp-content/uploads/2011/04/IdeaBookAwareness. pdfon 1/10/2014
22. Schneider, R. and Lester, L. (2001) *Social Work Advocacy: A New Framework for Action*, Belmont CA, Brooks Cole.
23. Singh, Surender (1986). Social Action in Horizons of Social Work. In Surender S. & K.S. Soodan. (ed). Harnam Publications.
24. Thomas, Gracious (2010). Existing Trends in Counselling Services in India. In G. Thomas (Ed.), *Substance Abuse and Counselling*, IGNOU, New Delhi.
25. Thomas, Gracious. (Ed: 2010). *Case Work and Counselling: Working with Individuals,* New Delhi: IGNOU.
26. Trecker, G. (1955). *Social Group Work: Principles and Practices*. New York: Association Press.
27. Trecker, Harleigh. (1948). *Social Group Work, Principles and Practices.* New York: Woman's Press.
28. Trecker, H.B. (1971). *Social Work Administration Principles and Practice*. New York: Association Press.
29. Public Interest Litigation retrieved from http://www.legalblog.in/2011/02/public-interest-litigation-definition.html#sthash.gyVLLfUN.dpuf on 27/11/2014.

7

Resource Mobilization

Sheeba Joseph

Social Work has been described as the profession that helps society work better for people, and helps people function fruitfully within the society. It uses various methods to achieve these objectives. Resource mobilization is considered to be an integral part of the helping process wherein the social worker has to mobilize the much needed resources for the betterment of the client/group/community. The genesis of resource mobilization not only dates back to ancient India, where philanthropic activities were a drama or religion but also to several societies and nations across the globe. The concept of charity has its roots in Vedic period. Even the Indian scriptures like Rig Veda mention philanthropic and religious acts like making water ponds for the community and dharamshalas and even providing free food for travellers. In fact, those who are well endowed are supposed to do more and more for the community at large, especially for the marginalized and deprived with the ultimate aim of salvation through the service of humanity. It is the pivot on which the Indian socio-culture revolves. The welfare of the least has been the main motivation behind the philanthropic activities of people and institutions all over the world including India. The entire voluntary sector / development agencies working for the vulnerable have taken up resource mobilization or fund raising to act as a catalyst for empowerment and self-sustainability. The efforts of the Associations of Fundraising Professionals (AFP) in the USA are well known among the philanthropists.

Resource mobilization involves helping the client with needed resources such as housing, clothing, food, furniture or financial support or healthcare (Hepworth, Rooney and Larson, 2002). Resource mobilization is acquisition of needed services, and it requires the knowledge of service networks. According to Patti and Resnik (1972), the three intra-organizational change components in social work practice are formulation of goals, mobilization of resources and intervention. Resources are the inputs that are used in the activities of a program. Broadly speaking, the term encompasses natural, physical, financial, human, community and social resources.

Definition

According to *Michael Norton* (2003), " Resource mobilisation is about an organisation getting the resources that are needed to be able to do the work it has planned. It is about getting a range of resources from a wide range of resource providers (or donors) through a number of different mechanisms."

Resource mobilization is a process of identifying the resources essential for the development, implementation and continuation of works for achieving the objectives. In real terms, resource mobilization means expansion of relations with the resource providers, the skills, knowledge, competence, and capacity for proper use of resources. Resource mobilization is a means to the end, the end being the fulfilment of the vision: a team effort that involves commitment to resource mobilization, acceptance for the needy to raise resources, and institutionalization of resource mobilization policies and budget allocation based on priorities. Resource Mobilization entails identification of resources as well as resource provider and mechanism to receive resources. It further entails expansion of relations with the resource provider; right use of resources; knowledge and skills to mobilize resources; human skills, service, information, equipment; seeking out new resources; institutional sustainability and lowering of financial risks. Resources are the financial and non-financial supplies that help to attain objectives. These include providing expertise, money, skills, time contributions and services of humans, equipment and materials.

Resource mobilization refers to a distinct perspective for understanding social movements, emphasizing the critical role played by material resources. Earlier studies of social movements tended to view them as spontaneous or hysterical reactions to high levels of frustration. Resource mobilization stresses rationality, and the importance of adequate funding, leadership, and organization. It is giving people the opportunity to give. It is not an end in itself but rather the process, whereby resources are transferred from those who are able to give to those who are in need. The mobilization of resources facilitates this process. Resources are the enablers of an activity that not only satisfies the need, but also satisfies the giver that their contribution has been wisely and effectively used.

This term is used as it is more comprehensive than the usual "fundraising". Fundraising suggests that someone else has funds and approaches need to be devised to access their funds. Resource mobilization is more than fundraising. Fundraising is only one part of resource mobilization, which is the process of getting a broad range of resources for an organization. One needs to understand that resource mobilization is not begging, but an effort to facilitate the well to do to share their mite for the needy. It is a concept where people help themselves or in other words it bridges the gap between needs and the resources for a particular cause. It gives opportunity to the people to give whatever they can.

In the context of social welfare organization, the following queries will be raised in the context of mobilising resources: how one will raise the funds needed to carry out its mission? Where are the required resources? How one does sustains the organisation and work? These are the key questions confronting organisations when they consider how to maintain their work and strengthen organisational sustainability. Developing a plan or strategy for resource mobilization can lead to creative efforts in using one's own local assets to gain support for the organisation. Multiple sources of funding can increase the independence, and flexibility to implement programmes and reduce reliance on external (or foreign) funding. With increased competition for scarce resources, thinking of, and creating options for new, diverse, and multiple funding streams will help the organisation manage its programmes.

Classification of Resources

Local resources are any contribution from within the local community that assists the implementation of an activity, project or programme. They include a wide range of financial and non-financial contributions from local community members, including individual citizens, institutions, organisations, businesses, or government authorities. Resource Mobilization includes various forms of self generated income, such as community contributions, fees for services and sales of publications. It also includes obtaining support from the government, the corporate sector as part of their CSR activities, trusts and foundations as well as from civilians.

It is essential to be aware of the availability of the various resources at the first place, which can then be mobilized for appropriate social work intervention for human development modalities. In the field of social work, optimum utilization of existing resources is a fundamental policy that all the social work practitioners must follow. Local resources are resources which are available locally which may or may not be identified by the community. Therefore identifying these resources by the professional and utilising these for the welfare of the people requires a lot of skill and competence. We may classify resources under various categories.

Classification of Resources

Types of resources	*Examples of resources available in the local area*	*Examples of resources that are not available or that are difficult to acquire in the local area*
1. Resources Categorized by their Physical Traits and Characteristics		
a) Human Resource (Women and Men)	Educated (literate) women and men, carpenter, mason, semi-skilled labour etc.	Engineer, Overseer, Doctor, Trained men and women.
b) Natural Resource	Forests, rivers, land, stone, etc. (depends on the area)	Water, arable land, etc. (depends on the area)
c) Physical Resource	Plough, spade, table, pick, etc.	Polythene pipes, GI pipes, corrugated sheet, and cement.
d) Financial Resource	Local funds	External funds

(*Contd.*)

Types of resources	*Examples of resources available in the local area*	*Examples of resources that are not available or that are difficult to acquire in the local area*
2. Resources Categorized as Internal or External to the Organization		
a) Internal resource	Membership fees, special contribution of cash and kinds, staff, board and general members of organization, volunteer members, equipment, land, office building, furniture, time contribution.	Time availability of board, general, volunteer members.
b) External resource	Influence of government offices. Technical and financial support of development organizations like NGOs.	Funds and equipment.
3. Resources Categorized by Geographic Location		
a) Local (community level) resource	Community, CBO, members, local forests, rivers, land, stone, locally made equipment etc.	Time contribution, money, and technical services.
b) Resources outside the community	National and international organizations working in the community, or with programmes that area available to the local community.	National and international organisations and resources located outside local area.

Adapted from Community Resource Mobilization Manual (Part I),(1997) LDTA, Kathmandu

Human resources could be a great source of local resource. In social work, it includes the manpower associated in the formation for social group, the client and the persons associated in the client system. In communities, the potential personnel associated with any project as part of community organization comes under human resource. If we take into account the secondary methods of social work, people who are involved in the social audit, manpower that is part of social welfare organization and also the masses who take part in any social action movements are included in human resources. Human resource also include potential learners, teachers/facilitators, leaders elected to local administrative bodies, influential personalities, religious leaders, parents, etc.

All the resources available in the organization for the smooth execution of any project or activities are called organizational resources. It includes manpower, infrastructure, finance and raw materials which are part of the organisation. Infrastructure resources are the physical infrastructures, existing material facilities, transportation, communication establishments, etc. to name a few. Although, donor agencies offering small and large grants to undertake social action programmes are the major financial resources for NGOs, social philanthropy is also considered to be an effective tool to mobilize financial resources at local level. The federal government of India has provision for local funds that are being disbursed through elected representatives both at state level called MLA (Member of Legislative Assembly/Council) development grants and MP (Member of Parliament) development grants. These funds are being used for local infrastructure developments including roads, various facilities such as schools and health clinics infrastructures as well as toilets. By mobilizing local resources to support projects, organisation and local contributors benefit in a number of ways

Aspects of Resource Mobilisation

According to Sekajingo (2007), the following aspects are beneficial for both local communities and organizations for resource mobilization.

Sense of Ownership: By contributing their time and resources, citizens, institutions, businesses, and others can assume greater ownership of activities that directly contribute to the positive development of their communities. The sense of "ownership" comes from the pride and accomplishment of knowing that they have contributed their share to make their community a better place to live.

Building Social Capital: Social capital refers to the value of social networks and the increased willingness of individuals and organisations to help one another as a result of these relationships. By seeking local support, the human service organisations (HSOs) are more likely to build long term relationships with other institutions and organisations. These relationships contribute to the social capital within the community and provide a better base for future work.

Sustainability: Mobilizing local resources increase the sustainability of community initiatives. As the rapport between HSOs and supporters develop, future endeavours are likely to become successful. As members of the community have with long term interests in developmental projects, local supporters are more likely to join their hands than the external donors.

Independence: Raising resources locally also gives an organisation more independence and flexibility to implement activities according to the felt needs of the community. Additionally, local support means that an NGO does not have to adjust their programmes to meet the needs and interests of external donors. They can plan the activities with a bottom-up planning with the full participation of targeted community.

Sekajingo (2007) states that as organizations look for strategies to mobilize resources, they should be guided by these two important principles and assess the various possible alternatives from these two standpoints.

1. Resources, particularly money, are not value neutral or value free. They bring certain baggage with them depending on their origin and culture. Some local NGOs/CBOs will have strong reactions to some kind of resources (like for instance, resources from politicians), but will accept the possibility of resources from businessmen. Other local NGOs/CBOs will have a different perspective. The important point

is to have a broad vision to explore a wide range of possibilities and to be non-judgmental towards the donors.

2. The HSOs world is likely to change. Some of these changes are already in place particularly the drying up of funds from foreign donors. Existing patterns of resources from foreign donors to HSOs will likely fall into one or more of the following categories:
   - They will not be available to local organizations in the future
   - They have significant disadvantages that outweigh their advantages
   - They seem less attractive in relation to some other resources.

Therefore HSOs need to pre-plan the source of resources before these changes happen. But before planning resource mobilisation work, it is useful to spend a short amount of time thinking about the range of resources that organisations can use. Some of the possible resources which can be mobilized within the community for any programme or projects are:

Financial Resources: These are probably the key resources that all human service organizations need to be able to function and carry out their work. Depending on the source, financial resources may be targeted to specific expenses or be used at the HSOs discretion. Financial resources can be raised from local citizens, business, local authorities, or others in a variety of forms and through many means, including:

- Donations in the form of cash
- Grants from local authorities or other community organisation
- User fees for participation in various activities
- Membership dues paid by members
- Fundraising events
- Sponsorship of NGOs and/or their activities by local business.

In-kind Material Donations: In-kind material donations can help reduce the costs of implementing an activity significantly. Examples of in-kind material donations include:

- Sports and recreational equipment for playgrounds or youth programmes
- Office supplies needed for the operation of an HSO
- Building materials for the construction/renovation of community buildings
- Use of a car or other vehicle to transport or visit beneficiaries
- Food and drinks to offer to volunteers or beneficiaries

In-kind Intellectual Services: In-kind intellectual services can be an extremely valuable contribution for projects that require expert and professional services such as legal, accounting, medical, education, psychological or counselling.

Space: One can also take the help of philanthropists who are willing to support any programme in the name of social cause such as the free use of a room, office building, community centre, school or playground for regular or special events.

Human Resources in the Community: For conducting certain programmes in the community like medical camps, tuition programmes, construction of roads, awareness campaign etc. it is important to identify the manpower in the locality especially the youth. For organising a medical camp in the community, mobilizing human resource include the efforts being made to locate a medical practitioner, nurse, pharmacist and a chemist from the local community. Try to pull these resource centres for the execution of the programme with peoples' participation. Submitting grant proposals or writing letters to local NGOs, other funding agencies seeking local individual supporter are other forms of mobilising funds.

NGOs or the social groups including the Self Help Groups (SHGs) can take up small business during the festival season or throughout the year such as: selling products like food supplements, medicines, books, clothes and providing paid services like counselling, tuition classes etc. Organisation of events such as fundraising, demonstrations, and musical concerts can both raise financial resources and increase public interest among community members. Meeting a person face to face at home or in an office for resources which could be beneficial for the project is another way of resource mobilisation. Through resource mobilisation one can instil the basic value of love for humanity among children and youth by sharing their mite with the underprivileged.

Appealing through social networking sites has become a very popular medium to mobilize funds/resources. Twitter, Facebook etc. can be used by making an appeal for a social cause. It has wider acceptance in the society and reaches very fast to the people in this world of advanced technology.

Challenges to Resource Mobilization

There are several factors responsible for dearth in resources across the globe. Some of the common reasons for ever increasing lack of resources are:

- Trends in steadily dwindling the resources,
- Reduced external dependency Vs. financial sustainability,
- Many organisations are seeking access to resources while resource levels are still the same in most societies,
- Strategic issues, lack of solidarity and networking among the NGOs and compromise of principles in order to get funding,
- Lose of faith in the activities of HSOs by the donors,
- Swindling of financial resources by organizations and involvement of middle men,
- Lack of accountability and loss of credibility has in some cases caused donors to shift funding to other organisations,

- Inability of the professionals to convince the stake holders about the need and impact of the proposals, and
- Competition among NGOs and VOs for resource mobilization.

Resource Mobilization Approach

The Resource Mobilization Approach (RMA) theory is not a very popular theory. The RMA is based on micro-economic and sociological theories developed by McCarthy and Zald during the 1960s. Kitschelt (1991) discusses in his critique on the RMA six basic prepositions of this approach:

1. Individuals know what they want to accomplish through collective action.
2. Individuals are able to calculate cost/benefit ratios of participation in collective action.
3. Grievances in society are ubiquitous, but social movement entrepreneurs and protest organizations are the catalysts which transform amorphous masses and their demands into concerted and purposive movements. Although social movements are not identical with movement organizations, the latter are the 'backbone' of collective struggles.
4. Knowledge, money, hours of labour and solidarity and legitimacy are the resources that enable movements to build organizations and launch effective struggles to attain their objectives. The way and the extent to which movements acquire these resources form their constituencies and shape their activities.
5. Movements act in contingent 'opportunity structures' that facilitate or dampen their efforts to mobilize, patterns their strategies, and influence their potential success. Because movement participants respond rationally to contingent opportunities, movements are not subject to a rigid international logic of development. Movements neither follow a prescribed 'natural history' of rise and decline nor do they involve 'iron laws' of co-optation and institutionalization in the existing social order.
6. Resource mobilization theorists employ the notion of 'social movement' in a very broad sense. It covers all activities, or even beliefs and preferences, to change society by collective mobilization. This broad notion of social movements also implies a broad applicability of all propositions that RM approaches develop in concerning the behaviour of social movements.

Elements to Strengthen Resource Mobilisation

Some of the key elements that will strengthen the resource mobilization process are:

- Clear sense and commitment to the vision and mission by individual or organisation.

- Proposing programmes and projects that will yield results.
- Evidence of past accomplishments.
- Effective management and leadership by board members and staff who will ensure the accountability and transparency of the organisation.
- Financial systems that will safeguard the resources raised, including adequate financial controls, timely auditing and submission of utilisation certificates that demonstrate good management.
- Solid reputation, credibility, and positive image.
- Mutual respect and knowledge sharing between the organisation and the community.
- Participatory development and the inclusion of women and marginalized communities.
- The ability to attract, create, and sustain new resources, especially from the local community.

Steps Involved in Resource Mobilisation Plan

A resource mobilisation process requires preplanning. The effectiveness of the strategy largely depends on two pillars: the programme (its quality, relevance, efficiency, effectiveness, impact, results and sustainability) and effective communication strategies. Let us examine some of the steps involved in the planning of resource mobilization.

1. *Assessing current situation*: The first step towards effective resource mobilization is to link it with the overall strategy of the organization. One should keep in mind the vision of the organization and a plan of action of RM that is in tune with the objectives of the organisation which must be clearly spelt out. A review of the existing mobilization efforts will help to avoid the repetition and lacunas if any. The activities should be planned systematically and the modus-operandi should be decided specifically. The expected deliverables is another area that requires clarification. An assessment of the current situation places the project within the broader context. There is also a need to prepare proposals keeping in view the immediate requirements and long term requirements both for project implementation and infrastructure development.

2. *Identifying Required Resources*: Secondly there is a need to enlist all the resources needed for the project and the potential sources for mobilisation. It is very vital to make sure the all the resources are considered for short term intervention and long term requirement. It includes manpower, finance, legal expenses, infrastructure, transportation, equipment, raw materials, etc. Social work skills and capacities of the individuals have to be identified and utilized for proper conduct of any programme or implementing any project. It is inevitable to compare the needs of the clients/group/community with the available resources and the gaps should be noted for installation of required resources through networking.

3. *Identifying Potential Sources*: The phase of identification of potential sources of needed resources is the third step. One has to identify the donors and partners of the project. As Chiam (2011) states the need to match their scope and interest with the requirement of the project. Resource mobilization environment search and donor mapping has to be done in the due course. Ethical issues are to be considered i.e., one needs to understand the underlying principles of the donor and the values of the organization. That is how the most likely donors are identified to tap the much required resources. Some of the sources of funding include national and inter-national donor agencies; governmental sources; individual donors; philanthropists and now the corporate bodies under CSR scheme. At times political parties and faith based organisations also provide grants.

4. *Strategies for Approaching Stakeholders*: It is very important to strategise the approach needed to be followed for networking with stakeholders. Here one needs to consider the support of the previous donors and work on building new relationships. Meanwhile the new donors who have been identified should be made aware about the track record of HSO to create a strong rapport. In the case of new donors the initial contact would be rather formal while for former donors the strategy would be informal because of the already existing relationship.

5. *Steps in Approaching Donors*: A system has to be followed while approaching the donors. As an initial step of targeting the associates, informal request can be made over phone, e-mails, meetings over lunch, tea, etc. In a formal environment, it is always appropriate to get an appointment with the donor for initial contact. To introduce the organisation to the donor, it is appropriate to send an introductory letter along with the details of the organisation and its objectives. Drafting a project proposal and submitting it to a donor in the prescribed format ensures better chances of success. All these efforts need to be properly coordinated and channelized. Usually organisation employ liaison officers and programme coordinators having social work background to deal with such assignments.

6. *Monitoring and Evaluation*: All the activities pertaining to mobilizing the resources must be recorded with high promptness at all stages. It is crucial to include metrics at each stage and the expected deliverables should be indicated for every activity. If there is no monitoring and evaluation, the purpose will be defeated. Ongoing monitoring helps to understand the current progress of the project and it can be improved and enhanced if some errors are identified at any stage. Evaluation helps to introspect on the reasons for success as well as for failures of every activity.

Principles of Resource Mobilization

Some of the basic principles of resource mobilization include:

Resource mobilization should be based on a robust situational analysis

Most donor agencies welcome project proposals prepared based on situational analysis. Plans that are clearly focused on results, by definition include an estimation of the scope and scale of the required response, and of the resources needed to implement that response. One of the important components of the strategic plan, is the costing of the plan. A good plan therefore provides justification for allocating resources. Need assessment study will help to have a better understanding about the current scenario of any issue. Moreover, the situational analysis should also provide valuable information on different actors currently involved in supporting or implementing the project. The analysis should provide the information on the levels of funding available currently and over the next few years and therefore on the gaps that need to be filled. The annual and five year plans of some governments and bilateral agencies speak volumes about the need for long term planning. It is also helpful in funding proposals to demonstrate that the sector has already some allocated resources by the agency as this would indicate commitment and increases the chances of sustainability.

For various welfare and developmental programmes considerable resources are available at the disposal of the government. Many of the interventions within a particular sector requires minimal resources. It is better to have linkages with different organizations to expand the resources for better execution of the project. This will facilitate in saving resources by avoiding duplication of the projects and intervention. Therefore there is a need for networking with other agencies operational in the same area to avoid duplication. One of the classic examples is the rescue and rehabilitation programmes during national calamities wherein a whole lot of people and agencies including the government get involved.

Build consensus and collaboration for resource mobilization

The resource mobilization activities should be planned and carried out in collaboration with all the actors within a particular sector. Coordination within the sector will help to minimize overlaps in funding requests, and to ensure that requests are aligned to the sector plan. Coordination with the other stakeholders, particularly the concerned departments, will help to ensure that duplications are avoided. This is required to build cooperation with the donors. One of the well-known examples is the local fund raising campaigns of the Helpage India especially from schools across the country.

Resource needs should be prioritized

Although the ultimate aim is to ensure the availability of resources to meet the needs, the reality is that existing resources are insufficient, and that donors providing resources very often have preferences for funding certain types of intervention, or for funding work in certain geographic locations or those that target certain population groups. In addition, each funding source tends to have its own cycle or calendar, meaning that some resources are likely to become available sooner than others. In view of this it is necessary to prioritize resource needs, so that some gaps can be filled as a matter of urgency and the remainder as soon as opportunities arise. For example, to meet experts towards certain unforeseen circumstances, ministries and agencies keep unassigned grants at the discretion of the head or the Executive Body of the Ministry or the funding agency. Very often donor agencies provide funds from such budgetary heads for emergency situations.

Resource mobilization activities should be meticulously planned

All the activities that are planned for the mobilization of resources have to be in accordance with the phases mentioned in the proposal and also the grant allotted by the donor agency. There is a need to be cautious about the deadlines of the funding agency. It therefore makes sense for the professional to make a resource mobilization plan well in advance so that one is certain about getting positive responses. It is also appropriate for NGOs to apply to different agencies so that even if one agency is unable to provide support as proposed one can pursue with other donors for positive response.

Good relationships are the foundation for effective resource mobilization

Networking and collaboration are essential for building trust. Trust is essential for resource mobilization. Good personal relationships are just as important as strong professional relationships between organizations. Personalities matter. Government is strongest when it invites open collaboration. The core social work values of integrity, importance of human relationship, social justice and service are relevant to the principles of resource mobilisation. Similarly the methods of networking and advocacy are the two associated methods for resource mobilisation.

Collaboration is part of networking which further enables resource mobilisation. When people with common interests get to know each other, they often choose to work together, establish organizations and create alliances among themselves. Collaboration helps organizations to solve common problems, overcome their differences and pursue the goals of their organizations. Credibility of the organisation made evident through integrity and loyalty to the profession matters a lot in the process of seeking collaboration with the aim of seeking resources.

Transparency builds confidence for resource mobilisation

Transparency serves three purposes: it deters violations of norms; it reassures actors that others are not misusing resources; and it may also reveal problems with the existing regime that actors have not recognized before. Transparency is fostered by consistent, timely, accurate and comprehensive reporting of activities by implementers. Some of the values of social work that make evident transparency in matters associated with the resource mobilisation include, responsibility and commitment, loyalty to profession, integrity, service and hard work. Although most of methods of social work have linkage with resource mobilisation, some of the prominent methods associated with transparency are advocacy, awareness campaign, group work, social work research, community organisation and social welfare administration.

Publicising successes is important for resource mobilisation

Analyze and tell others about successes. Be generous in publicizing donor contributions. Packaging good news and success stories are important. Acknowledging and appreciating the donors, is very important. The value of integrity, social justice and service before self, enables an organisation to be transparent by publicising success stories of the organisation. This practice would also contribute to the knowledge base of the profession and would motivate other agencies and professionals to adopt similar practices.

Accountability brings credibility to resource mobilisation

The increased level of interaction with donors at different levels shows that donors expect accountability. Increasing mobilization of resources from them requires increased accountability from among recipients of donor funds. Integrity of the agency and its functionaries are very important to attract the attention of donor agencies. This is all the more important when corporate bodies and philanthropists are searching for agencies having credibility.

Maximizing use of resources

Within the context of strategic approaches to planning, mobilizing resources is as much about making better use of available resources as it is about mobilizing additional ones. Thus, stakeholder/actor interventions are duty bound to put to good use resources mobilised, which is envisaged to motivate current and potential donors/supporters to the cause. Timely evaluation, periodic auditing and performance appraisal aimed at maximising outcome are essential to maximising the use of resources. Donor funds are meant to change the status of clients and their households. Continued access to donor funds will therefore have to be achieved through effective use of resources to give results and demonstrate the outcomes and impact. The results of evaluation would make it evident about the impact of interventions. The method of social work research and social welfare administration are of great importance in order to document result or outcomes of intervention.

Governments, development cooperation partners, the civil society and the private sector undertakings must come together and develop a common understanding to invest resources in addressing the problems of the targeted population. By promoting partnerships between communities, between public and private sectors, and between communities and international research organisations can further enhance the process.

Regardless of local circumstances, if the local community values the work that agency is doing, it will find ways to support the efforts further. The most important thing is to recognize that there are many ways to sustain and improve the work without large financial contributions. The organization's future ultimately lies in the support and acceptance by the local community, and depends on the ability of the agency to develop creative ways for the community to facilitate the services provided.

Conclusion

Mobilising resources is integral to all methods whether it is primary or secondary. It depends on the skill and knowledge base of the social worker, how he/she is able to identify and mobilize the resources of the community. It is important to note that all the resources that have to be mobilised is in accordance with the community participation. Resource mobilisation process must follow certain steps and categorisation keeping in view, the need of the agency and the targeted audience. There are certain challenges that are involved in resource mobilisation. Linkages with some of the other methods of social work such as social work research, community organisation, networking, social welfare administration and advocacy would be of great help for any successful campaign for resource mobilisation.

REFERENCES

1. Dean, H. Hepworth., Jo, Larsen., & Ronald, H. Rooney. (2002). *Direct Social Work Practice: Theory and Skills*. Australia; Pacific Grove, CA : Brooks/Cole-Thomson Learning.
2. Norton, Micheal. (2003). *Getting Started in Communication: A Practical Guide for Activists and Organisations*. UK: Sage Publications.
3. LDTA. (1997). LDTA reference manual for VDC-level training. Kathmandu, Local Development Training Academy (LDTA).
4. Sekajingo, Latifa. (2007). *Training Manual. A Handbook on Local Resource Mobilization for NGOs and CBOs*.
5. J.D. Mcarthy and M.N Zald. *Resource Mobilization and Social Movements*. American Journal of Sociology 82(1977): 1212-1239.
6. Patti, R.J. and Resnick, H. (1972). Changing the Agency from Within, *Social Work*, Vol. 17, No. 4, July 1972, pp. 48-57.
7. Kitschelt, H. (1991). Industrial Governance Structure innovation strategies and the case of Japan: Sectoral or cross sectional comparative analysis. *International Organization* 45 (04), 453-493. 203.
8. Gordon Marshall. "Resource Mobilization." A Dictionary of Sociology. 1998. Retrieved on November16, 2014 from http://www.encyclopedia.com doc/ 1O88-resource mobilization. html
9. Civil Society Resource Centre (A Project of Aga Khan Foundation) Women Empowered through Citizens' Community Boards (WECCB) Hum Qadam Project Participant's Manual Local Resource Mobilization and Social Entrepreneurship.

10. UNASO. *"Resource Mobilization – Trainers' Guide"*, Organisational Development Programme Resource Mobilization. Available at: http://www.unaso.org.ug [Accessed on14th April, 2010].
11. UNASO. *"Resource Mobilization – Participants' Manual"*, Organisational Development Programme Resource Mobilization. http://www.unaso.org.ug [Accessed on 14th April, 2010].
12. PDA and UNAIDS Joint Publication. *"UNAIDS Best Practice Collection 2001, Strategies to strengthen NGO capacity in resource mobilization"*, 2001. http://data.unaids.org/publications/IRCpub06/jc579strategies_ngo_ en.pdf.Undated [Accessed on 14th April, 2010].
13. http://siteresources.worldbank.org/extgloregparprog/Resources/grpp_sourcebook_chap13.pdf
14. http://www.unesco.org/new/fileadmin/Multimedia/Hq/Ed/pdf/EDUCAIDSpractical%20guidelines-%20chap%205.pdf
15. http://www.csrc.org.pk/humqadam/wpcontent/uploads/2011/07/LocalResourceMobilisationManual.pdf

8

Resource Mobilization and its Relation with Other Methods of Social Work

Sheeba Joseph

Social Work as a profession underwent significant changes ever since it started during the later part of the 19th century. It is a profession which provides services to relieve distress, prevent sufferings, remove social injustice and provide opportunities for social development. Mishra (2004) suggests four areas of information with which a social worker must be equipped. They are knowledge about the availability of services; knowledge about people and their motivations; dynamics and strengths; and knowledge about the society and its values, traditions, customs, taboos, problems, priorities and information of resources such as fiscal, material and manpower. It depends on the case worker how he/she integrates all these information for the betterment of the individual/group/community. In this chapter let us discuss the relation of resource mobilization as a method of social work with the other eleven methods of social work given in Figure 1.

Social Case Work and Resource Mobilization

Social Case Work is the oldest method of Social Work. Every individual, child or an adult in order to grow and develop, has various needs (psychological, physical and social) to fulfil. Very often, he/she fails to interact and adjust with his/her environmental conditions fully or partially. Social Case Work enables an individual to obtain a higher level of social functioning through an interpersonal transaction or face-to-face or person-to-person encounter. The worker helps the client to achieve some personal/social goals by optimally utilizing the available resources in terms of the strength of the personality of the client, his/her social system or material provisions available in the family, community, agency or his/her social support network as a whole. According to Bowers (1949) "Social Case Work is an art in which knowledge of the science of human relations and skills in relationships are used to mobilize, capacities in the individual and resources in the community, appropriate for better adjustment between the client and all or any part of his total environment". A person is the net product of interaction between biological, psychological and environmental (social and physical) factors.

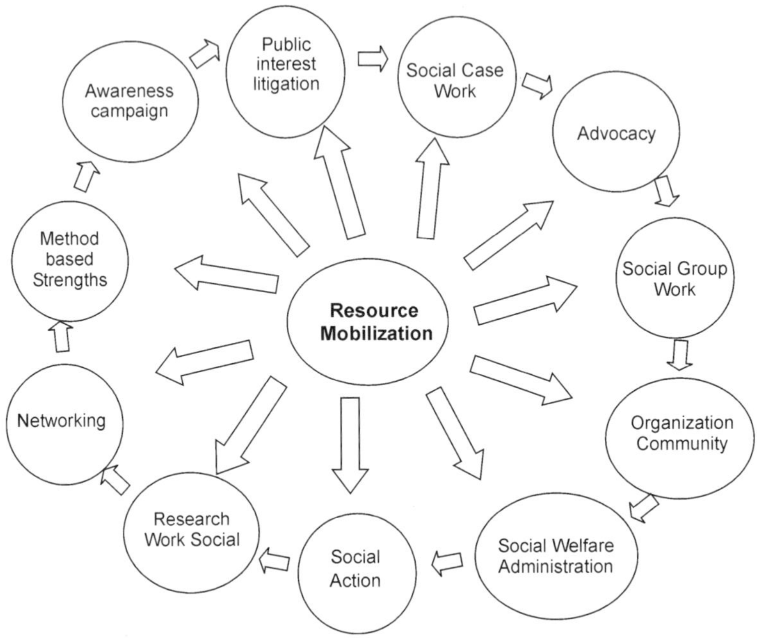

Figure 1

According to the principle of resource utilization it is the society's responsibility to provide necessary facilities for self-actualisation of its members. Therefore all the available resources within the community, agency and within the family support system of the client should be utilised to help the client. Resources may be in terms of money, material, power and influence, talents and capabilities, etc. The social case worker in course of the process will identify the resources available and try to mobilize it for strengthening the capacity of the client to make him competent enough to be productive in the society. Many a times, the client may not be aware about the various resources available, so the practitioners act as brokers by referring to resource systems such as public legal services, healthcare agencies, child welfare divisions, mental health centres, centres for elderly persons and family counselling agencies. Some social work agencies do not have the financial resources to help the client who is seeking help. Here, the social case worker can intervene and connect him/her to a source from where he/she can avail the service. Depending upon the problem of the client, the various resources are mobilised. Doremus (1976) suggests the 4 R's as a way of conceptualizing assessment in healthcare settings. The 4 R's are: Roles, Reaction, Relationship and Resources. The worker during the process of exploration and assessment will identify the internal and external resources that are useful for the helping procedure.

According to Hollis (1964) social worker is a provider of resources either as an advocate, source of knowledge, or as a person who has access to the resources of agency. For example, residential and day care services, foster care services, rehabilitation services, transportation services, medical aid, financial help, etc. The Case Worker in the process helps the client to enhance the resource identifying capacity and how to muster it. This will in turn facilitate the capacity of client towards mobilizing for himself/herself in the future. The worker should possess skills in resource identification and mobilization. This will help the client to optimally utilize the resources which will lead to successful restoration of the capability of the person.

Social Group Work and Resource Mobilization

Social group work, as one of the methods of the social work profession, was introduced during the first quarter of the 20th century. Konopka (1963) defines group work as a method of social work that is utilised in order to 'help individuals to enhance their social functioning through purposeful group experiences and to cope more effectively with their personal, group or community problems'. This definition shows a tradition within group work of helping individuals with problems. Brown provides a modernised and more comprehensive definition of group work (1994, p.8). He states that 'group work provides a context in which individuals help each other; it is a method of helping groups as well as helping individuals; and it can enable individuals and groups to influence and change personal, group, organisational and community problems' (original emphasis). In the principle of Social Group Work proposed by Trecker (1948), it is clearly stated that the group and the community resources should be utilized in relation to the group and individual needs for the benefits of group as whole. The group is always a part of the setting. This setting consists of the agency and the community. Thus the group must be understood as it is influenced by the setting. There is always a mutual relationship between the group and the setting. The worker will wish to see the group in this larger setting and will endeavour to help the group utilize all available resources. Thus, the worker plays a role outside the group as well as with the group. He will make his knowledge and experience available to the group. In this process, he acts as a liaison between the group and the community. In the group work process, the group members' capabilities have to be tapped for the fulfilment of goals. The group and the worker need to identify the power centre of resources which has to be mobilised for any programme or activity. Hence tapping the resources of the stakeholders and utilising in the right way for the betterment of themselves fulfil the goals of social group work. The activities of Self Help Groups (SHGs) in India is a suitable example of the linkage between resource mobilisation and social group work.

Community Organization and Resource Mobilization

Community Organization is one of the primary methods of social work which focuses on developing the capacities of local people in the community for solving their own problems. It tries to integrate and coordinate with the existing organizations/groups for helping people to identify their needs and fulfil them. Kramer and Specht (1975) stated: "Community organisation refers to various methods of intervention whereby a professional change agent helps a community action system composed of individuals, groups or organisations to engage in planned collective action in order to deal with special problems within the democratic system of values." According to their explanations, it involves two major interrelated concerns: (a) the interaction process of working with an action system which includes identifying, recruiting and working with the members and developing organisational and interpersonal relationships among them which facilitates their efforts; and (b) the technical tasks involved in identifying problem areas, analyzing causes, formulating plans, developing strategies and mobilizing the resources necessary to have effective action. This passage explains the relationship of community organization and resource mobilization.

The community organiser mobilizes all resources whether internal or external to avoid duplication of efforts. He/she utilizes these resources for the community. He/she also explores the talents and ability of different groups in the community which are very necessary for the development of community. To address a problem of the community while working as a professional requires resources. The resources may be in terms of manpower, money, material and time. On one hand, the worker is aware of the availability of the resources within the community or outside the community and on the other hand makes the people to identify the sources of resources and the way to tap such resources. Community mobilisation is a process in which relief workers and organisations work together with a community to address the community's needs. Efforts of this type may be initiated by members of the local community or by outside groups, but in either case, the goal is to support and strengthen the community's natively-available resources, encouraging ownership and continuation of the same, after the relief organisations have departed.

The goal of community mobilisation is to assist the affected community while it recovers. Following a crisis, the ability of the affected community to function independently will be compromised. Community mobilisation is about coordinating services and programmes cooperatively. The role of responding agencies is to strengthen and build on the affected communities' resources. It will include the affected community as an active and willing participant in the process of community mobilisation. It is a partnership between those affected and those responding. The affected communities need to be in control of the direction of their recovery. When they have ownership and responsibility for the programmes, they will be better prepared to sustain changes beyond the recovery period. In the process of community mobilization the worker consciously directs the channel in such a way that the resources existing in the community will be mobilized for a better tomorrow. Resource mobilization is a method which is constantly used by the worker in the course of community organization. Perhaps no other method will have a better linkage with resource mobilisation than the method of community organisation.

Social Welfare Administration and Resource Mobilisation

Administration is a process of direction coordination and stimulation in an agency designed to carry out some agreed purpose with economy and effectiveness in means employed (material and personnel) and with all possible regard for the claims of the individuals involved. Social work administration is securing resources in the form of materials, staff, clients and societal legitimating necessary for goal attainment and organizational survival. Social welfare administration covers welfare of all the disadvantaged sections of the society including the scheduled castes, scheduled tribes and backward communities. Social welfare administration has to play an important role in the administration of creative, preventive and promotive developmental and statutory social welfare services. One of the salient features of social welfare administration is equitable distribution of resources.

Resource mobilization as a method of social work, helps to identify the resources which are locally available, internal or external, and to mobilize it according to the needs of the underprivileged. Planning of the allocation of these resources is done with the help of welfare administration section. In the functions of social welfare administration, promotion of cooperative efforts has a significant place. In the present times, social welfare administration is a highly sophisticated method. For the participatory planning and management, the personnel who are working in the field need to have right type of knowledge, skills and attitude to work as social welfare managers. If the social worker is an NGO functionary, he/she should have the capability of identifying all possible means to coordinate with government agencies working at different levels. If the person is a government functionary then the person should be able to coordinate with other voluntary organizations or people from the development sector. Several schemes and projects which are implemented by the government as community development initiative could be grabbed with the ideas of various resource mobilization techniques.

The goal of every developmental project is to implement programmes for sustainable development. All the available resources of a state, community or agency are pooled together for better and coordinated utilisation. It harnesses the capabilities of human service personnel of different sectors to work together for a similar cause. In order to provide effective social welfare services to the needy and suffering, proper mobilization of human resource is very important. It will be accomplished with the help of proper planning and devising proper strategies. For any type of resource mobilization, proper administration is required or in other words we may say that both are inter-woven.

Social Action and Resource Mobilization

For some social action is an auxiliary method of social work. It is a method of mobilising masses in order to bring about structural changes in the social system or to prevent adverse changes in the situation. Richmond (1922) defined "social action as mass betterment through propaganda and social legislation". Social problems are part of society since time immemorial. Social Work, being a systematized body of knowledge, helps the humanity to overcome the gamut of issues they face. Social action is a mass propaganda to fight against any social evil or to fight for the rights of the people. Social action covers movements of social, religious and political reform, social legislation, racial and social justice, human rights, freedom and civic liberty. Previously social action was considered as a tool within the field of community organisation, but now it has been considered as a separate technique of social work (Siddiqui, 1984).

Social action has a definite set of goals and objectives like the other methods of social work. The goal of social action is relocation of resources and power to provide social justice and equality to all. The main objective is the appropriate shaping and development of physio-socio-cultural environment in which a better life may be possible for all the populace. Social action aims at solution of mass problems, improvement in socio-economic conditions, influencing institutions, policies and practices, initiation of new mechanisms or programmes, reorganization of power, resources (human, material and moral) and improvement in health, education, social, economic condition which can lead to social welfare. Certain strategies which are adopted by the social activists like dharna, morcha, slogans, emotional and powerful speeches and rallies create dramatic effects in social action. This is one way of pooling the resources for protesting against any social issues underpinning the Gandhian ideology of non-violence and satyagraha.

Mobilizing human resource is an integral part of any social movement. Most of the movements of the past witnessed tremendous support from the masses since they were influenced by the views of great leaders. They applied various strategies to mobilize them with proper planning. Social workers or actionists, during social action, make use of all the principles for achieving the overall objective of social justice and welfare. As Kitler (quoted by Tripathi,1988) told: Social Action as the undertaking of collective action to mitigate or resolve a social problem. According to him, five C's are important in social action and movement. They are cause, change agency, change targets, channels and change strategy. Advocacy is one of the forms that can be usually seen in social action. Social justice advocacy basically deals with power and relation and tries to bring a just society. As a method of social work, the interconnection and coordination between social action and resource mobilization brings success to any mass initiative.

Social Work Research and Resource Mobilization

Due to the complexity of social work practice, both on an individual and societal basis, social workers are often encouraged to further develop theories and hypotheses regarding the root causes of the problems faced by their clients. Research is underpinned by objectivity which is true essence of any scientific method. Social Work research is the application of research methods to find the causes and alternate solutions of a problem to help the client/group/

community that they confront in the practice of social work. The resource mobilization methods which is in tune with social work research goes through similar steps.

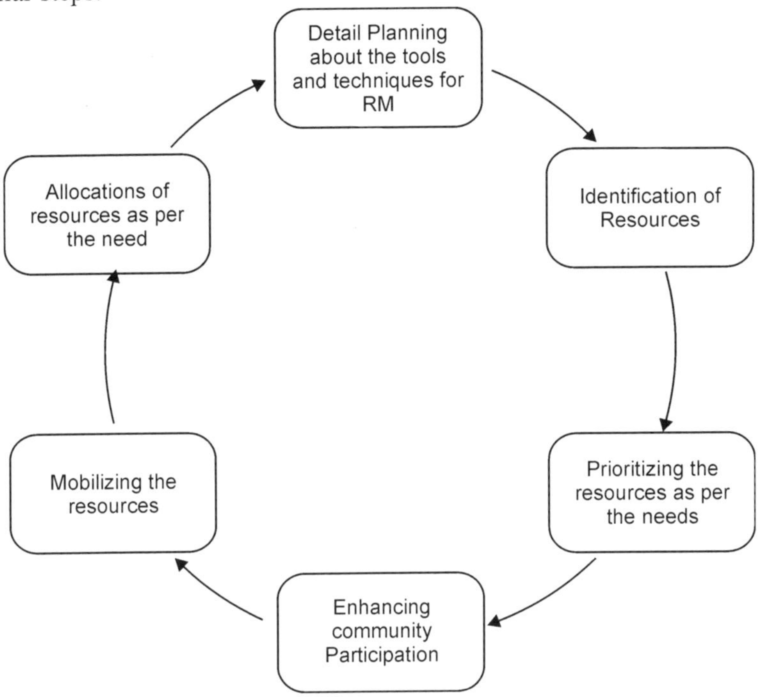

Figure 2: A Schematic Representation of Resource Mobilization

For mobilizing any resource, preplanning is required. We have to chalk out a plan of action regarding the tools and techniques for RM, how to identify the resources and rank them. The identification of resources requires the expertise of research. Based on the priority of the programme or activity/ project, it can be ranked and the survey will also help to understand the socio-cultural-economic-political background. This approach will help us to understand the system prevailing in community and device the strategies to pool the resources which can further enhance community participation. This approach is applicable if you are dealing with a client/group/community. Just like the research process, the resource mobilization as a method of social work has to be worked out systematically for grabbing it for optimum utilization. Social work research typically focuses on assessment of practitioner's work with individuals, groups, families, communities or appraisal. It offers an opportunity for all social workers to make a difference in their practice. The end results of social work research is another form of resource namely, the new knowledge which further enhances the effective practice of social work across the board. It also adds to the value of competence in social work.

Networking and Resource Mobilization

Social work profession stands for connecting with people, groups, organizations and agencies for providing better services to the client through the method of networking. The idea behind networking is to enhance connectivity and coordination for the betterment of help offered by the social workers. One of the main objectives of networking is to establish contact with people, experts and institutions engaged in same or related field. It can facilitate professional support for collaborative endeavours. Good networking helps to mobilize resources such as financial, material, technical and professional expertise. The growth and development of professional social work can also be fostered with the help of networking. It helps with the exchange of professional knowledge and experience among the professionals and between professional institutions and social welfare agencies. Resources can be mobilised with the help of proper networking since it helps us to understand the external resources. For instance, observing any UN declared days can be done in a large scale by an educational institution if they have networking with NGOs and other welfare organizations in the locality. Welfare agencies can allocate small grants and enable the students of social work to conduct various sensitization programmes to create awareness. Networking facilitates the mobilization of resources in professional social work in a big way.

In the professional social work practice, knowledge about the breadth of services and resources is a critical component of providing networking linkages. People may receive services from multiple service systems. The social worker can act as a link between all these systems. According to businessdictionary.com, linkages are relationships and interaction between tasks, functions, departments and organizations, that promote flow of information, ideas and integration in achievement of shared objectives. As per the Cambridge dictionary, linkages means the existence or forming of a connection between two or more things so that one thing happening or changing depends on the other thing happening or changing. Vertical linkages connect community units (people, groups, organizations) to units outside the community. The horizontal community is geographically bounded and is represented by many linkages between and among organizations and neighbourhoods that are located within the area, and, in most cases, serve the community. For example, the local nursing home may work with the neighbourhood school to develop an intergenerational programme for residents and children. This effort may also include a local bookstore that provides children's books, a bus driver who provides transportation, and a staff member from the local multigenerational center. These types of collaborative efforts, which are becoming increasingly common, illustrate the importance of the horizontal community as a concept. A linkage with the units within the community and outside the community helps the social workers to muster the resources. For illustration let us take the example of social work institutions that have linkages with many NGOs for appropriately carrying out the field work practicum of the trainees. The social workers utilize all these linkages to draw up capital for all their actions. Linkages help us to mobilize the internal and external resources i.e., resources within the community or outside the community. In short, it can be asserted that networking creates linkage between the needs and the resources.

Awareness Campaign and Resource Mobilization

Awareness Campaign is an organized, systematic effort through various communications media to alert the general population of a given area to anything of significant interest or concern (Rockwell International). Social Work as a profession always tries to create awareness among the people as a promotive, preventive, curative, and rehabilitative approach. Some of the recent specific examples for awareness campaign especially among developing countries include pulse-polio immunization campaign, laws, human rights, regarding various diseases such as HIV/AIDs etc. Campaigning is a creative and a technical process – an art and a science. It's all too easy to get 'too close' to the subject and to lose perspective. Thomas (1997) has given the wider application of social works methods to build awareness among the public regarding HIV/AIDS. It is impossible to practice social work by omitting awareness campaign. For instance whatever information social workers want to provide to the clients/group/community through the medium of communication is a part of awareness creation activities. To mobilize resources, we should create awareness among the public, without which community mobilization will be a mammoth task to do. We can pronounce that awareness campaign is an integral factor to mobilize resources. Most social work students involve in awareness creation activities as part of their extension programmes and field practicum. They execute the mission through nukkad natak, songs, signature campaign, leaflet and organizing panel discussion, seminars, FGDs, social networking sites, music concerts, drama etc. Several professionals mobilize significant amount of resources to further take this mission to a higher level where it can catch attention of policy makers. As it is mentioned earlier awareness building and resource mobilization are undividable elements of the same body. Awareness campaign itself requires resources and knowledge gained through awareness campaigns facilitate resource mobilisation.

PIL and Resource Mobilization

Public Interest Litigation (PIL) is one of the legitimate strategies used under social action. The concept of PIL is not new for social work professionals; nowadays it is used to protect the interests of the common people and also of the weaker section due to which it has come to limelight. The marginalised and the oppressed continued to fight for their civic rights; the emergence of PIL is a great hope for the disadvantaged and the common people as well. PIL emerged as a result of informal nexus of proactive judges, media persons and social activists. The Black Law Dictionary explains PIL as a "means of legal action initiated in a court of law for the enforcement of public interest or general interest in which the public or class of the community have pecuniary interest or some interest by which their legal rights or liabilities are affected". Collaborative litigation is a part of non-adversarial litigation. In this, the effort is made from various sections of society, the affected party, the court, the common people and the government official. They come together to ensure that basic human rights get implemented practically, so that a large number of people get social justice. Just like the other methods of social work, PIL also has different steps to achieve its objectives. For example in Narmada Bachao Andolan (NBA), PIL was used for obtaining the rights of tribal, rural and displaced people and also for the cause of ecology/ecosystem. In the case for the filing a PIL, the main resource which is the human resource was mobilised and continue to be utilised all over the world.

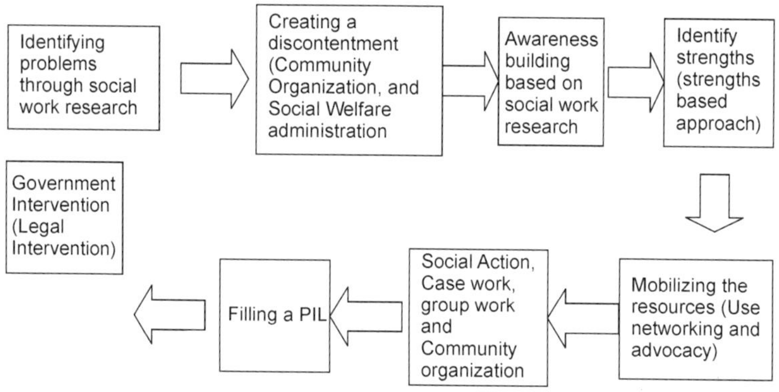

Figure 3

Figure 3 shows how various methods are interwoven, i.e., one method supplement the other for the effective implementation of any activity. Once again, it is reiterated that these methods are inseparable and one cannot be taken out as it is part of the same whole.

Advocacy and Resource Mobilization

Advocacy has been described as being 'at the heart of social work' (Sheafor and Horejsi, 2003: 57), a key function of social work practice in terms of helping service users and carers to become independent from service providers and in the process developing the skills to advocate for themselves (Haynes and Mickleson, 1997) and an important element of social work practice (Payne, 2000a). Advocacy therefore works to ensure that service users and carers, who are often denied these basic rights and opportunities, are empowered not only to regain voice and agency but also to be recognised as citizens. This is reflected in a definition of advocacy by the Scottish Executive, which states that: Advocacy is a crucial element in achieving social justice. It is a way to ensure that everyone matters and everyone is heard – including people who are at risk of exclusion and people who have particular difficulties in making their views known (SIAA, 2010: 4). According to Hodgson's (1995) model of advocacy identifies two elements of advocacy: Case or issue-based advocacy (where work is focused with individuals or small groups such as families in a task-centred way). Systemic or cause advocacy (where knowledge from individual cases contributes to collective advocacy for systemic change to legislation, policy or practice). Advocacy as a method of Social work helps to assist clients in upholding their rights to receive resources and services or to actively support causes to change programmes and policies that have a negative effect on individual clients or client groups (Sheafor and Horejsi, 2003: 57). Adams et al. (2009a) note that three dimensions of social work can be seen in the international definition, which also equate to Payne's (2006) account of approaches to social work: Promoting social change, Promoting problem solving, Empowerment and liberation. Social work advocacy is weaved through these dimensions.

The first dimension promoting social change relates to transformational social work whether with individuals, groups or communities. At an individual level, it involves advocacy on behalf of service users' and carers' needs within health and social care services. Social work advocacy also involves enabling people who use services to understand the oppression and disadvantage they face and to use this knowledge to promote change. In work with groups or communities, social work brings people together for mutual help and support to promote social transformation through changing structures and challenging inequality and injustice in society. This aspect of social work advocacy is less about direct advocacy and more about supporting self- or collective advocacy with service users and carers and attempts to mobilise people to challenge the impact of oppression in society (Payne, 2009b). Advocacy promotes equality, social justice and social inclusion. It can empower the people to speak up for themselves. So through the process of advocacy, a social worker is mobilizing human resource for a just society. It can help the people to be more aware about their rights and to exercise those rights and they can also be involved and can influence the decisions made for them regarding their future. Other methods to be used include awareness campaigns, resource mobilization, group work, strengths based practice, social work research, social welfare administration, networking, and community organization. Once again, it can be propounded that resource mobilization and advocacy as methods of social work are amalgamated.

Strengths Based Practice Method and Resource Mobilization

A strengths-based approach is a philosophy for working with individuals, families, groups, organisations and communities (O'Neil, 2005). It is an ecological perspective that recognises the importance of people's environments and the multiple contexts that influence their lives (Saint-Jacques, Turcotte, and Pouliot, 2009). This perspective recognises the resilience of individuals and focuses on the potentials, strengths, interests, abilities, knowledge and capacities of individuals, rather than their limits (Grant & Cadell, 2009). It is in this way that a strengths-based approach is seen to differ from traditional deficit models. As outlined in Saint-Jacques, et al. (2009) the strengths-based approach is based on six key principles: Every individual, family, group and community has strengths, and the focus is on these strengths rather than pathology. The community is a rich source of resources. Interventions are based on client's self-determination. Collaboration is central with the practitioner-client relationship as primary and essential. Outreach is employed as a preferred mode of intervention, and all people have the inherent capacity to learn, grow and change. Strengths Based Practices (SBPs) concentrate on the inherent strengths of individuals, families, groups and organisations deploying peoples' personal strengths to aid their recovery and empowerment (Pulla, 2012). Resource mobilization as a method of social work is utilizing strengths based approach to identify the strength of clients/group/community for mobilizing every possible resources. In all these methods, we can see every single method is helping the other to restore the capacity of target population for effective functioning.

The extent of the success of any resource mobilisation campaign would depend on the strengths of various individuals, experts, activists, agencies and groups involved. The clients - individuals, group, family and community - have their own strengths. The worker and the agency too have their own strengths which are both qualitative and quantitative. Along with the advanced media technology and social networking every resource mobilisation campaign can be made successful by the professionals.

Conclusion

In each and every method, one or the other way resources are mobilized and resource mobilization as a method acts a vital component in the execution of professional social work strategies in every society.

REFERENCES

1. Brown, A. (1994). *Group work* 3rd Edition. Great Yarmouth: Ashgate Publishing.
2. Haynes, K. S., & Mickelson, J. S. (1997). *Affecting Change: Social workers in the political arena* (3rd ed.). New York: Longman.
3. Hodgson, G. M. (eds.) (1995). *Economics and Biology*. Edward Elgar, Hants, UK: Brookfield.
4. Konopka, G. (1963). *Social Group Work: a Helping Process.* Englewood Cliffs, N.J. : Prentice Hall
5. Lal Das, D.K. (2000). *Practice of Social Research: A Social Work Perspective*, Jaipur: Rawat.
6. Brandon, B. and Brandon, T. (2001). *Advocacy in Social Work.* Birmingham: Venture Press.

7. P.D. Misra, Bina Misra. *2004. Social Work Profession in India*. New Delhi: D.K. Agencies.
8. Richmond, Mary Ellen (1922). *What is Social Case Work? An Introductory Description,* New York: Russell Sage Foundation.
9. Payne, M (2006). *What is Professional Social Work?* Bristol: Policy Press.
10. Payne, M. 2009. A Critical reflection and Social Work Theories in R. Adams, L. Domenelli, and M. Payne (eds). *Clinical Practice in Social Work*. Basingstoke: Palgrave ; Macmillan, pp. 91-104.
11. Schnieder, R. and Lester, L. (2001). *Social Work Advocacy: A New Framework for Action*. Belmont, CA: Brooks/Cole.
12. Sheafor, B. W, and Horejsi, C. R. (2003). *Techniques and guidelines for social work practice* (6th ed.). Boston, MA: Allyn & Bacon.
13. THOMAS, Gracious. (1997). *AIDS, Law and Social Work*. New Delhi: Rawat Publications.
14. Harleigh B. Trecker. (1948). *Social Group Work: Principles and Practices*. New York: Woman's Press.
15. Wilks, T. (2012*). Advocacy and Social Work Practice*. Maidenhead: Open University Press.
16. Hollis, F. (1964), *Casework: A Psychosocial Therapy.* New York: Random House.
17. *Doremus*, Bertha. (1976). 'The *Four R's*: *Social* Diagnosis in Health Care', *Health and Social Work,* Vol. 1, No. 4, Nov. *1976*, pp. 121139.
18. Elizabeth Segal, Karen Gerdes, Sue Steiner.(2009). An Introduction to the Profession of Social Work: Becoming a Change Agent. *Cengage Learning*, 16-Jan-2009 - Social Science.
19. Grant, J. G., and Cadell, S. (2009). Power, Pathological Worldviews, and the Strengths Perspective in Social Work. *Families in Society*, 90(4), 425- 430.
20. O'Neil, D. (2005). How Can a Strengths Approach Increase Safety in a ChildProtection Context? *Children Australia*, 30(4), 28-32.
21. Payne, S., Large, S. and Hawker, S. (2000). 'Elderly patients' perceptions of the readability and content of written information in palliative care', *Generations Review,* Vol. 10, No. 4, 2000, pp. 6-7.
22. Saint-Jacques, M., Turcotte, D., and Pouliot, E. (2009). Adopting a Stengths Perspective in Social Work Practice with Families in Difficulty: From theory to practice. *Families in Society*, 90(4), 454-461.
23. Adams, W. K., Paulson, A., & Wieman, C. E. (2009). What Levels of Guidance Promote Engaged Exploration with Interactive Simulations? PERC Proceedings.
24. http://www.eionet.europa.eu/gemet/en/concept/114
25. http://www.campaignstrategy.org/articles/12basicguidelines.pdf
26. http://www.pearsonhighered.com/assets/hip/us/hip_us_pearsonhighered/samplechapter/0205838782.pdf
27. http://dictionary.cambridge.org/dictionary/business-english/linkage
28. http://www.childrenyoungpeopleandfamilies.org.au/__data/assets/file/0013/62401/Research_Paper_6_Strengths_Based_Practice.pdf retrieved on 3rd December 2014.

9

Public Interest Litigation (PIL)

P.D. Mathew

One of the most important developments in the history of legal system in the recent years is the introduction of Public Interest Litigation (PIL) which enables social workers in mitigating the plight of the poorest of the poor. Until the emergence of PIL, justice was a remote reality for the illiterate, underprivileged and exploited masses. This has been largely due to three major difficulties: (i) lack of awareness amongst people; (ii) lack of assertiveness due to their low socio-economic status; and (iii) lack of an effective machinery to give them legal aid. It is only when the poor become aware that the wrong done to them is a legal wrong and that there is a legal remedy available to them, they will seek a legal redressal. Even if they are aware of their legal rights, the poor do not have the means nor the will to go for expensive litigation. Wherever a large number of people are victims of a common injustice or common exploitation, it is not possible for each one of them to file separate petitions and seek remedies individually. These are some of the major obstacles the poor face in the pursuit of justice.

The reinterpretation of the concept of 'locus standi' by the Supreme Court of India has removed one of the major hurdles faced by the poor and has paved the way for easy access to courts of justice. According to the traditional interpretation only a person who had suffered a legal wrong himself could take recourse to the court of law for relief. The new position is that if a legal wrong is done to a person or a class of persons who, by reasons of poverty or any other disability, cannot approach a court of law for justice, it is open to any public-spirited individual or a social action group to file a petition on his or their behalf. This new approach to bring justice to the poor and the oppressed, will give meaning to the constitutional objectives of socio-economic justice for all which is also one of the values (social justice) of professional social work.

PIL and Social Work

A social worker should be sufficiently equipped with the knowledge of the available sources of relief – medical, economic, psychological, legal — for those who are in trouble. Professional social workers whether they have just entered the profession or have been working for a number of years have an indispensable partnership with law. By virtue of the nature of social work and peoples' expectations as human service profession, legal knowledge is imperative for social workers. They should know the laws connected with everyday matters such as adoption, inheritance, begging, prostitution, offences against women, children, and other disadvantaged group as they will be often required to fall back on their legal knowledge in the process of helping their clients. A social worker working in the field of women welfare in India must have knowledge about the family laws, the Dowry Prohibition Act, the Prevention of Immoral Traffic Act and other such laws available for the welfare of women. Likewise those working with children must have knowledge about the Juvenile Justice Act and other laws protecting the interests of children. We can, thus say that PIL which comprises areas of laws fundamental to the welfare rights of the poorest of the poor are essential for the practice of social work.

It is expected of a social worker to know the application of law for addressing the problems of their clients. They should be sufficiently equipped with not only the knowledge of these laws but also the process and procedure as it relates to their practice. Here, we have to understand that the knowledge of PIL law that a social worker must possess is significantly different from the one usually possessed by the legal practitioners. The social worker uses law to empower the vulnerable and disadvantaged sections to reform social institutions, and to ensure social justice rather than to win or lose cases. They need to know about various legislations so that they can use them in the best interests of the clients/agencies. If social workers are adequately aware of these laws, they can work more easily for the target groups. By knowing these laws, they will be strengthening the efforts of the government in delivering welfare and relief to those in need of it.

Union and State Governments have constituted rights commissions, vigilance bodies and have provided an elaborate scheme of legal aid for the poor in order to provide access to justice for everyone. PIL is concerned as not just a representation by lawyers in court proceedings but a movement to empower the people with legal literacy, to mobilize them for legal action and to enable them with free legal aid to settle disputes. In short, social workers have an equally important role in PIL as that of lawyers. Courts and legal aid authorities are increasingly using the social workers as court commissioners to gather evidence in PILs and to monitor and report on court orders in the matters of relief and remedies.

Meaning of PIL

Public Interest Litigation means a legal action initiated in a court of law for the enforcement of public interest or general interest in which the public or a class of the community have pecuniary interest or some interest by which their legal rights or liabilities are affected. Therefore, PIL is a proceeding in which an individual or group seeks relief in the interest of general public and not for its own purposes.

PIL is a strategic arm of the legal aid movement and is intended to bring justice within the reach of poor masses. It is a devise to provide justice to those who individually are not in a position to have access to the courts. It was initiated for the benefit of a class of people, who were deprived of their constitutional and legal rights because they were unable to have access to the courts on account of their socio-economic disabilities.

Today millions of poor particularly those of the oppressed sections of society are looking at the courts for getting justice and improving their life conditions. Responding to the demands of the changing times and needs of the people, the courts are making efforts to become the courts of the poor and the struggling masses in this country. Fortunately, this change is gradually taking place and PIL is playing a major part in bringing this change. For social workers who are change agents PIL has come as one of the methods of social work during present times.

Origin of PIL

The term "PIL" originated in the United States in the mid-1960s. In the nineteenth century, various movements in that country have contributed to public interest law, which are a part of the legal aid movement. The first legal aid office was established in New York in 1876. In the 1960s the PIL movement began to receive financial support from the office of economic opportunity. This encouraged lawyers and public spirited persons to take up cases of the under-privileged and fight against various issues like—dangers to environment, harms to public health, exploitation of vulnerable masses, exploitation of consumers and injustice to the weaker sections. In England PIL made a mark during the years of Lord Denning in the 1970s. He as a petitioner brought several public issues to the court.

PIL had begun in India towards the end of 1970s and came into full bloom in the 1980s. Justice V.R. Krishna Iyer and Justice P.N. Bhagwati, have delivered some landmark judgements which opened up new vistas of PIL.

Some of the Supreme Court Judges in India felt the need for initiating PIL because they observed that the protection of law had so far been available only to the rich and the politically powerful. The civil and political rights of the poor people existed only on paper and not in reality. The poor and the illiterate were not able to understand their legal problems and did not have legal access to justice through the traditional type of litigation because of its high cost, complicated and slow procedures. Hence they believed that the time has come for the courts of the rich to become the courts also of the poor and the oppressed masses. They wanted to make the judicial system an effective instrument of social justice. Justice Bhagwati has encouraged PIL as chairperson of the committee for implementing Legal Aid Schemes.

The Apex Court in India realized its constitutional power of intervention which could be used to mitigate the misery arising from repressive practices of government, lawlessness and administrative negligence and indifference.

Judges, committed to the cause of social justice, recognized that they could play a proactive role to tilt the balance of governance in favour of the have-nots.

Nature of PIL

According to Justice V.R. Krishna Iyer, PIL is a process, of obtaining justice for the people and of voicing people's grievances through the legal process. The aim of PIL is to give to common people access to courts and obtain legal redressal against injustice done to them. Justice P.N. Bhagwati, opined that "PIL is not in the nature of adversary litigation but it is a challenge and an opportunity to the Government and its officers to make basic human rights meaningful to the deprived and vulnerable sections of the community and to assure them social and economic justice which is the signature tune of our Constitution. The government and its officers must welcome PIL because it would provide them an occasion to examine whether the poor and the downtrodden are getting their social entitlements or they are continuing to remain victims of deception and exploitation at the hands of strong and powerful sections of the community. When the court entertains PIL, it does not do so in a caviling spirit or in a confrontational mood or with a view to tilting at executive authority or seeking to usurp it, but its attempt is only to ensure observance of social and economic rescue programmes, legislative as well as executive, framed for the benefit of the have-nots and the handicapped and to protect them against violation of their basic human rights, which is also the constitutional obligation of the executive. The court is thus merely assisting in the realization of the constitutional objective *(Bandhua Mukti Morcha Vs. Union of India,* AIR 1984 SC 802). In PIL unlike traditional dispute resolution mechanism, there is no determination, or adjudication on individual rights. While in the ordinary conventional adjudication, the party structure is merely bipolar and controversy pertains to the determination of legal consequences of past events and the remedy is essentially linked to and limited by the logic of the array of the parties, in public interest action the proceeding cut across and transcend these traditional forms and inhibitions. The compulsion for judicial innovation of the technique of public interest action in the constitutional premise of a social and economic transformation is to usher in an egalitarian social order and a welfare state (Bakshi, 2000: 189-193).

Essentials of PIL

The main presumption behind PIL was that radical changes in society would come about through the courts of justice if fundamental rights of weak and poor citizens are enforced effectively. The new technique fashioned by the architects of PIL would bring about far reaching changes in the judicial system of the country. Public enterprises are owned by the people and those who run them are accountable to the people. The accountability of the public sector to the Parliament is ineffective. In such cases the court would be under duty to interfere (*Fertiliser Corporation V/s Union of India,* AIR 1981, SC 434).

There are three new elements incorporated in PIL: (a) Liberalisation of law relating to "locus standi", (b) Adoption of simple procedure in entertaining PIL petitions, and (c) Expansion of the meaning and scope of Articles 14, 21 and 32 of the Constitution.

Justice Bhagwati in S.P. Gupta's case pointed out the essentials of PIL, as under:

a) There must be a legal wrong caused to a person or to a determinate class of person, on whom burden is imposed in violation of law or without legal authority.
b) The wrong must arise from violation of any constitutional or legal right.
c) The wronged person (or determinate group of persons) must be unable to approach court for relief by reason of (i) poverty, (ii) helplessness; or (iii) social or economic disability or socially or economically disadvantaged person.
d) If the above conditions are satisfactory, then any member of the public can seek judicial relief for the above wrong.
e) But the court should be anxious to ensure that the person initiated the proceeding to acting bona fide to get redress for a public grievance and not to pursue personal gains or from malicious motives.
f) If the case is otherwise appropriate for PIL then the court can act even on letter addressed to it (*S.P. Gupta vs. Union of India*, AIR 1982 SC 149).

Thus it is an appropriate method of social work intervention to provide justice to the poor.

Constitutional Provisions

The new and liberal interpretation of the fundamental rights found in Part III and the Directive Principles of State Policy in Part IV of the Constitution of India gave the present movement for PIL a radical thrust. They are drawn from the revolutionary documents like the American Bill of Rights and the Universal Declaration of Human Rights. Articles 32 and 226 of the Constitution give power to any citizen to move the Supreme Court or High Courts whenever there is an infringement of a fundamental right.

Article 32 (1) guarantees the right to move the Supreme Court by appropriate proceedings for the enforcement of the fundamental rights. Article 32(2) states that the Supreme Court shall have the power to issue directions or orders or writs, including writs in the nature of habeas corpus, mandamus, prohibition, quo warranto and certiorari, whichever may be appropriate for the enforcement, of any of the rights conferred by Part III of the Constitution.

Article 226 states that notwithstanding anything contained in Article 32, every High Court shall have power, throughout the territories in relation to which it exercises jurisdiction, to issue to any person or authority, including writs in the nature of habeas corpus, mandamus, prohibition, quo warranto and certiorari; or any of them, for the enforcement of any of the rights conferred by Part III (fundamental rights) and for any other purpose.

The Supreme Court and the High Courts have equal powers to issue writs, orders or directions for enforcement of the fundamental rights. The Supreme Court expanded the meaning and scope of the fundamental rights in favour of the weaker sections of society. The meaning and scope of Articles 14, 21 and 32 of the Constitution were given a wider interpretation in favour of the weaker sections. The right to life was interpreted to mean a right to livelihood as well.

Similarly, the right of equality under the law guaranteed by Article 14 was interpreted to provide a right against executive and administrative arbitrariness in any decision making.

New Interpretations of 'Locus Standi'

The Latin words "locus standi" signify the legal right of a person to file a suit or conduct a litigation in a court of law. According to the traditional Anglo-Saxon concept of 'locus standi' means only the person whose rights were violated could sue for judicial redress. No one could file a petition in the court on his behalf. This doctrine was evolved in an era when the courts were mainly concerned with the rights of the individual. The old doctrine of 'locus standi' had not been found to be adequate to meet the needs of a developing society. In the new age of collective rights, it has been felt that the traditional interpretation of 'locus standi' should be changed to bring justice within the reach of the poor masses. According to the new interpretation given to this doctrine by the Supreme Court when the rights of an individual or a class of persons are violated and if by reasons of poverty or disability they cannot approach the court themselves, any public spirited-person or institution, acting in good faith, and not out of vengeance, can move the court for judicial redress.

The strict rule of 'locus standi' was first relaxed in *S.P. Gupta vs. Union of India* (AIR 1982 SC 149). The seven-Judges Constitution bench, by a majority, ruled that any member of the public acting bona fide and having sufficient interest in instituting an action for redressal of public wrong or public injury, but who is not a busy body or a meddlesome interloper, could move the court. The court will not insist on strict procedures when such a person moves a petition on behalf of another or a class of persons who have suffered legal wrong and they themselves cannot approach the court by reason of poverty, helplessness or social backwardness.

The important part of this judgment dealing with the issue of 'locus stand' is that it may, therefore, now be taken as well established that where a legal wrong or a legal injury is caused to a person or to a determinate class of persons by reason of violation of any constitutional or legal right or any burden is imposed in contravention of any constitutional or legal provision or without authority of law or any such legal wrong or legal injury or illegal burden is threatened and such person or determinate class of persons is by reason of poverty, helplessness or disability or socially or economically disadvantaged position, unable to approach the court for relief, any member of the public can maintain an application for an appropriate direction, order or writ in the High Court under Article 226 and in case of breach of any fundamental right of such person or determinate class of persons, in this Court under Article 32 seeking judicial redress for the legal wrong or injury caused to such person or determinate class of persons."

Regarding 'locus standi' the Supreme Court in the Judges transfer case [*S.P. Gupta vs. Union of India,* AIR 1982 SC 149 and (1994) 4 SCC 305] ruled that any member of the public having "sufficient interest" can approach the court for enforcing constitutional or legal rights of other persons and redressal of a common grievance.

Persons Disqualified to File PIL

The following persons are not entitled to file a PIL case: (a) a person without sufficient public interest; (b) a person acting for self-gain or personal profit.; (c) a person with political involvement; and (d) a person with malafide intentions.

A third party who is a total stranger to the prosecution which ended in the conviction of the accused has no 'locus standi' to challenge the conviction and sentence awarded to the convicts through a PIL. It was upheld by the Supreme Court in *Simaranjit Singh Mann vs. Union of India*, 1992 (4) SC 65. In this case the two assassins of General Vaidya were found guilty of murdering him. They were awarded death penalty which was confirmed by the Supreme Court. The President of Akali Dal filed a PIL under Article 32 challenging the conviction and the sentence on the ground of violation of Article 22, 21 and 14 of the Constitution. The court held that the petitioner has no 'locus standi' to file the petition as he was a total stranger to the prosecution and more than that he was not even authorised by the convicts. The fear expressed by certain people regarding the liberal view of the Supreme Court on 'locus standi' is that it would lead the court being flooded with writ litigation and therefore they should not be encouraged.

To the above criticism the court declared, "No State, had the right to tell its citizens that because a large number of cases of the rich are pending in our courts, we will not help the poor to come to the courts, for seeking justice until the staggering load of cases of people who can afford rich lawyers is disposed off" (AIR 1983 SC 339).

Issues Related to PIL

The following issues can be taken for PIL.

1. Basic amenities such as roads, water, medicines, electricity, primary school, primary health centre, bus service, etc.
2. Rehabilitation of displaced persons
3. Identification and rehabilitation of bonded and child labourers
4. Illegal detention and arrest
5. Torture of people in police custody
6. Custodial deaths
7. Protection of prisoner's rights
8. Jail reform
9. Speedy trials of undertrials
10. Atrocities against SCs/STs
11. Neglect of inmates of government welfare homes
12. Children in custody
13. Adoption of children
14. Corruption charges against public servants
15. Maintenance of law and order
16. Payment of minimum wages
17. Legal aid to the poor
18. Starvation deaths
19. Indecent television programmes
20. Environmental pollution
21. Unauthorised eviction of poor people from slums
22. Implementation of welfare laws
23. Violation of fundamental rights of weaker sections

In addition, PIL can also be filed in violation of or infringement of human rights.

Examples of PIL

1) Demands of Asiad Workers for their Rights under Labour Laws

Delhi Administration in 1981 had employed over one lakh labourers through contractors for the construction of Asiad projects. The government agencies and the contractors did not care for the observance of the labour laws related to the contract workers. They were noteven paid the minimum wages. The report of a freelance journalist V.T. Padmanabhan of their exploitation by the contractors which appeared in the Mainstream (August 1981) accompanied by a letter written by the President of the People's Union for Democratic Rights (PUDR) was sent to the Supreme Court. The Court accepted the letter and appointed ombudsmen to study the working conditions of Asiad labourers.

The decision of the court on this case was a landmark judgment which enlarged the scope of locus standi, fundamental rights and liability of the State (*Peoples' Union for Democratic Rights vs. Union of India*, AIR 1982 SC 1477).

2) Eviction of Gudalur Farmers

This PIL was filed in the Supreme Court against the State of Tamil Nadu by a local advocate, Mr. M.J. Cherian, on behalf of the poor farmers of Gudalur who have been cultivating their lands for several years. The petitioner alleged that persons who had for many years been cultivating the land were sought to be summarily evicted without adhering to the principles of natural justice contained in the State Forest Act. It was stated in the petition that the forest officers and the police were committing atrocities on the Gudalur farmers.

The Supreme Court by an interim order, stopped the destruction of crops and forcible eviction of farmers. The Court finally ordered that the claims of the farmers for grant of pattas to the lands in question should be re-examined by a competent authority. Those farmers whose claims were not substantiated ultimately could make representations on humanitarian and compassionate grounds. The court also ordered the State Government to consider their case sympathetically.

3. Liberation of Pichola Bonded Labourers

About forty bonded labourers working in Pichola in Bhiwani district described their miserable conditions in which they were living, through a letter addressed to the Supreme Court. They wrote "We are all Adivasi Bhils, with great difficulty we are given wages from Rs. 3 to 5 a day which is just enough for our food rations. Drinking water is supplied once in three or four days. Our huts are worse than those used for keeping animals. We want to go away from here now itself but our Master and his goondas tell us that we cannot leave unless we pay back their loan which is Rs. 2,200 to Rs. 8,000 per family. Our master enters our huts and molests our young daughters and also beats them up. Please save us." Swami Agnivesh, Chairman of the Bandhua Mukti Morcha forwarded this letter to the Supreme Court.

A division bench headed by Justice P.N. Bhagwati appointed two Commissions to enquire into the conditions of these labourers and report to the court. The expenses of the Commissioners were met by the Committee for Implementing Legal Aid Schemes. Through the interim orders of the Court, several groups of bonded labourers were released from the contractors.

4. Case Against Custodial Violence

In 1983, Sheela Barse, a well known journalist, addressed a letter to the Supreme Court complaining of custodial violence committed against women undertrials while they were confined in police lock-ups in the city of Bombay. The court appointed Ms Armaity Desai, from Nirmala Niketan, College of Social Work, to investigate the matter and submit a report. On the basis of Ms Desai's report, the Supreme Court bench consisting of Justice Bhagwati, Justice R.S. Pathak and Justice A.N. Sen issued directions to the State of Maharashtra to take steps to protect the prisoners in police lock-ups against torture and ill-treatment.

5. Petition for Speedy Trials of Juvenile Undertrials

In this writ petition filed in 1985, Sheela Barse highlighted the inhuman treatment meted out to juveniles. The petition prayed for the release of 1,400 children detained in jails and for speedy trials of juvenile under trials. It also requested the court for a uniform juvenile justice system. It was a direct outcome of the exposure of this issue through media and public interest litigation that a Juvenile Justice Bill was passed in 1986 which laid down a uniform legal framework and guidelines to the states to try juvenile delinquents. The decision to shift children from jails to observation homes providing educational and vocational training facilities was also taken at the state level (*Sherla Barse vs. Union of India*, AIR SC 2211).

6. Ban on Harmful Drugs

Dr. Vincent Panikulangara, Advocate and General Secretary of Public Interest Law Service Society (PILSS), Cochin, filed a writ petition in the Supreme Court in April 1983 seeking a ban on harmful and ineffective drugs. He pointed out that a committee appointed by the Government recommended to ban 20 fixed dose combinations of drugs including some of the commonly used drugs. This was to have effect on about two thousand drugs used in connection with several diseases. Some of them are banned or are withdrawn from the market in other countries. However, because of the unethical practices of the multinational drug companies, such drugs were still existing in our country.

The petitioner sought an order from the Court to ban the drugs that are found to be harmful or ineffective on the ground that the existence of such drugs in the market affects his fundamental rights to life under Article 21 of the Constitution of India. He also pointed out that though the Directive Principles of State Policy cannot be enforced by a court, government actions contrary to the Directive Principles can and must be prevented by judicial actions. The Court rejected the plea on the ground that it was for the Government to lay down the drug policy.

The judgement, however, recommended the setting up of a Central enforcement machinery to regulate the manufacture of drugs and punish the defaulters.

Other Examples of PIL

Of the numerous cases on the subject, the following cases are from India worthy of studies:

i) *S.P. Gupta vs. Union of India*, AIR 1982 SC 149, 194 (Scope and basic approach)
ii) *D.C. Wadhwa vs. State of Bihar*, AIR 1987 SC 579 (Locus Standi)
iii) *Ratlam Municipality vs. Vardichand*, AIR 1980 SC 1622 (General)
iv) *Fertilizer Corporation vs. Union of India*, AIR 1981 SC 344 (Locus Standi)

v) *People's Union for Democratic Rights vs. Union of India*, AIR 1982 SC 1473 (General)
vi) *State of Himachal Pradesh vs. Parents*, AIR 1985 SC
vii) *Shivaji Rao vs. Mahesh,* AIR 1985 SC 910 (Mode of entertaining).

Procedure to File PIL

No person is bound to follow all the prescribed procedures and formalities of a writ under Article 32, when he files a public interest litigation, because procedure, according to the Supreme Court, is but a handmaiden of justice and the cause of justice should never be allowed to be wasted by any procedural technicalities.

"It is true that there are rules made by this Court prescribing the procedure for moving this court for relief under Article 32 and they require various formalities to be gone through by a person seeking to approach this Court. But it must not be forgotten that procedure is but a handmaiden of justice and the cause of justice can never be allowed to be thwarted by any procedural technicalities. The court would therefore unhesitatingly and without the slightest qualms of conscience cast aside the technical rules of procedure in the exercise of its dispensing power and treat the letter of the public minded individual as a writ petition and act upon it" (*S.P. Gupta vs. Union of India*, AIR 1982 SC). The Supreme Court held that it was empowered to appoint socio-legal commissions or devise any procedure and forge any tools it considers appropriate for the enforcement of fundamental rights of the poor (AIR 1987 SC 1087).

The Supreme Court has enormous power under Article 32 to enforce fundamental rights of the citizens. In the case of Shriram Foods and Fertilizer Industries the Court held, "Article 32 does not merely confer power on the Court to issue a direction, order or writ for the enforcement of the fundamental rights but it also lays a constitutional obligation on this Court to protect the fundamental rights of the people and for that purpose this court has all incidental and ancillary powers including to forge new remedies and fashion new strategies designed to enforce fundamental rights. It is in realisation of this constitutional obligation that this court has innovated new methods and strategies particularly for enforcing the fundamental rights of the poor and disadvantaged who are denied their human rights and to whom freedom and liberty have no meaning."

PIL can be filed in the Supreme Court and High Courts in the following ways:

- Sending registered letter petitions with relevant facts and documents to the Chief Justice of the concerned Court.
- By directly filing the PIL in the court through the Free Legal Service Committee of the Court.
- Directly filing the case with the help of any lawyer.
- Filing the case through NGOs or PIL firms.

Steps to be Followed While Filing PIL

While filing a PIL the following points are to be taken for consideration:

1. Discuss the legal issue with the affected people thoroughly.
2. Find out whether the matter infringes on the fundamental rights of the people or not. It is also important to specify which fundamental rights have been infringed.
3. Help the people to decide whether legal action should be taken in the court to enforce their rights or to prevent the violation of their rights.
4. Write out a petition with all the facts and details, dates, etc.
5. Specify in the petition the type of relief wanted by the people.
6. Get the signatures of all the affected people, if possible.
7. Collect all the available documents, newspaper clippings, photographs, investigation reports, certificates and affidavits related to the issue and attach them to the main petition as annexures.
8. If possible, consult a socially conscious lawyer or the members of the local legal aid society before sending the petition.
9. Send the registered petition to the Chairman of the High Court Legal Services Committee of the respective High Court or to the Chairman of the Supreme Court Legal Services Committee, New Delhi-110 001.

PIL and Role of Social Worker

PIL can be used as an effective method of intervention by the social workers. In this process, provision and operation of appropriate services and by contributing to social planning.

They work with, on behalf or in the interests of people to enable them to deal with personal and social difficulties and obtain essential resources and services. Their work may include, but is not limited to, personal practice, group work, community work, social development, social action, policy development, research, social work education and supervisory and managerial functions in these fields. PIL can be used by professional social workers as a tool for social advocacy, empowerment to ensure basic human rights, dignity, and conducive environment. In other words, the overall thrust of social work will be on developmental, remedial and rehabilitative dimension with non-elitistapproach. Thus PIL works as tool for social reform, social welfare, development and change while reaching out to the poorest of the poor who are neglected and powerless to address their own problems.

Conclusion

The Constitution of India guarantees fundamental rights to every citizen. The exercise of these rights is necessary for his/her overall development. The State has an obligation to enforce these rights. When these rights are violated by the State and its agencies, citizens have the right to take the matter to the constitutional courts for enforcement. But in the past, deprived sections of society could not make use of the constitutional provisions to get adequate justice through these courts due to ignorance of their legal rights and lack of means.

Following the new trends in Public Interest Litigation (PIL) in Western countries, the Supreme Court of India expanded the concept of 'locus standi' to enable public spirited persons and organisations working for the welfare and development of the weaker sections to approach the constitutional courts to seek justice on their behalf. For this the Supreme Court has expanded the scope of fundamental rights and simplified the proceedings. The main assumption behind PIL is that radical changes could be brought in society through courts of justice if fundamental rights of poor citizens are violated.

Today, public spirited persons can file writ petitions in the Supreme Court under Article 32 or in High Courts under Article 226 to get adequate orders to enforce their fundamental rights. Many PILs filed in the Supreme Court in the recent past on matters related to basic amenities, rehabilitation of bonded labourers, illegal detention of women and children, custodial death, environmental pollution, unauthorized eviction of people living in slums, spurious drugs, etc., have helped the victims of human rights violations to get justice. It is now left to the social activists and non-governmental organisations interested in the development of the weaker sections of society to make the best use of the recent development in the judicial system in India to enforce the fundamental rights guaranteed by the Constitution and to bring adequate socio-economic transformation in society.

REFERENCES

1. Peiris, G.L. (1991), 'Public Interest Litigation in the Indian Subcontinent: Current Dimensions, '*International and Comparative Law Quarterly*, January 1991.
2. '*Public Interest Litigation: A Retrospect and Prospects*', Indian Social Institute, PUCL (Delhi Chapter) and Centre for Public Interest Litigation, 1994.
3. Susman, Susan D. (1995), 'Transformation of Standing in Public Interest Litigation', *Legal News and Views*, November 1995.
4. Gangrade, K.D. (1978), *Social Legislation in India,* Concept Publishing Company, New Delhi
5. *The Planning Social Legislation: It's Role in Social Commission Welfare,* (1956) Government of India, Delhi.

10

Public Interest Litigation and its Relation with Other Methods of Social Work

N. Ramya

The international definition of social work is generally used as a basis for considering what social work does. The definition states: "The social work profession promotes social change, problem solving in human relationships and the empowerment and liberation of people to enhance wellbeing. Utilising theories of human behaviour and social systems, social work intervenes at points where people interact with their environments. Principles of human rights and social justice are fundamental to social work" (IFSW and IASSW, 2001). This definition recognises the complexity of social work profession. Due to globalization, modernisation and technology advancement, the present society has also become more complex. Owing to these changing scenario, Social work profession has undergone a major transformation. In democratic setup, services are offered under the framework of the legal system. Hence, social work profession requires an in-depth understanding of law and legal system. The aim of law and legal system is to achieve justice in the society. Thus, law and legal system are very important components of social work profession.

In the history of legal system, the most important development in the recent years is the introduction of Public Interest Litigation (PIL). PIL plays vital role in the civil justice system in most countries. It is one type of litigation wherein the interest of the public is given priority over all other interests with an aim to ensure social and collective justice. It offers justice to disadvantaged, oppressed and marginalized sections of society. It provides an avenue to enforce, diffused or collective rights. It enables civil society not only to spread awareness about human rights but also allows them to participate in decision making process of the government. It contributes to good governance by keeping the government accountable. The most important contribution of PIL in India is to bring courts closer to the poorest of the poor, the disadvantaged and marginalized sections of society such as prisoners, destitute, child or bonded labourers, women, and scheduled caste/tribes. It thus helps social workers to approach the court for the interest of the public in general as well as the disadvantaged or under-privileged segments of the society in particular for enforcing their rights.

The traditional social work methods such as case work, group work, community organisation, social welfare administration, social research and social action were developed over long period of time. All these methods are being deployed to address problems of individuals, family, community and society as a whole. However, in the modern society, social problems such as child labour, bonded labour, prisoner's right, protection of environment, corruption-free administration, right to education, sexual harassment at the workplace, relocation of industries, rule of law, good governance etc. are complex in nature. These complex problems either directly or indirectly affect the individual and the society at large or could not be effectively addressed through traditional social work methods. The cotemporary methods advocated by the Founder Director of School of Social Work at Indira Gandhi National Open University (IGNOU) which include awareness campaign, resource mobilisation, networking, strengths based practice, PIL and advocacy have given new ray of hope to address the contemporary social problems. This chapter explores the relationship between PIL and the other eleven methods of social work.

Social Case Work

Social case work is one of the earliest methods of professional social work. According to Mary Richmond, the case work is defined as "an art of doing different things for and with different people by cooperating with them to achieve at one and at the same time their own and the society's betterment." Thus, case work method aims to find solution to an individual's problem. On the contrary, the PIL is mainly used as a tool to address injustice to the society at large. However, there is strong interrelationship between case work method and PIL. Case work is primarily concerned with the adjustment and development of the individual towards more satisfying human relations. It helps to diagnose the root cause of problems. Better family life, improved education, better housing, more hospitals and medical care facilities, protected economic conditions and better relations between religious groups help the individual in his adjustment and development. Sometimes, due to certain factors, internal or external, the individual fails to avail the existing facilities. Legislative and policy gaps in the governance system could also lead to an individual's problems. Such issues could be effectively handled through PIL. For example, Individual hardship of the under trial prisoners of Bihar prison was published in Indian Express (one of the prominent dailies in India) had triggered a public spirited advocate to file PIL. In this case, *Hussainra Khatton vs. State of Bihar*, the Supreme Court recognized the right of speedy trial as a basic fundamental right. This led to the release of more than 40,000 under trial prisoners. Similarly, another individual case that triggered judiciary to fill the legislative gaps was of *Vishaka* which laid down detailed guidelines on sexual harassment at the workplace. The petition originated from the gang-rape of a grassroots level social worker. The Court invoked the text of the Convention for the Elimination of all forms of Discrimination Against Women (CEDAW) and framed guidelines for establishment of redressal mechanisms to tackle sexual harassment of women at workplace. Even though a particular petition may fail to secure relief in a wholesome manner or be slow in its implementation, PIL is nevertheless an important step towards systemic reforms. Thus, the method of case work not only addresses the problems of individuals but also helps to bring meaningful social change through legal and constitutional provisions. It may be noted that in several countries, registered organizations have come up exclusively to fight for justice through PIL.

Group Work

Social group work is a method that helps persons to enhance their social functioning through purposeful group experiences and to cope more effectively with their personal, group or community problems (Marjorie Murphy, 1959). The Social worker plays a vital role in this method. Social worker identifies problems and organises the affected individuals to help themselves to find solutions for their problems. According to Brown (1994), the group work provides a context in which individuals help each other; it is a method of helping groups as well as helping individuals; and it can enable individuals and groups to influence and change personal, group, organisation and community problems. Sometimes group work helps social worker to identify the problems which could be resolved through legal remedy. For such cases, filing PIL in the court of law is a promising solution for enforcing legal rights of the aggrieved individuals. For example, PIL was filed, on behalf of the poor farmers, against forcible eviction and atrocities committed by the forest officers and the police on the Gudalur farmers in the state of Tamil Nadu in South India. The court intervened and stopped the destruction of crops and forcible eviction of farmers In another PIL of *Ratlam vs. Vardichand* case, a group of aggrieved citizens had sought direction against the local Municipal Council for removal of open drains that caused stench as well as diseases. The Court recognizing the right of the group of citizens asserted that the centre of gravity of justice is to shift from the traditional individualism of *locus standi* to the community orientation of public interest litigation. Thus, the method of social group work helps to identify the larger legal issues which can be resolved through PIL. Both these methods are complementary to each other.

Community Organisation

Community Organisation method has interrelationship with other methods which brings supplementary and complementary effect. Murry G.— Ross (1967) defines community organisation as a "process by which a community identifies its needs or objectives, gives priority to them, develops confidence and will to work at them, finds resources (internal and external) to deal with them, and in doing so, extends and develops cooperative and collaborative attitudes and practices in the community". Kramer and Specht (1975) states that Community Organisation refers to various methods of intervention whereby a professional change agent helps a community action system composed of individuals, groups or organisations to engage in planned collective action in order to deal with special problems within the democratic system of values. One of the best examples for this method is the Narmada Bachao Andolan movement. It is one of the most popular movements in modern India. This movement was started in the year 1970 against Narmada River Valley Project. The movement has undergone several transformations. At the initial stage, Dr. Medha Patkar, a professional social worker, worked towards proper re-habitation of displaced people through community organisation. Several PIL were filed on re-habitation and environmental issues through planned collective action and community organisation. In another PIL case of Shriram Food & Fertilizer Industries, M.C. Mehta, an eminent lawyer, filed a PIL to claim compensation for the losses caused. Several people died in vicinity of industrial cluster due to release of hazardous gases. The court directed those industries to close down the manufacturing activities and processing of hazardous and lethal chemicals. Thus it is found that community organisation and planned collective action helps to address larger legal issues through PIL.

Social Action

Social Action has been described as a method concerned with mass solution of the mass problems. Social action often brings relief to a large number of individuals with similar afflictions possibly quicker than is otherwise possible. Social action and social legislation are complementary to each other in fulfilling the objectives of social justice, welfare, and development. Social action plays a vital intervention role for new law, repeal or modify an older one, and an honest implementation of existing ones. According to Hill (1951) social action is an organised group effort to solve mass social problems or to further socially desirable objectives by attempting to influence basic social and economic conditions or practices. Baldwin (1966) defined social action as an organised effort to change social and economic institutions as distinguished from social work or social service, the fields of which do not characteristically cover essential changes in the established institutions. The relationship of this method with PIL can be explained through *Parmanand Katara vs. Union of India* case. In this case, the court held that it is a paramount obligation of every member of medical profession to give medical aid to every injured citizen as soon as possible without waiting for any procedural formalities. In this case, mass solution for mass problem has come into reality through PIL. In another case, the mass social action of Narmada Bachao Andolan movement, through PIL, got direction from the court for proper rehabilitation of displaced tribal population.

Social Welfare Administration

It is basically the execution of social policies, social programmes and social legislations by philanthropic, religious and charitable organizations which provide services and benefits for the general population in need. In a recent ruling the Supreme Court of India through PIL filed by B.L. Wadere and Almitra Patel held that large area of public land was covered by the people living in slum area. As the growth of slums tended to increase, the court directed the concerned departments to take appropriate action to check the growth of slums and to create an environment worthy for living. Similarly, through PIL, the Supreme Court ordered government to convert government owned buses to use compressed natural gas (CNG) as an environment friendly fuel to address the issue of environmental pollution. Subsequently, it was extended to auto rickshaws for addressing pollution problem in Delhi. In recent years, through PIL, the Supreme Court has taken on the mantle of monitoring forest conservation measures all over India, and a special "Green Bench" has been constituted to give directions to the concerned governmental agencies to maintain judicial supervision in order to protect the forests against rampant encroachments and administrative apathy. Through PIL, Right to Education Act,2009 was passed in India in which Right to Education has been recognised as fundamental right under Article 21-A of the Constitution.

Social Work Research

It is through the application of research method in social work that creates additional knowledge and skills for social workers to solve problems that they confront in the practice of social work. The objective of social work research is to search for answers to questions raised regarding interventions or treatment-effectiveness in social work practice. It attempts to provide knowledge about what interventions or treatments really help or hinder the attainment of social work goals. Thus, social work research is the systematic and professional investigation of social problems and social work practice to enhance the quality of social work practices. Social work professionals have to undertake an in-depth study on various legal issues and identify infringement of any fundamental human rights so as to take up the matter through court of law for restoring legal rights through PIL. In several PIL cases, social workers have undertaken research methods such as quantitative and qualitative analysis of various data to prove the cause of social problems. For example in the Shriram Foods and Fertilizer case, quantitative data collected proved that the hazardous gases and chemicals released from the industries had directly caused the disease and death which paved way to file a PIL against the infringement of basic rights and sought relief for victims. Social work professionals, NGO functionaries and legal experts extensively use the outcomes of social work research for filling PIL.

Resource Mobilization

Resource mobilization is a one of the new methods being promoted as cotemporary methods of social work. It emphasises the importance and need for resources for social movement, welfare programmes and socio-economic development. Resources include knowledge, money, media, labour, solidarity, legitimacy and internal and external support from various services. Resource mobilization is a process of raising different types of support for an organization for cause. It can include both cash and kind support. For example under community organization programme, a professional may require resources for making certain infrastructure for the community for their frequent meetings. The resources may be in terms man power, money material and time. The social worker by making use of this method is aware of the availability of the resources within the community or outside the community and on the other hand makes the people to identify the sources of resources and the way to tap such resources. Obviously, resources are required for filing PIL. It is both in terms of money for engaging legal professionals and in terms of manpower to collect necessary data to prove cause of social problems. Social workers are by and large working for underprivileged people. They do not have enough resources to approach the concerned authority to enforce their rights. Therefore, resource mobilization is prerequisite for approaching authorities including the Court of law for enforcing legal rights through PIL. Under certain special circumstances, the channel of PIL can be sought for court's intervention for resource mobilization to cater to the needs of the most vulnerable and the deprived in difficult circumstances.

Networking

Networking is defined as "the exchange of information or services among individuals, groups, or institutions; specifically: the cultivation of productive relationships for employment or business" (Merriam-Webster Dictionary, 2012). This is one of the new methods being adopted by social work professionals. It is the concept of exchange of information and services through various communication media. The benefits of networking are long -lasting and continuous. Networking is a tool, whether through social media outlets or face to face meetings provides opportunities to talk with people, exchange ideas and gain knowledge. For example, an NGO working against Koodankulam Nuclear Power Project (KNPP) in the state of Tamil Nadu in South India had to network with various groups of people, organizations and donor agencies to file PIL against KNPP. Finally, government was forced to implement a development package for the people living in and around KNPP vicinity.

For initiating PIL against any cause, institution or government, one has to have wide network with the affected clients, their supporters, decision makers, legal experts and the affected community itself. Network would help in pooling resources from various sources including media publicity, research inputs, and responses from experts who had to force similar situations.

Strengths Based Method

Strengths based approach is considered as one of the methods which has focused a deficit oriented approach to the possibilities or what works. In contrast to a deficit approach, the strengths-based perspective offers a way to assess, treat and empower children and youth to assist them in achieving their highest potential (Racco, A., 2009). It operates on the assumption that people have strengths and resources for their own empowerment. It recognises that for the most part of life, people face adversity, become resilient and resourceful and learn new strategies to overcome adversity. Thus, strengths based approach is using client's personal strengths and in discovering resources in the environments to fulfill the client's needs and to enhance the client's resilience (Norman, 2000). It is an alternative to the conventional methods. PIL can play complementary role to the Strengths based methods. PIL filed in the field of protection of environment, corruption free administration, right to education, rule of law, good governance and accountability are attempts to enhance resilience. Strengths based approach in-fact helps to identify the positive aspects which have capacity to enhance resilience. Enforcement of such positive aspect is possible only through PIL.

PIL can help the clients to draw strengths from one's own hidden energies. Social work professionals can facilitate clients to become aware of the supports and reliefs that one can get by approaching the court of law through PIL. This is another way of educating the clients about the strengths available within one's own reach to address various problems being confronted by them.

Awareness Campaign

Awareness Campaign as a method of social work contributes significantly to other methods of social work. It has strong interrelation with traditional and contemporary methods of social work practice. Awareness Campaign is an organized, systematic effort through various communication media to alert the general population of a given area to anything of significant interest or concern. This method also has complementary effect on PIL. The social worker engaged in the process of resolving problems can highlight the problems of the affected people through various media. Some time, socially sensitive lawyers may take up these issues through PIL to address the policy gap, ensuring enforceability of legal rights and enhance the scope of fundamental rights. For example, *Hussaianra Khatoon vs. State of Bihar* (1979) was filed through an Advocate, based on the newspaper article published in Indian Express regarding the hardship of under trail prisoners of Bihar prison. Similarly, in the case of *Hindustan Times vs. Central Pollution Board*, a newspaper cutting was taken as complaint by the court of law. Anna Hazare's movement against corruption had followed well planned awareness campaign to achieve their objectives. Awareness campaign had played crucial role to the PIL cases being filed before the Supreme Court of India.

Awareness campaign method can certainly facilitate people from all walks of life to seek remedial measures from a court of law through PIL. In a democratic society like India with wide geographical coverage and home to nearly 1.25 billion people, the issues and problems confronting the poorest of poor are far too many. One of the most hopeful means or methods of social work intervention is to seek directions from a court of low through PIL when the rights of people are being compromised. The method of awareness campaign can go a long way in ensuring better and satisfying response to the exploited and the oppressed through PIL.

Advocacy

The dictionary meaning of Advocacy is: "the act of pleading for, supporting or recommending". It is an ongoing process aimed at changing attitudes, actions, polices and laws by influencing people in power systems and structures at different levels for the betterment of those affected by the issues. Advocacy is defined as "the process of working with and/or on behalf of clients to obtain services or resources for clients that would not otherwise be provided; to modify extant policies, procedures, or practice that adversely impact clients, or to promote new legislation or policies that will result in the provision of needed resources or services" Hepworth and Larson (1986). Advocacy requires a series of well-planned and interconnected areas to be implemented over a period of time. It is about promoting change and challenging injustice at both individual level and systemic levels. PIL is related with Advocacy as well. PIL is also promoting social changes and challenging injustice. The only difference is that PIL can be used when fundamental and enforceable rights are infringed, but in case of Advocacy, it can be used in other social problems as well. But both are complementary to each other in the contest of social work.

In a broader sense, PIL facilitates advocacy. PIL can promote policy changes as well as policy formulation in the context of social issues particularly those affecting the marginalized and the poorest of the poor. Social work professionals can move the court of law to address problems arising out of industrial disaster, food adulteration, environmental pollution including river/ water pollution caused by industries, safety of women, acid attacks, relief to those assisting victims of accidents, undertrials, bonded labours, child labours, sex workers, disabled, and so on. In several cases, courts not only give immediate relief to the victims but also direct the governments for amendments of legislations or enacting new legislations in order to provide justice to the affected and punishment to those violating human rights.

Conclusion

PIL plays an invaluable role in advancing constitutional philosophy of social transformation and improving justice. PIL has come of age to be considered as one of the methods of social work profession. It is an ideal form of "Indirect social work practice" for providing justice to clients at large. Furthermore, PIL can be used only when rights are infringed or when legal provisions are missing to address certain human rights problems. It always plays complementary and supplementary role to the other methods of social work. However, it is a growing and promising area to address complex social problems through constitutional and legal methods. Through Judicial Activism, the courts are proactively protecting the rights of citizens from legislative and administrative apathy particularly to underprivileged and poor voiceless people. Therefore, social work professionals should make use of PIL as one of the new methods to address the emerging complex social problems at large.

REFERENCES

1. Dassi Archana (2010). Social case work Practice in Indian context. In G. Thomas (Ed.), Case Work and Counselling: Working with Individuals. New Delhi, IGNOU.
2. Johns, Robert (2014). *Using the Law in Social Work* (6th Ed.). Sage publication, New Delhi.
3. Misra, P.D. (1994). *Social work, Philosophy and Methods*. New Delhi. Inter-India publications, New Delhi.
4. Neera Agnimitra (2010). Community Organization: Concept, Value Orientation and Assumptions. In G. Thomas (Ed.), Community organization management for community development. New Delhi, IGNOU.
5. Varghese Joseph (2010). Social group work as a method of social work. In G. Thomas (Ed.), Social Group work: working with Groups. New Delhi, IGNOU.

WEB REFERENCES

1. Deva Surya (2009). Public Interest Litigation in India: A critical Review, CJQ Vol 28 (I) retrieved from http://ssm.com/abstract=1424236.
2. NASW, July 2012. Careers. Social workers.org/documents/networking.pdf
3. Pulla, V. (2012). what are strengths based Practice all about? In Pulla, V. Chenoweth, L., Francis, A., Bakaj, S. eds. papers in Strengths Based practice, New Delhi: Allied Publishers.
4. Public Interest Litigation. Law Teacher retrieved from http:/www.lawteacher .net/ litigation-law/essays/public interest Litigation php.retrieved on 18th December 2014.
5. Racco, A. (2009). What is strength-based child and Youth care anyway? Cyconline, 127 retrieved from www.cye-net.org/cyc-ontesy cyconline-racca.html.
6. Sharma, Kusum, Growth of Public Interest Litigation in India, delivered lecture on 5th February 2013 at Amity University, Noida U.P.
7. Singh Aradhana, Public Interest Litigation, PIL. NGOs India retrieved from http:/ www.ng.osindia.com/resources/pil.Php on 18th December 2014.

8. Sood Mehta Avani (2009) Article: Part II Equality, Social Exclusion, and Women's Rights: Redressing Women's Rights Violations Through the Judiciary.
9. Srivastava, Anjali (2013) India: Public Interest Litigation: A New Horizon. retrieved from http://www.mondaq.com/india/x/273102/trials+appeals+compensation/public+Interest+ Litigation+A+Horizon on 18th December 2014
10. http://www.fundsforngos.org/free-resources-forngos/resourcemobilization retrieved on 26th December 2014.
11. http://SW741 advocacy.tripod.com.retrieved on 23rd December 2014.
12. http://www.campaignstrategy.org/articles/12basicguidelines.pdf.retrieved on 24th December 2014
13. http://humanrightsindia.blogspot.in/2012/09/human-rights-advocacy-for-social.html.retrieved on 23rd December 2014.

11

Networking

Nita Kumari and Rafat Aara

The history of professional social work shows that the methods to deal with the social problems evolved according to the nature of the problems as well as the levels of service delivery viz. micro, mezo, macro. The earliest methods were case work and group work and later the other methods of social work intervention were formulated. In this age of globalization, the nature and characteristics of social problems are complex and therefore new methods and techniques are needed to respond to some of the emerging problems. There are times when social workers find it necessary to network with people and institutions in order to render best possible help to the client system which is much needed and timely. Networking involves making contact with the third person or institution in order to get help of varying nature – monetary, expertise, facilitation, etc.

Let us examine the case of Rani, a domestic help, who could not take her disabled husband to the hospital for regular treatment, as the hospital timings clashed with her work schedule. Hence she requested the social worker to help her in getting an appointment with the physician for her husband so that she could accompany her husband after her duties are over. The social worker through her network contacted the social worker of that hospital and requested him to help Rani for giving her time as per her need. On the request of social worker, the physician agreed to meet the patient at a convenient time when Rani could take her husband for treatment. In this case, the social worker could help the client through his healthy and cordial professional network. This is something unusual in Indian situation. An ordinary person that too a person such as a 'domestic help' is able to get an appointment with a physician as per her convenient time.

Definition

According to dictionary.com "networking is a supportive system of sharing information and services among individuals and groups having a common interest". In Oxford Dictionary, 'networking is a system of trying to meet and talk to other people who may be useful to you in your work.'

In a November 2012 blog post, Miser described a new definition of networking as "the process of developing and activating relationships to increase the business, enhance knowledge, expand the sphere of influence or serve the community (http://msw.usc.edu/mswusc-blog/social-work-networking/).

In social work, networking implies the establishment of cooperative and collaborative relationship with likeminded people and institutions for mutual development and support for rendering help to the clients.

Importance of Networking in Social Work

Networking helps the professionals who establish contacts with other people and institutions working in the same or related fields. Through a properly planned networking, information can be shared with other people and help can be sought. It can be one of the important sources of making benefits from new contacts. Often people are not aware about the existence of several options in addressing a problem at hand. In such situations networking becomes very helpful. For example positive people's network which is a very well tested practice by people living with HIV/AIDS across the globe extends the much needed support to the group members.

Social workers seek membership in different national and international associations and come in contact with other professional social workers. Through network a social worker can make connections, and build enduring, mutually beneficial relationships. Through networking a professional can use contacts to acquire information, advice, and referrals for people in need as well as for financial and technical support.

In social work, networking is of utmost importance as a worker has to refer a client for other services which can be facilitated through other people who are working in different departments. For example, a child who is from a poor family and unable to get admission to a school could be helped by a social worker in an ideal school. The social worker can make use of the contacts he has with people who are working with educational departments or related to that school in various capacities and can find out how the help could be rendered to the child in getting the admission.

Objectives

The objective of networking is to increase the connectivity and coordinate between people and institutions working in the same area or in different areas. Through networking people can share ideas and information and can generate new knowledge. The general objectives of networking in social work are:

(1) To establish contact with people, experts and institutions engaged in same or related fields,
(2) To arrange professional support for collaborative endeavours for social work intervention,

(3) To mobilise resources of varying nature: financial, material, technical and professional expertise,
(4) To enable the growth and development of professional social work, and
(5) For the exchange of scientific knowledge and experience among the professionals and between professional institutions and social welfare agenesis and their personnel.

Essentials of Networking

The purpose of social work is to enhance the problem solving and coping capacities of the people; link people with systems that provide them with resources, services and opportunities; promote effective and human operation of these systems and; contribute to social development and social policy (Pincus and Minahan, 1973:9). Some of the essentials of networking include:

(i) Data Base

A professional social worker must have a data base of people and institutions which should be periodically updated. This data base could be saved in one's mobile, laptop, notepad as well as in the e- mail id, so that one can have access to these at any given time. The data base may contain details such as the names, address for communication, mobile and landline, e-mail ID, areas of expertise as well as other required information. For a professional, details of donor agencies, social and welfare agencies, banks, multimedia communication agencies, press, T.V., radio, police, physicians, taxi, people who matter including elected representatives, people in district, state and central administration, religious leaders, teachers, people in various service departments etc. would be of great importance.

(ii) Building Sustainable Relationship

Human relationships are of paramount importance in social work. Social workers believe in building a long term and sustainable relationship with people and institutions with whom they come in touch with during their study, work or attending a seminar/workshop/conference and utilize these relationships whenever needed. They believe in building relationship based on commitment and trust, which are keys to a long term relationship. Networking plays an important role in building long term relationship. Similar to other methods of social work, networking too gives importance to human worth and dignity of each individual involved. It always believes in giving respect to everyone and believes in respecting the cultural sentiments. It is essential to keep in touch with such people and institutions, through various communication net works like phone, e-mail, personal visits, and invitation for programmes and events as well as for various types of collaboration.

(iii) Communication

As discussed before, building long term relationship is an important aspect of networking and communication is the key to maintain long term relationship. Individuals and groups communicate with each other regularly on common grounds, and try to find solutions to various problems being faced by a member.

In the process of networking, communication facilitates the people to share experiences, interests, concerns, and support each other, to take decisions, and work together to help the people in need. Effective communication plays a vital role in building positive relationship and networking. To develop positive networking through effective communication, it is very important to establish trust. Effective communication among and between people depends on the quality of relationship. When negative emotions dominate in such relationships, communication is likely to be less effective in comparison to the situations where there are positive feelings of respect, trust and friendliness. Therefore the essential task in the networking method of social work is the development of an atmosphere in which people feel comfortable and are able to express themselves. In the networking process, one should feel at ease and to be given an opportunity to communicate back with comfort and confidence. If good communication exists between everyone involved in the process of networking, it may prevent misunderstanding and unnecessary concerns. If communication is effective, people and institutions involved are more likely to contribute to and offer best possible support and services.

(iv) Mutual Development and Support

Mutual development is about helping each other. It is about working together with what one has. It always begins with helping, understanding and learning. Through networking one can help oneself by helping others. Networking gives an opportunity to learn new skills and knowledge by interacting with each other. It benefits all the people who are connected.

Let us take the example of a child who was in great need of blood while he was hospitalized. The social worker contacts some blood donors from his data base or approaches some institutions or groups where voluntary blood donors could be identified and help sought. This is possible only through mutual support and proper net working with such institutions and individuals

(v) Shared Confidentiality

Confidentiality is the preservation of secret (and very often personal or private) information concerning the client. This becomes shared confidentiality in the professional relationship which will enable the worker to mobilize the required assistance for the good of the client. Confidentiality is based upon a basic right of the client; it is an ethical obligation of the caseworker and is necessary for effective casework service. The client's right, however, is not absolute. Moreover, the client's secret is often shared with other professionals within the agency and in other agencies; the obligation then binds all equally (Felix P., Biestek, S.J., 1957).

In the Indian context shared confidentiality is the norm of society especially with regard to most issues involving the females. Usually a female in India visits a physician accompanied by the parents, particularly mother, sister, husband, mother-in law and in several cases close friends or neighbours. Same is the case when she has to visit a case worker, a psychologist or a counselor. Most problems are known and shared among close family members. Joint families and extended families usually find solutions to the problems on their own. Keeping in view the value of cultural sensitivity, the aspect of shared confidentiality in matters of client system must be recognized and facilitated. This is essential while seeking various types of assistance through networking.

Functions of a Network Method

Networking is a systematic process of establishing and maintaining relationships with people who have the resources or capability to help one to further one's personal or professional goals. As a method of social work, networking has great potential impact on the enhancement of manifold social work interventions. Major functions of network in the social work scenario are:

Opens doors to variety of resources inside and outside the profession

The method of network enables social work professionals to identify various resources like expertise, funds, materials etc. within the social work profession, other allied professions and in the larger society. This will enhance the quality of social work intervention. The resources could be of different nature: contacts for implementing various methods of social work; material and financial resources; manpower and referral services; curriculum; research results; knowledge on various types of clients including indigenous people as well as best practices traditionally existing in various communities.

Widening support to client system

Networking is a matter of creating useful linkages, both within and among people, groups, communities, organizations, and societies, in order to mobilize resources as well as to support the profession through different ways. This will help in enabling social work intervention with the clients- individuals, groups, families, and communities- to provide various types of assistance in the best interest of maximizing results. Networking will help in supporting the practice of various methods of social work.

Facilitate effective referrals

The method of networking will facilitate effective referral of clients to appropriate professionals and agencies and to ensure effective social work intervention. In several western countries professional agencies are available for referring clients for case work. In most developing countries there is an absence of such agencies especially since social work does not have professional status and or council. Absence of code of conduct or ethics in these countries further dilute the process of referral services.

Ensuring quality based social work education

The method of networking can facilitate social work professionals, organisations, social work associations and schools of social work to highlight issues, challenges and strategies for enhancing quality social work education in the country. It will also help in ensuring minimum standards in social work education, and formulation of the national council on professional social work. Above all, networking is essential for the professionals as well as others for enhancing the knowledge base and skills of the profession.

Types of Network

Networking occurs at a variety of levels. At the level of social work practice it is a matter of creating reciprocal relationships with other members of society, institutions and the larger society. The major types of network are:

Formal Network

Formal network means a professional group designed to promote networking among its members. The networking among professional social workers through associations of social work can be viewed as part of formal network. Such associations can be at the state, regional, national and international levels.

Informal Network

Informal net work means the personal relationships that one has developed over a period of time with wide variety of experts and organizations. Professionals can depend on this type of network and can expect support while providing services to clients.

Internal Network

Professional relationships and contacts developed in the workplace can be termed as internal network. The networking in the same organisation or in the same school of social work, is an example for the internal network. Similarly the alumni associations are potential groups for internal networking.

External Network

Professional relationships and contacts developed outside the workplace is called external network. Relationships and networks developed through participating in international conference/ seminars etc. are examples for external network. Usually social work professionals are invited as members experts and to working groups in governmental and non-governmental agencies. There is no limit for identifying and benefiting from such networking experiences.

Hermania Ibarra (2008) speaks of three types of professional networks:

Operational Network

Operational network means network with the people one directly work with to get one's job done. Most professionals including social workers have to develop these relationships to enhance their professional intervention.

Personal Networks

Personal networks are well explained with the examples of alumni, professional, social and affinity groups. These groups/associations allow social workers to meet diverse groups of like-minded professionals and others, and learn from each other.

Strategic Networks

Strategic network means maintaining contacts with peers and senior people in one's professional field. It is very necessary for professional development. Strategic networks are crucial for sharing ideas about best practices, learning new approaches and keeping tabs on developments in business and technology.

Networking as a Method of Social Work in the Indian Context

The problems being confronted by the Indian masses who form about twenty percent of the world population are diverse in nature. With globalization the country is also facing a fast changing social scenario which requires timely intervention with new strategies, ideas and methods. Networking is one such method which the social work profession must extensively practice for the benefit of the client system. Networking as a method of social work can be used in the macro as well as micro settings. It aims at solving the problem by minimizing the gap between the client and the resources. Networking can be an effective method to address the developmental needs of the Indian population.

Illiteracy, malnutrition, ill health, corruption, economic deprivation and destitution of a large section of the population are some of the problems that the social workers have to confront and such problems can be addressed through effective networking to a great extent. Social workers can take help of media in addressing several of these problems. Media can expose corruption and educate the public and policy makers about the urgency in bringing about the much needed changes. Educational campaigns can be introduced in order to inform citizens of their rights and remedial measures with regard to various issues. Networking along with some of the related methods of social work such as group work, community organization, social work research, PIL, resource mobilization and advocacy can bring about positive changes and outcome.

Social Work and Social Networks

In social work the term 'network' or 'social network' is used to denote an interconnection or web of likeminded voluntary organisations (VOs)/ community based organisations (CBOs)/non-government organisations (NGOs) to address common goals by working in a coordinated and effective manner. As the government is encouraging development through the voluntary sector, there is an unparallel growth of NGOs which has taken place in recent years. Therefore it becomes necessary that these NGOs come together to strengthen themselves for addressing the issues effectively. These social networks address macro issues affecting the masses. Social network abide by commonly agreed upon code of conduct while carrying out various activities. These social networks are highly useful for the social work professional because they provide organised platforms for mobilization of required resources, and formation of healthy public opinion and promotion of well-being of people, especially the weaker and vulnerable sections of society, help in promoting socio-economic development and assist in speedy eradication of social evils which impede human development and effective functioning of people (S. Surendra, 2010).

For instance, at present Wada Na Todo Abhiyan and People's Budget Initiative are two social networks carrying out advocacy activities with the government of India. These networks have a headquarter which maintains contact with all its partners, facilitate training and capacity building exercises as well as knowledge sharing, through regular meets. The aim is to strengthen the partner NGOs so that the cause can be voiced effectively. Social network thus becomes a tool for networking in social work.

Approaches and Models of Networking in Social Work

(i) Social Networking Sites

With the advancement in information technology, the communication pattern of people have drastically progressed and changed. Distance and national boundaries are no more any barrier to communication. Internets have provided an efficient means for communication. It has also provided a platform for people connecting from different parts of the globe. One such example is the various social networking sites which have paved the way for likeminded people, to communicate individually as well as in groups, e.g. Facebook, Twitter etc. These sites have become very popular lately as a means to connect to people. Social networking sites are very informative and make people aware about various events which are going on in the world at large. Social networking sites enable individuals to communicate with a large number of people. Likeminded people can form an online group to voice their concern. Various organisations and universities host their LinkedIn or Google official group page, Facebook page, twitter feed and its own YouTube link, so as to connect with large number of people. In order to disseminate information to people in large scale, instantly, they post the information to different group pages. The people who are members of that group receive the information instantly at one go. Similarly it can be used effectively as a tool for networking by the social workers for rendering help to individuals, groups or voice the concern of a larger population. At present it has become an effective means to start online campaigns for social issues, raise awareness for a particular cause, motivating people to come together to fight for the rights of the under privileged or whose human rights have been violated.

(ii) Seminar/Conferences/Workshops

Various national and international organisations of social workers have a number of ways for the professionals, to network in different areas of social work such as women and child welfare, youth welfare, old age, HIV/AIDS etc. Some of these organisations are NASW, NAPSWI, APSWI and many more. These organisations also provide an opportunity to network with each other by conducting seminars and conferences for the members and provide a platform to interact and build a long term relationship with the people. Attending conferences and seminars is an ideal way to network with the people. Such conferences provide information about the current practices in various fields as well as continuing education. These seminars provide an opportunity to network with colleagues and hear and interact with speakers on contemporary issues and challenges that are relevant in the field of social work. The prominent speakers in the seminar share their personal insights and experiences. For example NAPSWI organises national seminar every year in the field of social work and HIV/AIDS, which provide an opportunity to the social workers to build a long term relationship, as well as provide information in the field of social work and HIV/AIDS.

(iii) Networking of Schools of Social Work

Schools of social work can play an effective role in networking with different stakeholders of the society to mobilize human and material resources. They can collaborate with different non-governmental organizations, government agencies as well as international organizations working in the area of social development, and take initiatives for policy changes and drafting of new policies through advocacy. Various programmes, activities and schemes can be carried out as extension activities by these schools. Besides this, various schools of social work can network with each other to exchange expertise for the professional development of the students and faculty. The effort of the school of social work (SOSW) at IGNOU is worth noting in this regard.

SOSW was established on 16thAugust 2007 with the approval of the President of India in the capacity as visitor of IGNOU. The school offers about a dozen programmes of study from certificate to doctorate degree, and it also has a recognized research centre for MPhil and PhD at Rajgiri College of Social Sciences at Kochi in Kerala. It is housing two chairs of study, namely, Mother Teresa Chair and CBCI Chair. Many programmes of study have been developed in collaboration with these chairs. Besides this, the School has a Centre for Tibetan Studies. The school has extensively used networking with voluntary organizations, institutions of higher education within India and abroad, as well as experts from various walks of life to develop academically sound and socially relevant indigenous programmes of study in social work to provide knowledge to the society.

With the aim to provide direct intervention in the field, the school has adopted a slum community, namely, Tigri, which is situated in South Delhi. Tigri is one of the largest slum clusters of Delhi which also acts as a practicum lab for students and scholars of the school of social work. Extension activities are also carried out for inmates in Tihar Jail which is the largest jail in India housing over 11,000 persons. The school has a history of addressing emergency situations across the country including floods or earthquakes. It distributes clothes collected from neighbouring communities to about 84 night shelters in Delhi. In providing these extension services, and to ensure that the services reach out to the needy, strong networking skills with different stakeholders are provided.

The school organizes an annual national seminar on 'social work response to HIV/ AIDS' in different parts of the country which provides a platform for interaction of professionals from across the country. Over 300 participants take part in these seminars each year. It has more than 200 study centres within India and 12 other countries offering programmes in social work and HIV/AIDS and more than 1500 qualified social workers are involved in counseling, supervision and evaluation of practicum at these study centres. Besides these, the school has rich collaborative programme with various institutions within India and abroad which include WHO, UNICEF, NACO, AIDS Healthcare Foundation USA, Florida State University (USA), James Cook University Australia, apart from several universities and about 400 schools of social work in the country. Thus the school mobilizes resources for programme development and delivery through networking and collaboration.

On similar lines networking can be practiced by NGOs/CBOs other schools of social work and social work agencies to provide their services effectively, keeping in view the values of human relationships, patriotism, teachership, loyalty to the profession, service, integrity, hard work, competence, responsibility and commitment as well as cultural sensitivity.

Conclusion

Social work is primarily a helping profession which involves a set of values, principles, methods, tools, techniques and code of ethics. Networking has emerged as one of the methods in social work practice that helps individuals to exchange information, share experiences, mobilise resources for the needy and so on through cooperation and coordination. This exchange of ideas or information could be possible through direct or indirect means. Through networking various techniques can be developed to reach the unreached. The scope and areas of social work intervention is much large in India and networking method would be of great importance in this regard.

REFERENCES

1. Acosta Gabriela (2013). 5 Career Tips: Networking in the Social Work Profession. Retrieved from http://msw.usc.edu/mswusc-blog/social-work-networking/ on 11/6/2014.
2. Pincus, A. and Minahan, A. (1973). *Social Work Practice: Model and Method.* Ithaca, Illionois: Peacock Publishers.
3. Singh Surendra (2010). Introduction to Social Work Concepts-I, In G. Thomas (Ed.), Introduction to Social Work, BSWE-001, Vol. 1, New Delhi: IGNOU.

12

Networking and its Relation with Other Methods of Social Work

Nita Kumari

A network refers to an association of individuals, groups and community that come together to share resources, information, knowledge and skills. Through networking each member's strengths can be identified and increased and skills can be sharpened. This will help them to respond better to injustice, share information and services among individuals, groups and communities having common interest. Social networking is very important in the profession of social work as social workers are called upon to deal with human beings who are faced with problems in their social, economic and emotional context. The professionals have to create useful linkages, both within and among the communities, organizations and societies, in order to mobilize resources and for helping individuals, groups and communities.

Networking is closely associated with other methods of social work popularly known and being practiced across the globe namely, social case work, social group work, community organization, social welfare administration, social action and social work research. Based on the initiatives of professor Gracious Thomas to create awareness and education on HIV/AIDS among other issues in a developing country like India for almost three decades, six more methods of social work are being promoted as contemporary methods. They are advocacy, awareness campaigns, networking, public interest litigation, resources mobilization and strengths based practice (Koteswer Raju, 2014). These are some of the contemporary methods through which social work can be practiced. Removing these methods would be like one has removed the soul from the body. In fact these contemporary methods are the unique assets for the social work profession. The social work professionals working in different areas can meaningfully practice these methods. Let us examine how networking method is associated with other methods of social work.

Social Case Work and Networking

Social case work is one of the primary methods of social work and involves dealing with problems of individuals. It strives towards better adjustment and development of an individual, in order to help the client attain more satisfying human relations. Sometimes due to certain internal or external factors, a client may not be in a position to adjust with the environment and fail to avail existing facilities. In such situations, social case worker helps an individual to adjust with the situation.

According to Mary Richmond social casework is "the art of doing different things for and with different people by cooperating with them, to achieve at one and the same time, their own and society's betterment" (Richmond, 1922). The needs of the individuals are not limited to their material wants only, as the material benefits alone cannot ensure human satisfaction. Satisfaction is achieved when material comforts are accompanied by fulfillment of emotional needs.

Social caseworker seeks to find a lasting solution to the client's problem by restoring his/her self-esteem. A caseworker studies the client in totality i.e. in relation to his/her environment, past experiences, relation with significant others, understanding of the problem and problem solving capacity and helps to understand himself/herself. During case work many a times the social worker has to make referral services. Networking with different individuals, groups, and organizations can make the service delivery more efficient.

For example PLHAs often come under shock, feeling of anger, guilt, sorrow, despair, revenge, suicide and such other emotions. In such situations it is very necessary to unburden the client from such feelings and indicate that even these will have to be looked at in a positive way. The caseworker in such a situation can use his/her networking skills and can refer the client to an expert counsellor or even a psychiatrist where the latter listens carefully and facilitate expression of repressed feelings by the client. He/she respects his/her worth and dignity as an individual human being. A caseworker helps the patient to adjust to the reality situation and motivates the patient to be associated with other PLHAs groups. He/she also offers referral services to other suitable resources. Caseworker also helps an individual to reach a new level of integration by introducing new ideas and new ways of living.

In fact positive people's network is very popular among many societies across the globe. In this globalized world with technological advancement, networking among likeminded people is an asset not only for the immediate satisfaction of emotional needs, but also for other helps. Positive people's network has been known for supporting people to find avenues for seeking entertainment, learning opportunities and education, find job, week-end relaxation, legal remedies, advocacy for the cause of the HIV infected and affected, creating awareness, getting involved in preventive education and some even becoming brand ambassadors.

Networking efficiencies can help the professional in helping the client to find health care services; educational facilities supported with scholarships or loan; remedies for farmers by approaching donor agencies and government machineries; clients in correctional settings to appropriatelyaddress their cases through efficient legal professionals; poor village women to improve their financial situation through self help groups (SHGs); and helping displaced clients and refugees as well as client in many more similar contexts. If the worker has a sound networking capacity, he/she will be in a much better position to help the clients through the social case work method.

Social Group Work and Networking

Group work involves intervention in problems at group level. A group is formed of members facing same problem and the group worker facilitates the group in finding solution to their problems. According to Trecker "social group work is a method through which individuals in groups in social agency settings are helped by a worker who guides their interaction in programme activities so that they may relate themselves to others and experience growth opportunities in accordance with their needs and capacities to the end of the individual, group and community development" (Trecker, 1955).

The definition of Trecker needs to be adapted to the national situation. In advanced western countries, client approach the agencies and they are referred to the practitioners. Similarly Trecker talks of groups of individual in the context of agencies which are very often impossible in a developing country like India. Therefore the professionals are challenged to adapt to situations where clients are to be gathered, motivated to stay on and work together to attain certain set goals.

One of the best examples is the Self Help Groups (SHGs) which have gained momentum in India in recent years. SHG is a small voluntary association of people at local level. These people generally belong to same socio-economic background. The SHG is formed with the purpose of solving common problems of the group members through mutual help. The SHG promotes small savings among its members and the savings are kept with the bank.

In the process of forming a self-help group, professional social worker makes meaningful intervention by building good networking with the village authorities and the target group and explain to them about the what, why and how of self-help groups. He/she does networking with financial institutions, government agencies and departments, local market and traders, resource persons from various fields including agricultural experts, financial managers, cooperative body specialists etc. The worker also motivates and facilitates the president (group leader) of the self-help group to approach people and institutions that matter; keep the group together; help study the situation; suggestions for improvement; to be honest etc.

A social group worker is also instrumental in organizing the HIV support groups and educational groups and guides the group work process. In the educational groups the information is disseminated about the disease, prevention and treatment. They educate the group members about the pattern of progression and its debilitating effects in near future. They are also taught about adherence to the treatment process like taking medicines without failure and educate to avoid those behaviour patterns that may worsen the condition.

In the support groups the group members provide the necessary social and emotional support to the patients. It is an important platform for the HIV/ AIDS patients where they can express themselves freely and share their problems to help each other. Through social group work, the HIV infected individuals are helped to change their attitude for the rest of their life that helps in living a positive life and coping with the situation. Various such groups with common interest and goals come together for support and information sharing through networking.

Community Organization and Networking

Community organization is a macro method in social work. It involves interventions aiming at addressing the problems at the community level by involving the members of the community in the process. According to Ross "community organization is a process by which a community identifies its needs or objectives, orders (or ranks) these needs or objectives, develops the confidence and will to work at those needs or objectives, finds the resources (internal and/or external) to deal with these needs or objectives, takes action in respect of them, and in so doing extends and develops cooperative and collaborative attitudes and practices in the community" (Ross, 1955).

The professional community organiser possesses required qualities and skills to work with the people and conveys information to the community people in an effective way. The social work community organiser has essential knowledge, skills about the principles, process and steps of community organization and applies the same while working in the community.

In relation to HIV/AIDS, through this method the information is disseminated about the disease, modes of transmission, ways of prevention and various programmes and services available for people living with HIV/ AIDS. The community organiser brings together the people of a community for necessary action in order to prevent and control the spread of HIV/AIDS. He/she organises awareness camps related to health, governmental programmes and human rights, to improve the knowledge and understanding of the people. He/she conducts street plays, puppet shows, lectures etc. to disseminate the information among the general public. The community organiser also educates the people in community about HIV/AIDS, keeping in view their religious beliefs, social taboos, attitude of the community in its cultural and environmental contexts. They are the best persons to work closely and change the attitude of the people in the community in reducing stigma and discrimination towards people living with HIV/AIDS.

Through networking diverse members of the population build relationships, share resources, and work together in an organized way for social change. Through networking people can have connections with other individuals or groups who face similar problems and issues and want to work together toward solutions. These social connections allow individuals, groups, and organizations to find allies, access tools, share practical wisdom, and build collaborative strategies. Networking thus helps those working for social change to share resources and information, devise an agenda, and engage in collective action.

For example, local activists and those working in the field of health and sanitation will find it useful to make contact with other grassroots organisers to coordinate efforts, learn what has already been done on the issue, and discuss what has and has not worked. Likewise, it is important for organizations to make contacts with other agencies, groups, and individuals that might support their work in direct or indirect ways.

Therefore, it can be said that networking is very important to deal with different groups in the community, to identify key persons or to bring resources of the community and facilitate the utilization of the resources and identify new or outside resources. Depending upon the issues, a social worker is able to meaningfully make interventions for community development through community organization. The worker's networking strategies and extent of networking with experts and individuals that matter with regard to a particular issue will result in organizing the community. For any field of intervention such as health, education, socio-economic developmental projects, legal matters etc. the worker must have adequate abilities for networking. Networking involves possession of adequate information about individual experts, administrators, community and religious leaders, panchayat (local body at village level) level functionaries, financial institutions, academics, political leaders, donor agencies, law enforcing agencies etc. to name a few. It also involves the temperament and personality traits of the worker for negotiation and accommodating the views of other people. One needs to be working with people following democratic principles. Knowing well the intellectual level of the people, their cultural background and extent of socialization within the family are essential for any successful intervention through networking. At the end of the day, we may say that a well-planned networking system should be in place for any sustainable community organization and development programme.

Social Welfare Administration and Networking

Social welfare administration is another method of social work. According to Walter A. Friedlander (1958) "administration of social agencies translates the provisions of social legislation of social agencies and the aims of private philanthropy and religious charities into the dynamics of services and benefits for humanity". In order to fulfil the objectives of agency, networking can be used to implement certain programmes. Networking plays an important role to raise funds from the community and grants can be mobilized from the government.

Social welfare agencies play a pivotal role in rendering services to the needy population. They can network with people or organisations who have professional competence to achieve desired objectives. They can call on people who have in-depth knowledge and can make use of available resources together with active community participation in order to achieve the goals of the organization. For example organization working with elderly can network with other organisations or experts who can provide them in-depth knowledge of various government schemes and programmes run by the government. They could be given information about how to avail such facilities and whom to contact when in need.

Depending upon the objectives of each agency, the worker must plan and design his/her networking strategies. This requires meeting people, visiting institutions of similar nature, participating in seminars, conferences, training programmes as well as organizing similar programmes wherein experts and likeminded people from various walks of life can come together and share their expertise for the benefit of all concerned.

The success of social welfare administration largely depends upon the networking skills of the social worker. He/she begins networking within the agency and among its staff and various stakeholders. For example the social worker while working with the prisoners need to do net-working with other agencies that can provide training to help clients, so that they can be trained in occupations which can lead to a career and economic self-sufficiency; provide referral services to various organizations that can provide emotional and psychological support to the prisoners; and network with the families or caregivers who can provide support and supervision when the offender re-enters the community.

Social work is rooted in humanitarianism and based on certain values. A social worker while working with the clients-individuals, families, groups and community or network with other stakeholders to provide much needed support should strictly follow the principle and values of the profession. He/she should respect the people and should believe in the worth and dignity of the individuals. He/she should be honest and dedicated while helping the client. He/she should be non-judgmental and non-possessive in his/her approach. He/she should accept, care and show concern for the client in a non-dominating way. He/she should motivate, encourage and guide the clients whenever needed.

Social Action and Networking

Social action is an individual, group or community effort within the framework of social work philosophy and practice that aims to achieve social progress, to modify social policies and to improve social legislation and health and welfare services (Friedlander, 1977). Nanawati (1965) considered social action as "a process of bringing about the desired changes by deliberate group and community efforts. Social action does not end with the enactment and signing of social legislation, but that the execution of the policies was the real test of success or failure of social action. Singh has given a broad definition of social action by stating that social action is a process in which conscious, systematic and organized efforts are made by some elite(s) and/or people themselves to bring about change in the system which is instrumental in solving problems and improving conditions which limit the social functioning of weaker and vulnerable sections (Singh, 1986).

Social action involves a large number of people to fight for a particular cause. A leader who takes a lead in the process of social action brings together all the likeminded people and this process involves an effective networking. For example by networking with the people in the field of HIV/AIDS, social worker can raise the voice on behalf of the people living with HIV/AIDS. It is widely accepted that the rights of the PLHAs are being violated across the board. They are being stigmatized and discriminated in the health care setting. Through advocacy, social workers influence, motivate and encourage democratic powers to take decisions for the welfare of PLHAs. They fight to bring desired changes in the policies with the aim to ensure equitable distribution of resources in the social system, protecting their rights and providing justice. Social action is one of the most effective methods of social work, which social workers can use in fighting for the rights of the PLHAs by networking with influential personalities.

Networking in social action provides valuable opportunities for discussion and reporting back. They enable representatives to learn from others and possibly expend their sense of collective identity and accountability. To cite an example, networking has been effectively used by Medha Patkar while taking up the issue of Narmada Bachao Andolan. She has been doing networking with adivasis, farmers, environmentalists, human rights activists, government authorities and non-governmental organizations in order to provide justice to the affected population. She also involved well known and influential personalities like Amir Khan from bollywood and Booker Prize Winner Arundhati Roy and many more. She does campaigning on various issues that include undertaking or adopting strategies like hunger strikes, dhranas, holding meeting with the people, writing to the authorities, taking help of media, etc.

In the process of social action it is very important to be loyal towards the issue and the people involved as well. Networking is important with social media to communicate with the outside world and to pressurize the authorities. Through networking different parties can be engaged in the process of social action, each with their own roles, responsibilities and ways, to make their voices heard and create social pressure.

Social Work Research and Networking

Social work research is the systematic investigation of the problems confronted by the social workers in the field of social work. According to Thomas, social work research is a systematic, critical and careful investigation of a social phenomenon. The findings of social work research may help the social worker, the agency/organization and the policy makers to plan effective programmes based on the needs of a particular community (Thomas, 2010).

Networking plays an important role during the investigation of the problem. Networking helps an individual to seek information from variety of sources that could be useful while drawing conclusions. Networking among scholars and institutions allow those in professional's communities to share existing knowledge about the development and enhance their education and research skills. This can also bridge some of the knowledge gaps.

For example, networking is very important while conducting a study with the tribal population. It is not an easy task to collect data from the target population due to a number of challenges. The researcher needs to do networking with the officials like tribal officers, block development officers, cooperative societies etc.; non officials like local political leaders, village leaders, youth/women's club presidents etc. Researcher should have strong network with the people to conduct home visits. Transportation could be one of the biggest challenges while going for collecting the data in such areas. If researcher has strong networking with the people it would be easier for him/her to take the help of the villagers to reach out to the target population.

During the process of research, a researcher should respect the people and their cultural background. They have their own tradition which should be given due importance by the researcher. Building and maintaining trust of the target population is very important for the researcher. It requires considerable time, effort and commitment. Through effective networking skills, researcher can win over the situation and maintain the trust of the people.

Social networking could be an effective method to provide useful information about the different dimensions of the problems like HIV/AIDS and facilitate effective planning, policy formulation and implementation of the programme. As the issue of HIV/AIDS is very sensitive, the people involved in this area can assess the problem in a broader way with professional competence and suggest appropriate action plans. The results of the research need to reach professional social workers across the board as well as people involved in policy formulation and implementation. Only through a well-planned networking system, full utilization of the research results can be expected. This will also enhance the competence of the profession as well as professionals.

Advocacy and Networking

Advocacy is a principled activity that encompasses three broad principles of independence, empowerment and inclusion (Dunning, 2010). Dunning (2005) says that advocacy 'generally involves people making a case for themselves and advancing their own interests, or representing others and supporting them to secure and exercise their rights on an individual or collective basis'. According to Cohen, advocacy is the pursuit of influencing outcomes-including public-policy and resources allocation decisions within political, economic, and social systems and institutions-that directly affect people's current lives (Cohen, 2001).

Advocacy is the process of raising the voice on behalf of the needy population who lack political power and economic resources. Advocacy is one of the important methods used by social workers that promote equality, social justice and social inclusion of the disadvantaged groups in a society. As an advocate, social worker can network with other people and or agencies in order to represent or persuade the members and prepare them to represent their issues to the concerned authorities in order to bring about an effective solution to their unmet needs. They can speak on behalf of the target groups to gain access to services or to improve the quality of services provided. Through advocacy the social workers can address the root cause of the problem and fight for their rights.

Networking is the method which strengthens members' skills in mobilizing support for an issue, a useful skill when advocating with opinion leaders, policy makers, and the public. Through networking different people and groups can work together toward a shared goal by coordinating strategies and pooling resources. They can communicate and collaborate on a shared advocacy strategy. In networking, communication plays an important role in bringing together members and establishing a common advocacy agenda. Networking can improve the quality and the quantity of work and spread responsibilities by allowing individuals and groups to contribute ideas, expertise, and resources. When advocacy efforts are successful, all members get benefits.

Take the example of International Rivers Network (IRN) that works with environmental and Human Rights groups around the world in cooperative campaigns. This network campaigns against the construction of large dams and aims to promote "community-based river development." They have adopted a two-pronged approach, combining work on changing global policies with campaigning on specific key projects around the world. Their involvement depends on requests from like-minded NGOs or individuals from project affected communities. They mobilize international support from their network of activists and experts, raise funds and generate publicity through the media. IRN also undertakes research and provides project critiques, analysis of alternatives and activist briefings, to support advocacy and public efforts (Schaap and Steenbergen, 2001).

Awareness Campaigns and Networking

Awareness campaigns are designed to educate the public about specific issues. Generally, people become involved in a campaign or other forms of social action because they feel strongly about an issue that directly affects their lives or the lives of those they care about. All awareness campaigns aim to provide information and knowledge to influence the individual attitudes and behaviour towards a particular issue or problem. Knowing the results of his/her behaviour and realizing the importance of these results might convince that person to change a certain behavioural pattern.

An awareness campaign can include everything from inviting speakers/ experts to deliver talk to film screenings to showcases and demonstrations. For such campaigns networking plays a very important role. For example networking can be done with the people or organisations who are involved in the field of HIV/AIDS or with thevariety of media with the intent of educating the public so that they may be more conscious of the harms that are posed towards themselves as well as others. Networking could be done with other dance, drama, and folk theater as well as televisions, radio and print media in order to sensitize the public on various sensitive issues.

Awareness campaigns provide the much needed information to the people by which they can acknowledge the injustice or inequality done with them. For instance, through awareness campaigns the PLHAs can be made aware of their own rights and to exercise those rights. They could be encouraged to speak for themselves. HIV-positive people are often discriminated against because of fears of infection and because the infection is negatively associated with certain behaviours such as promiscuity, different sexual orientation, drug addiction etc. Social workers can raise the issue of stigma and discrimination through awareness campaigns and information can also be disseminated for approaching authorities on such issues. PLHAs can be sensitized about various schemes and programmes run by the government.

Networking is the creation of strategic relations of like-minded individuals, social groups and institutions. Through these networks information is exchanged, advocacy efforts are strengthened and involvement is stimulated. A lot of networking today is done through the internet. Other forms of networking include the formation of platforms of interested parties for campaign planning. Networking efforts aim at finding partners with similar interests. Networking campaigns can be designed in a participatory manner that can help stay closer to the ideas, constraints and opportunities of the target audience.

Campaign planning is always the art of finding a balance between maximum reach and maximum involvement. Using Networking skills, participatory approaches can help enhance involvement while mass media can help expand the campaign reach. Public participation in campaigns ensures an exchange of ideas and knowledge of priorities to and from the initiating organization. Further, public participation also helps broaden the initiated awareness movement by involving more people in an active manner. Networking is one of the important ways to involve the public in awareness campaigns.

One of the successful examples of awareness campaigns and networking is Pulse Polio immunization campaign in India. It was established by the government of India to eradicate poliomyelitis (polio) by vaccinating all children under the age of five years. In order to fight against the polio virus, government has done networking with various international institutions, state governments and non government organizations to achieve its objectives.

Resource Mobilization and Networking

Resource Mobilization is a process, which identifies the resources essential for the development, implementation and continuation of works for achieving the organization's mission. Resource mobilization means expansion of relations with the resource providers, the skills, knowledge and capacity for proper use of resources. These resources could be internal (material, space, money, manpower etc.) and external (funding, advice from the experts, other technical assistance etc.). It also means seeking new sources of resource mobilization and right and maximum use of the available resources.

For instance the social worker can mobilize the resources for effective service delivery to take place in providing quality care to PLHAs. The resources could be generated for people living with HIV/AIDS especially when majority of patients can not pay for the services. Besides providing monetary support for providing patient care, funders may be approached to support other essential activities such as setting up and running training programmes and research and information dissemination. In such situations networking can be done to mobilize resources from external sources.

Similarly a social work agency can help an amputee who is poor and who is a patient in a government hospital to get monetary help through networking with social work department of the hospital for buying artificial limbs. In order to mobilize resources it is very important to have sound networking with various national and international organizations, experts, leaders of the community, media etc. Through networking an organization can implement its programmes very effectively. It is useful in attracting and managing the human, financial, and physical resources for the sustainability of an organization. Good networking also helps to build trusting relationships among multiple stakeholders and allows for the sharing of resources so that individual groups and communities/institutions can bring important social, economic, and political changes for the welfare of the society.

Public Interest Litigation (PIL) and Networking

Public interest litigation (PIL) is a form of legal action initiated in a court of law for the enforcement of public interest or general interest in which the public or a class of the community have pecuniary interest or some interest by which their legal rights or liabilities are affected. Therefore, PIL is a proceeding in which an individual or group seeks relief in the interest of general public and not for its own purposes (Mathew, 2010).

Through PIL, justice can be provided to the individuals who are not in a position to fight for their rights due to their ignorance and socio-economic disabilities. A social worker can render help to PLHAs who are deprived of their constitutional and legal rights. Professionals can approach the constitutional courts to seek justice on behalf of PLHAs if their human rights are being violated and they have been discriminated on the basis of their positive status.

Guarding against human rights issue requires the active sharing of information and cooperation among human rights partners and local actors. In order to accomplish the task, networking is needed with civil society groups that include NGOs, FBOs, women's groups, youth organizations etc. Networking among human rights monitors and local organizations help to build relationship of trust. It enhances sharing of high quality information among various human rights groups, religious groups, trade unions, and hospitals. Networking allows all of these actors to share information and advice, which can lead to constructive thinking and bringing out new solutions to the problem.

Strengths based Practice and Networking

Strengths based practices (SBPs) concentrates on the inherent strengths of individuals, families, groups and organizations deploying peoples' personal strengths to aid their recovery and empowerment. Strengths based practice is being recognized as a method of social work in the contemporary society by professionals. Strengths based practice does not ignore the problems and difficulties of the clients. Rather, it attempts to identify the positive aspects and resources that are available with the clients and work on strengths to help the clients to alleviate their problems.

Every individual has some strengths and resources for their own empowerment. Through SBPs a social worker can help the PLHAs to identify and build on their strengths so that they can retain or regain independence in their daily lives. With the use of this approach PLHAs can improve their self-care abilities, increase their confidence and self-esteem which would help them to independently carry out their daily living activities. Social workers can also network with other organizations or PLHAs network to pool in resources to help the client, whenever needed.

Strengths-based practice is a collaborative process between the client and the social worker. It allows them to work together to determine an outcome that draws on the person's strengths and assets. For instance a drug abuse or prisoner who lost his/her self-confidence can be made aware about his/her strengths and capabilities and can be rehabilitated back in the community. In such cases social worker has to do networking with his/her family, friends, and relatives in order to facilitate unparalleled insight into the strengths, talent and challenges of their loved one. Social worker can also network with different organization in order to provide training to the person based on his/her skills. Networking is helpful in improving the level of social functioning for the target group.

Conclusion

Through networking, social workers can establish coordinated and collaborative relationships in order to have access to the resources of various social systems. They can network with human service organizations, other social structures like business and industry and influential community leaders in order to render help to the targeted clients.

REFERENCES

1. Cohen, D., De La Vega, R., Watson, G. (2001). *Advocacy for Social Justice.* Bloomfield, CT: Kumarian Press Inc.
2. Dunning, A. (2005). *Information, Advice and Advocacy for Older People: Defining and Developing Services*. York: Joseph Rowntree Foundation.
3. Dunning, A. (2010). A Scoping Study of Advocacy with Older People in Wales for the Older People's Commissioner for Wales. Older People's Commissioner for Wales, Cardiff.
4. Friedlander, W.A. (1977). *Introduction to Social Welfare*. New Delhi: Prentice Hall.
5. Friedlander, W.A. (1958). *Concepts and Methods of Social Work*. New Delhi: Prentice Hall.
6. Mathew, P.D. (2010). Public Interest Litigation. In G. Thomas (Ed.), Social Work Intervention with Individuals and Groups. New Delhi, IGNOU.
7. Nanavati, M.C., (1965). Social Action and the Professional Social Work. *Social Work Forum*, III (2), 26-29.
8. Pulla, V. (2012). What are Strengths Based Practices all About? In Venkat Pulla, Leseley Chenoweth, Abraham Francis and Stefan Bakaj (Eds.), *Papers in Strengths Based Practice*. Allied Publishers Pvt. Ltd.
9. Richmond, Marry (1922). *What is Social Casework*? New York: Russel Sage Foundation.
10. Ross, M. G. (1955). *Community Organization: Theory and Principles*. New York: Harper and Brothers.
11. Schaap, W. and Steenbergen F. Van (2001). Ideas for Water Awareness Campaigns. Stockholm, Sweden: The Global Water Partnership.
12. Retrieved from http://etameta.nl/wp-content/uploads/2011/04/IdeaBook Awareness.pdf on 1/10/2014
13. Singh, Surender (1986). *Social Action in Horizons of Social Work*. In Surender S. & K.S. Soodan. (ed). Harnam Publications.
14. Thomas, Gracious (2010). Existing Trends in Counselling Services in India. In G. Thomas (Ed.), Substance Abuse and Counselling, IGNOU, New Delhi.
15. Trecker, G. (1955). *Social Group Work: Principles and Practices*. New York: Association Press.

13

Strengths Based Practice Method

Aneesh Kurian

Some would say that the strengths based practice challenges our personal/ professional conventions and habits that we as social workers followed for several decades. The strengths based perspective is a significant alteration of thinking for professional social workers (Blundo, 2001). At the heart of the strengths perspective is a belief in the basic goodness of humankind, a faith that individuals, however downtrodden or debilitated, can discover strengths in themselves that they never knew, existed (Blundo, 2001). The strengths perspective demands a different way of looking at individuals, families and communities (Saleebey, 1996) seeking to develop in clients their natural abilities and capabilities. It means that everything we do as a social worker will be predicted, in some way, on helping to discover and embellish, explore and exploit client's strengths and resources in the service of assisting them to achieve their goals" (Saleebey, 1997). Strengths Based Practices (SBPs) concentrate on the inherent strengths of individuals, families, groups and organisations deploying peoples' personal strengths to aid their recovery and empowerment (Pulla, 2012). Over a period of time social work professionals have begun to realise that strengths based practice qualifies to be viewed as one of the methods of professional social work. Professor Gracious Thomas is one of the proponents of the same who has been extensively involved in promoting strengths based practice as a method of social work during the third millennium.

In short, a new paradigm has emerged in the social work perspective with strengths based practice shifting focus from deficits to strengths. This paper considers the strengths based "approach" as a method of social work profession. The philosophical assumptions and the value base of strengths based method is adjacent to that of social work profession. The strengths based method has lot of potential in filling the gap of social work practices especially in developing countries and particularly so while working with the poorest of the poor. The strengths based method is more than a mere shift from the deficit focused social work to strengths based social work practice. The strong philosophical assumptions, principles and techniques of the practice/assessment and the potential of change it brought to the profession suggests that strengths based practice has the right to be considered as a 'method' of social work profession.

Development of Strengths Based Method

A strengths based approach operates on the assumption that people have strengths and resources for their own empowerment (Pulla, 2012). Strengths can be internal strengths or the strengths evident in the environment accessible to the client/individual. Strengths based method has its roots in the humanistic philosophy which emphasises the potential of the individual. The strengths approach entails a fundamental view of human beings as being capable of change (Saleebey, 2002) which is the central focus of social work practice. The strengths based method originally developed in mental health practice concepts (O'Hanlon and Rowan, 2003), and is adapted for a broad range of social work practice contexts.

The deliberate efforts to incorporate strengths perspective as an approach to social work practice began in the early 1980s at the University of Kansas' School of Social Welfare (Saleebey, 2008). In 1989, Weick, Rapp, Sullivan, and Kishardt coined the term "strengths perspective" to address a system in which practitioners recognize the authority and assets a client possesses in the client's frame of reference to their life story (Eimers). Though strengths based practice is evident in social work literature and practices, now a days one can trace the roots of strengths based practices in the core values and principles of social work profession.

If one is closely observing the principles and values of social work one can trace the roots of strengths based practices in all of them. Identifying and affirming strengths is key to the value stance of the social work profession and may provide an alternative practice approach for professionals who find the values consistent with their own professional view (Rankin, 2007). The strengths perspective as a philosophical principle of social work practice emanates from social work values: self-determination, empowerment, inherent worth and dignity, hard work, cultural sensitivity, competence, integrity, and loyalty to profession. The belief in the dignity and worth of each individual and the corresponding belief in individual and collective strength as potential for effective change were over shadowed in the problem focused approach. The strengths perspective makes it easier for social workers to uphold the social work values, even when dealing with clients in very serious situation or facing a problem. This perspective enables clients, who often lack confidence and feel like failures when seeking services, to have improved self-esteem and feel confident of themselves.

According to Saleebey, the strengths perspective assumes four views: (1) All clients and environments possess strengths that can be marshalled to improve on quality of life. (2) Motivation should occur with a consistent emphasis on self-defined client strengths. (3) It is only through exploration between family and the helping person (listener and teller relationship) that discovery of client strengths can occur, with an emphasis on the definition of lying ultimately in the client's hands. (4) "Blaming the victim" is counteracted by the prominence of the client's strengths even in the most adverse of environments, which leads to the fifth assumption that all environments, no matter how unfavourable, contain utilizable resources (Saleebey, 1992).

Strengths Based Practice as a Method of Social Work Practice

Theory is an essential ingredient in practice that guides the way in which social workers view and approach individuals, groups, communities and society. Theory helps to predict, explain and assess situations and behaviours, and provide a rationale for how the social worker should react and intervene with clients who have particular histories, problems or goals. Methods are the specific techniques and approaches that social workers utilize in their work with clients to accomplish tasks and reach specific goals. Theories often inform social workers of the type of method that is most appropriate for use with a client. A method is what the social worker actually does when working with a client.

'Strengths based practice' in simple terms present approaches that promote resilience as opposed to dealing with deficits' (Pulla V., 2006). In the same way it is a method as it has specific techniques to assess the strengths of the clients and to tap those strengths to reach the goals. This method equally benefits from the strengths of the worker as well as that of the profession's ethics, values, principles and the lessons learned over a period of one century. Thus strengths based method pose a journey basing its foots in the strengths of the clients, the worker and the profession while moving towards goal achievement. Saleebey (1992) suggests that strengths based practice is not a model of practice but rather a collation of principles, ideas and techniques. At the same time the visibility of principles, ideas and the techniques and the practice evidences makes it rational to call the strengths based practice as a "method" of social work. The potency and the energy it brought to the social work practices are enormous. It refreshed and rejuvenated the problems focused approach and shifted the focus to the strengths which are adjacent to the mission and vision of social work.

The theoretical and philosophical assumptions and the process of assessment and help draw it near to a method rather than a mere approach or perspective. Strengths based method concentrates on the inherent strengths of individuals, families groups and organisations deploying peoples' personal strengths to aid their recovery and empowerment. Strengths based practices are empowering alternatives to traditional methods with individuals, groups or organizational work. The worker has to help the clients to identify what resources are available with them. The role of the social worker is not limited to let the people to identify their strengths but to help them to identify their inherent capacity to learn, grow, change and to direct it towards facing the challenges in an effective way. The inherent worth, experience, knowledge and commitment of the worker gives further impetus in the process of helping the client in addressing the issues. And this makes the strengths based practice a method of social work.

The Principles of Strengths Perspective

The principles of strengths based method are different from that of problem focused approaches. Saleebey (2002) speaks of certain principles of the strengths perspective which are given below:

1. Every Individual, Group, Family and Community has Strengths

It means that individual or family comes for help and the community around us posses assets, resources, wisdom, and knowledge which are not fully known to the client as well as the worker. Strengths based method is based upon the assumption that clients who are already in possession of various competencies and resources come for help that may be made possible by the worker to improve their situation.

2. Trauma and Abuse, Illness and Struggle may be Injurious but They may Also be Sources of Challenge and Opportunity

This principle enables the worker to look for strengths even in the adverse and downtrodden situations. Saleebey admits that there are traumas that can overwhelm the coping capacities of any child or adult, which require extra-ordinary measures to help such individuals getting back on track.

3. Assume that You do not Know the Upper Limits of the Capacity to Grow and Change and Take Individual, Group and Community Aspirations Seriously

This principle urges the worker to go beyond the set parameters in the process involved in helping. We cannot know the limits of the client's capacities and that it cannot be assumed.

4. We Best Serve Clients by Collaborating with Them

Saleebey cautions that we make a serious error when we "subjugate client's wisdom and knowledge to official views." He suggests that ultimately a collaborative stance may make us less vulnerable to the more political elements of helping: paternalism, victim blaming or victim-creating, and preemption of client views.

5. Every Environment is Full of Resources

This principle shapes perspective of the social workers to see the strengths hidden in the environment: the family, community groups, associations, institutions and so on. Saleebey explains that such resources usually exist outside the usual matrix of social and human service agencies, which are unsolicited and untapped.

6. Caring, Caretaking and Context

Here Saleebey speaks of caring in the family, caring extended by the care givers and the need of care everybody expect from the others.

Features of Strengths Based Practice

Empowerment: Empowerment is the practice approach embedded in the strengths perspective and consists of a variety of techniques used by the social worker to stimulate strengths within the client and in his environment. Oppression, discrimination, injustice, and experiences of powerlessness are the very circumstances that call for the application of empowerment-based social work practice (Miley et al. 2004). To address these issues of oppression, injustice, and powerlessness, strengths-oriented social work practice incorporates empowerment as both a concept and a process.

Focus on Resources: Strengths based practice sees the individual and environment as rich in resources. Strengths-based practice assumes every individual, group, family, and community has strengths and resources (Saleebey, 2006). The worker's role is to facilitate the client to explore the hidden resources within the reach of the client and in the environment. It believes that environment is a major source of resources, opportunities and potentials. The identification and use of resources, at one's disposal therefore becomes essential for strength based method.

Different Perspectives: In strengths-based practice method the situation is viewed from several perspectives looking for different choices and alternatives. This gives several choices and options for the client as well as the worker. The worker helps to clarify choices and encourages the individual to direct the process. The task in strengths based practice is client-directed. Individuals are encouraged to generate solutions and alternative courses of action (Rapp et al., 2005) and the worker is supporting the individual in the process. In the globalised world of today, opportunities and alternatives are several and one can have choices.

Collaboration: Strengths-based practice assumes that we best serve clients by collaborating with them as well as with various individuals, institutions and agencies. This requires adequate information as well as networking on the part of the worker who will be able to facilitate the client accordingly whether as an individual, family, group or community. In order to augment collaboration in a diverse society, one has to be having democratic approach, cultural sensitivity as well as service mentality which are some of the core values of social work. It is imperative that one must adopt a non judgemental attitude for successful collaboration.

Positive World View: The strengths based method views the individual and the environment through its strengths aspects. The process of help is to be integrated with an individual's strengths such as talents, assets, resources, skills and the strengths in the environment. Focus is more often on the current situation rather than past pathology although, the past can be explored for talents, resources, and assets. The professional practicing strengths based method should have the conviction that every problem has solutions, provided those involved in the process aspire for the same.

Faith in Change and Growth Potential: Strengths-based practice method assumes that the worker does not know the upper limits of individuals' capacity to grow and change. The strengths based method believes that every individual posses strengths and the growth potential and are subjected to change. Individuals often feel bound by past experiences, assessments, diagnoses, or judicial responses. By purposefully avoiding labels and by having high expectations the worker can focus on the strengths and empower individuals to believe in their own capacity to obtain their goals.

Spirituality: To be human means to be spiritual. Human beings have longings and aspirations that can be honoured only when the person's spiritual capacity is taken seriously (Gratton, 1995). Spirituality is often defined as a relationship with God. Specifically, spiritual beliefs and practices strengthen the ability to withstand and transcend adversity and are virtual wellsprings for healing and resilience. Compassion, love and forgiveness – themes in most religions – contribute to personal and interpersonal healing. Commitment to a faith can initiate a sense of meaning, renewal and hope for the future. Religious commitment may encourage concerns for the welfare of others and, for some, foster a zeal for addressing injustices (Rinkin, 2007). Usually in social work practice spirituality or religion is not seen as strengths or resources in a client's situation. But the strengths based method can explore the strengths of spirituality not only with an individual but also with a family, group or a community. In a country like India the strengths of spirituality is enormous. Most people are well oriented with spirituality and regularly practice religion into which they were born. The practice of yoga/meditation also will help in taping the strengths lying within the individuals.

Communication Skill: Satisfactory interpersonal relationship between a social worker and the client is the foundation of success in strengths based social work practice. Communication in social work does not happen spontaneously but with purpose (Coulshed Veronica & Ormae Joan, 2012). Effective communication skill helps the social workers to develop a working relationship with the clients and in identifying their strengths.

Self-Awareness: Self-awareness is a priceless ingredient to the effective practice of strengths based method. Self-awareness refers to awareness of the forces operating in one's environment. The social workers help the clients to expand their awareness of their needs or wants, emotions, motives, beliefs and identify their strengths. Introspection on the part of the worker is an essential aspect. It helps the worker to identify his/her strengths and the effectiveness of working towards potential goals through the method of strengths based practice.

Strengths Based Practice and Values of Social Work

Although the strength-based approach does involve an emphasis on strengths and capacities, it also integrates the values of social work. The twelve values of social work profession cited below are essential for strengths based practice method.

Service: Value of service is the driving force behind social work interventions. Social workers are social doctors who elevate service to others above self-interest and are specialized in serving the society including the marginalized, disadvantaged, downtrodden and neglected from various stratas of the society. The method of strengths based practice enables the social workers to identify the strengths, capacities, abilities and resources of the target population. The inculcation of strengths based practice method in social work service/intervention will uphold the dignity and worth of the client.

Social Justice: Ensuring social justice to the marginalized and the disadvantaged is a priority for social work profession. The value of social justice urges social workers to continually be aware of, and address the structural, social, political and economic realities that marginalize and disempower people. Strengths based practice method helps in exploring the strengths and resources of the client, the worker and the agency. Strengths based practice ensures the inclusion, collaboration, respect, the sharing of resources, and human rights of the clients system.

Respect for Dignity and Worth of the Person: Strengths based practice will be effective when social worker shows respect for human dignity and worth of all persons without any discrimination, respecting strengths, abilities and capacities of everyone from various class, caste, sex or religion. Strengths based practice reminds that every individual has strengths and capacities of their own whether rich or poor. A professional must respect strengths of the clients in various forms like cultural differences, religious beliefs, goals, desires, education, experience, expertise etc. Strengths based practice believes in the right to self-determination of clients and value it as one of the primary principles of social work interventions.

Importance of Human Relationships: Relationship is very important for strengths-based method. The relationship is clearly attuned to increasing the hopefulness of the individual, family or group (Rapp et al., 2005). To be accepting, empathetic, warm and genuine makes relationship the basic source of finding strengths in the individuals. Relationship is also empowering in that it increases individuals' perceptions of their abilities, increases choices and options, and increases confidence to choose (Rapp & Goscha, 2006). The value of the importance of human relationship is central to the method of strengths based practice.

Competence: Value of competence is directly linked to the strengths based practice. One of the prime goals of social work intervention is to enhance the competence of the clients to deal effectively with the demands of challenges of daily life. The method of strengths based practice expects every social worker to enhance one's competence in his/her area of specialization. It also means that a worker has to continually strive to enhance his/her professional knowledge, skills and attitudes through seminars, conferences, training workshops, exposure and exchange programmes for updating the professional self.

Integrity: Value of integrity is a great 'strength' for social work and social work practice. The expression of integrity through sincerity, honesty trustworthy behaviour etc. will help the social workers to identify and pool the strengths and resources of the clients – individuals, groups, families and communities – in the helping process. Social workers involved in this helping profession must be honest, disciplined, responsible, committed and keep high behavioural standards.

Hard Work: Strengths based practice believes in the value of hard work. Practice makes one perfect and hard work is essential for sincere efforts and practice. One has to come out of the comfort zones to identify the core strengths and abilities one possess. Social workers have to be hard working professionals. The values of hard work helps the social work profession to maintain high standards in its interventions.

Cultural Sensitivity: Strengths based social work practice becomes more appropriate when cultural sensitivity is evident in the approach. It respects clients' cultural orientation as a source of strength and appreciates the differences. The social worker has to gain an understanding of the clients' perception/differences as well as their environment as a source of strength.

Commitment and Responsibility: The strengths based practice assumes client's commitment to the helping process and stresses client's responsibility. A client's commitment and responsibility should not be taken for granted by the worker. The worker also should be committed to the helping process.

Teachership: Teachership is a divine profession and every social worker performs several duties of a teacher whether one is a practitioner or an academic. The value of teachership urges the social workers to spread the strengths based practice among the colleagues and to build a practice framework based on the positive note of strengths than on the deficits.

Loyalty to the Profession: Loyalty to profession is essential among the social work professionals to ensure the effective practice of the social work profession. In a way loyalty to profession among the professional social workers is a great strength in the process of enhancing the status and practice of social work profession.

Patriotism: Values of patriotism help in identifying and using the country specific resources and strengths and provide indigenous/ cultural specific intervention. Patriotism is a great strength for social work practice as it urges the professionals to provide their maximum efforts to the advancement and development of one's country and its people through identifying and promoting its strengths and resources.

Implication of Strengths-Based Method

Strengths based practice method urges social workers to focus on the strengths, abilities and resources of the client system rather than on the deficits. It is important to understand that strengths-based approach is not about denying that people do experience problems and challenges. When the problem becomes the starting point with an emphasis on what one is lacking, a dependency is created on the helping professional and the role of the professional is limited to identifying the causes of the problem and to eliminate the problem. In the strengths based method focus is on one's strengths and resources (internal and external) of the client-individual, group, family or community. In the helping process even though problems and issues are acknowledged, strengths are identified and highlighted.

Empirical research suggests that strengths-based interventions have positive psychological impact, particularly in enhancing individual well-being through development of hope. Strengths-based practices are effective in developing and maintaining hope in individuals, and consequently many studies cite evidence for enhanced well-being. There is an emerging evidence of the use of strengths-based approaches with children, young people and families. Early and Glenmaye (2000) found that the use of the strengths perspective in families not only helped the family identify resources for coping, but also helped them use existing strengths to sustain hope and a sense of purpose by setting and achieving goals in line with their personal aspirations, capabilities, and visions of a possible life. Strengths based approaches may lie in encouraging people to stay involved in treatment programmes, most notably for those with substance misuse problems. It can also be a very good method in bridging the gaps in the social work practices. The strengths based practices open a variety of avenues for practicing social work among the disadvantaged and disabled as it focus on their strengths not on deficits. Empowerment oriented strengths based method give a great ray of hope to the population who face physical, mental and resource related challenges.

Conclusion

Social work has to adapt to the needs of the people and demands of society. A new paradigm has emerged in the social work perspective focusing from deficits to strengths. In social work literature, there has been a great deal of discussion about strengths-based approach. The strengths approach provides techniques and tools to help social workers focus on and identify strengths and abilities of clients as well as strengths of families, and communities. The strengths perspective emphasizes the personal and community assets of a client rather than their deficits and offers possibility, promise and hope for the future. The strengths based method is a potential method of social work and can be applied to a wide range of interventions including individuals, family, group and community.

REFERENCES

1. Coulshed, Veronica., & Ormae, Joan. (2012). *Social Work Practice.* London: Palgrave Macmillan.
2. Gratton, C., (1995). *The Art of Spiritual Guidance.* New York: Crossroads.
3. Miley, K.K., O'melia, M. & Dubois, B. (2004). *Generalist Social Work Practice: An Empowering Approach.* Boston: Allyn and Bacon.
4. McCaskey, W. (2008). *The Strengths Approach.* Victoria: St. Luke's Innovative Resources.
5. O'Hanlon, B. & Wilk, J. (1987). *Shifting Contexts: The Generation of Effective Psychotherapy.* New York: The Guilford Press.
6. Pulla, V. (2006). Strengths Based Strategies, in Pulla, V. & Montgomery, (Eds). *Strengths based Strategies, resilience as opposed to deficits: working with strengths.* Brisbane Institute of Strengths Based Practice, Australia.
7. Pulla, V. (2012). "What is strength based practice all about?" In Pulla, V., Chenoweth, L., Francis A., Bakaj S. (Eds.). *Papers in Strength based Practice.* New Delhi: Allied Publications.
8. Pouline, John.,(2010). *Strengths base generalist practice: A collaborative approach. Wodsworth,* Cengage learning, USA.
9. Saleebey, D., (Ed.). (1992). *The Strengths Perspective in Social Work Practice.* White Plains, NY: Longman.
10. Saleebey, D. (Ed.). (1997). *The Strengths Perspective in Social Work Practice.* New York: Longman.
11. Saleebey, D. (Ed.). (2006). *The Strengths Perspective in Social Work Practice*(4th ed.). Boston: Pearson Education, Inc.
12. Rapp, C. A., & Goscha, R. (2006). *The Strengths Model: Case management with people with psychiatric disabilities (2nd ed.).* New York: Oxford.
13. Early, T.J., Glenmaye, L.F. (2000). Valuing Families: Social Work Practice with Families from Strength Perspective. *Social Work,* 45 (2): 118-130.
14. Graybeal, Clay., (2001). Strengths-Based Social Work Assessment: Transforming the Dominant Paradigm in Families in Society: *The Journal of Contemporary Human Services*82(3), 233–242.
15. Saleebey, D. (1996). The Strengths Perspective in Social Work Practice: Extensions and Cautions. *Social Work,* 41, 296-305.
16. Saleebey, D. (2008). Commentary on The Strengths Perspective and Potential Applications in School Counseling. *Professional School Counseling,* 12(2), 68-75.
17. Rapp, C. A., *et al.* (2005). The future of strengths-based social work. *Advances in Social Work,* 6(1), 79-90.

18. Blundo, R. (2001). Learning Strengths-Based Practice: Challenging our Personal and Professional Frames. Families in Society, 82(2), 296–304. Retrieved from http://www.academia.edu/2324023/Papers_in_Strengths_ Based_Practice.
19. Eimers, Lauren A., Strengths Perspective and Solution-focused Approach to New Conversations. Retrieved from http://able-differently.org/wp-content/uploads/ 2012/01/AStrengthsPerspectivewithPicsandIntro.pdf
20. Saleebey, D. (2010). The strengths perspective. Strengths Institute, University of Kansas School of Social Welfare. Retrieved from: http://www.socwel.ku.edu/ strengths/about/index.shtml
21. Rankin, (2007). Exploring and Describing the Strength/Empowerment Perspective in Social Work, in IUC Journal of social Work, Retrieved from www.bemidjistate.edu/academics/publications/social_work_journal/issue14/ articles/rankin.htm
22. Wormer, Katherine., (1998). "Social Work, Corrections, and the Strengths Approach" A paper presented at the Canadian Association of Social Workers National Social Work Conference, Canada. Retrieved from/sTRENGTH% 20BASED%20%20-%20SW/Social%20Work, %20Corrections,% 20and% 20the%20Strengths%20Approach.htm

14

Strengths Based Practice and its Relation with Other Methods of Social Work

Aneesh Kurian

Generalist practice is popular in any democratic society. Several schools of social work across the globe do teach and promote integrated method of social work which is known popularly as generalist practice. The six 'contemporary' methods of social work are also relevant to the client system across the globe as the professional can draw benefit from those methods while working with different types of clients be it individual, group or community. Strengths based practice method has much to offer to other methods of social work especially in the globalised world of the day as it can enable various types of clients in the system. Strengths based method expects a different way of viewing the individuals, families, groups, institutions and communities. The strengths perspective can cover all the practice arena of social work profession ranging from individual to community. It can encompass all the social work methods in its wider practice framework. If the social worker identifies and focuses on the strengths namely, the capacities, talents, competencies, possibilities and resources rather than on the deficits of the individual, family, community or any other stakeholders, the practice automatically becomes strengths based practice. An effort is made to link the strengths based method to the other methods of social work profession namely, social case work, group work, community organization, social work research, social action, social welfare administration and the 'contemporary' methods advocated by Gracious Thomas which include awareness campaign, resource mobilisation, public interest litigation, net working, and advocacy. All these methods of social work relies on similar assumptions namely, the dignity and worth of the client, the resources possessed by the client to deal with one's problems, the inherent capacity that the client possesses for growth and development and the ability to choose wisely for the management of their own affairs.

Social Case Work

Social case work is one of the methods of professional social work which is aimed at helping individuals, in finding solutions to their problems. Social case work is very much linked to the strengths based practice. Strengths based approach helps social case workers to make use of policies, programmes, and strategies in cultural context to identify and draw upon the strengths of individuals, families, and communities. Strengths based practice involves a shift from a deficit approach, which emphasizes problems and pathology, to a positive outlook of the client system. The approach acknowledges each individual, family and community as a unit with unique set of strengths and challenges, and engages them as a partner in developing and implementing the service plan, which could even be different from the traditionally followed problem focused case work approach. Helen Haris Perlmam in her book (Social Casework: A Problem Solving Process, 1957) has discussed the dynamic components, which make up the casework situation namely, the person, problem, place, worker/professional and process. It means a person with a problem comes to a place where the professional social worker helps him/her through the systematic process of social case work. The strengths based method reminds the case worker that the person not only comes with the problem but also with a set of strengths which can be tapped as a great source of resource. In the process of helping the client, the strengths of the worker and the agency also are of great importance.

While examining the linkage of strengths based practice method with social case work method we need to view the situation in environmental and cultural context. While in most western countries clients have the facilities to approach agencies for case work, counselling and referral services, most developing countries do not have such options. In a huge country like India with over one thousand two hundred million people having diversity of cultural background, the task of professionally addressing issues of individual clients are really challenging. The traditional family background, the environmental context including the rural, tribal and slum cluster population along with the diverse class, caste and religious background of the clients, play crucial role in the case work process.

In this context, the relevance of strengths based practice method in addressing the problems of individual clients is of utmost importance. Traditionally the strengths of clients, families, extended families, friendly neighbours as well as locality based religious communities helped clients in resolving several problems faced by them. However, in the fast changing social scenario the nature of problems being confronted by individuals became diverse which require shift in approaches and engagement of supportive methods to meaningfully address the problems. The strengths based methods enables the case worker to make use of the strengths of the clients, their families and communities in the process of case work. Therefore strengths based practice method is of great relevance in the present day context. Along with contemporary methods, there is a need to imbibe the twelve core values of professional social work in order to help the clients in finding solutions to the emerging problems and challenges.

Social Group Work

Social group work helps the individuals to enhance the social functioning through purposeful group experience and cope more effectively with their problems. Strengths based method helps the group worker to enhance the strengths of the group members through effective group experiences. Each member of the group gains from the strengths of the other members in the group. The problems are the results of lack of strengths. If the strengths are identified and emphasised, the problems will fade away in course of time. All the members of the group posses strengths in one domain or the other. It helps them to learn from the other members. The process of group work, the interaction pattern in the group, group morale etc. will contribute to the strengths of the group as well which will benefit each group member. Similarly the strengths of the group worker (particularly his/her several years of learning and work experience) and the agency's strengths will also influence the group members.

Some of the recent initiatives of the government of India to empower people include the women's reservation bill, women's representation in local governance, economic empowerment of women through self help groups, women's induction in security forces, enhancing the capacities and ensuring conducive environment for the disabled population, facilitation of prison inmates to pursue school and university offered programmes of study, skill development programmes for youth, promotion of positive people's net work, peer education and awareness campaign among the sex workers etc. show the extent of emerging roles of social group work and strengths based practice method. The strengths based method helps the group worker to practice a 'strengths based social group work' making use of these government initiatives and other related resources. Strengths based group work practice among the diverse population of women, children, adolescence, disables are of need of the time especially in the developing countries. Accordingly the professionals are expected improve their wealth of knowledge and information about such areas of intervention and the strategies required to be adopted.

Participation in seminars, conferences, exposure visits, faculty, practitioner and student exchange programmes, enhancing cooperation among members of national and state level associations of social work professionals, skill development programmes, involvement in policy formation, appraising social issues through print and visual media as well as drawing the attention of the elected representatives and the judiciary to make timely interventions can be viewed in the context of strengths based method. These initiatives are very important for social work professionals in the present day context for which the role of social group work and strengths based practice method are very important.

Community Organization

Community organization is one of the core methods of social work, used to intervene in the life and developmental process of a community whether rural, urban or in the tribal setting. In case of community organization method, the community is the client. Just as in any other methods of social work, community organisation also strives to solve the problems and fulfil the needs of its 'client', namely, the larger community. In the helping process, community organisation as a method of social work, relies upon the strengths of the community. The main purpose of community organisation is to utilise the latent potentialities of the community, to optimise the use of its indigenous resources, to develop its capacity to manage its own life and affairs and to enhance its ability to function as an integrated unit. The strengths based method is very supportive and very much linked to community organisation. Community is a vessel of resources/ strengths. The approach focuses on what the communities have to offer and contribute to the renewal process rather than just on problems and the indicators of deprivation. Community's strengths assessments can be useful for planning support for community groups and community enterprises such as training, advice, funding and mobilising resources. It will also provide a baseline description for the rationale for programmes for community development and community-based projects. Community development through community organisation can benefit immensely much from strengths based method as one can find numerous strengths within the individuals and families of each community along with strengths available in various operational sectors of the community and society.

The inter relation between community organisation and strengths based practice method is more relevant for a democratic society like India which comprises of a diversity of population and wide geographical spread. The professional who is groomed to work with the people for their overall development has to enlist the strengths of various stake holders within the community as well as those in the administration and others with service profession.

In order to maximise people's participation, organisation of the community at various levels is essential. Family visits, research and professional assessment of the problems along with all potential resources and strengths of the community and those associated with the development process, is very essential for successful community organisation initiative. Apart from the spontaneous response to addressing emergency issues, strengths based method enables social workers there to plan, design, develop and implement a plan of action for community development, based on the strengths and needs of the community. The scope of strengths based practice method in the organisation of a given community whether rural, urban or tribal is of utmost importance. It will boost the morale of the people. In fact the very essence or aim of social work is to "help people to help themselves" by the professional through the strengths of the community known and unknown to them. In this process the worker who is well aware of the socio-economic and cultural background of the community, helps and enables the community to benefit from their own innate abilities and strengths for their own development.

Social Action

The inherent theme behind social action is alteration of the social institutions and redistribution of power and resources for social justice and empowerment. As a method of social work, social action mobilizes the general population to bring about structural changes in the social system. Strengths based method adds more viability to social action as it operates on the principle of strengths. It helps to find the innate strengths even among the downtrodden and the devastated or disadvantaged people. Social action as a method of social work rests heavily on other methods such as case work, group work, community organization and research. The contemporary methods of social work namely, strengths based practice, public interest litigation, awareness campaign, resource mobilization, networking and advocacy are very much involved in the process of social action. Social action is an organized effort to change or improve social and economic institutions through organization and mobilization of the community. This peculiarity of social action to operate from strengths and focus for more strengths through social change bring it closer to strengths based method. Some of the strengths visible for any social action effort include the strengths of the individuals, groups, and community in terms of their extent of knowledge, wisdom, and understanding, the number of people available, communication skills, local resources, networking with people and organizations from across the board, as well as local leadership.

The depository of knowledge, information and experience of the professional, facilitates social action method to enhance the capacities of the affected groups to come together, organize themselves and work towards the realization of their set of goals.

We have several convincing examples from recent times which have enabled communities and nations from social action movements. The non-violent efforts of Mahatma Gandhi and later by Nelson Mandela in getting freedom and independence from foreign occupation for India and South Africa are clear examples of the effects of social action. The efforts of social activists to address the issues of corruption, right to information act, numerous cases of public interest litigation, issues pertaining to rights and dignity of women, proper wage for labour, addressing issues of child labour etc. are examples of successful social action initiatives in which the strengths based practice method also facilitated the process.

The efforts of social activists like Anna Hazare has drawn the attention of the world community. Various changes that Anna Hazare could bring about not only in his own village and panchayath (local governing province within a sub- district) but across the state of Maharastra are examples of the outcome of strengths based practice method. The model village which has drawn the attention of several visitors even from aboard, the health and education schemes and other developmental initiatives speak volumes about the importance of both social action and strengths based practice method for people's development.

Social Welfare Administration

Social welfare administration promotes social work practice in administration. It plans, administrates and implements special programmes to different sections of the society through social work processes which is a unique service profession unlike medicine, legal assistance etc. It also aims at the effective implementation of the regular and special programmes of social welfare agencies keeping in mind the core values of social work. Social welfare administration as a method of social work translates social welfare policies, programmes and social legislation into social work practice with special emphasis on code of ethics of the profession. Strengths based method can be found very much linked in effectively designing and implementing social welfare programmes. Strengths based method will help local self-governments, central and state governments, non-governmental organizations, inter-governmental agencies, corporate sector and private organizations to plan their developmental programmes based on need and implement the programmes. The strengths of individuals, groups, families, communities, agencies, organizations, committees or departments are effectively enhanced through the practice of social welfare administration which upholds the dignity and worth of the person, integrity and importance of human relationship and above all with a service mentality particularly to the needs of the poorest of the poor and the disadvantaged sections of the society.

Social welfare administration extensively benefits from strengths based practice method. The professionals working in various agencies are trained to manage programmes, projects, various functionaries as well as the clients that include individuals, groups, families and community.

The strengths based method helps to find the strengths of the professional, target group and the agency and its functionaries, and to make use of them in the process of planning and implementation of the programmes. The strengths of the professionals include the extent of knowledge and experience in social work, areas of specialization, extent of the commitment of the professional to the assigned task, loyalty to the profession, sense of responsibility, hard work, service mind as well as integrity to name a few. The target groups too have their own strengths which include the level of education, knowledge, value system, sense of belongingness, material and financial resources, expertise in various skills etc. The agency and its functionaries should have capacity for networking practically with every sector under the sun. Additional strengths would also include the ability to pool resources from governments and donor agencies as well as from community sources. The experiences of teachers, technicians, medical professionals, spiritual leaders and political leaders would also be of great help for effectively practicing social welfare administration along with strengths based method.

Social Work Research

Social work research primarily deals with social issues, profiles of client system, need based studies for developing project proposals and examining the what, why and how of the problems faced by professional social workers, social work agencies and community in its practice with social work functions. Social work research adds new knowledge to the social work theory and practice and improves the efficiency of professional social workers and their projects and programmes. It will strengthen the practice of different social work methods and the use of alternative intervention techniques or change or modification of programme. The strengths based social work method is directly connected to social work research as it brings strengths to the profession and its practice arena based on the outcome of research on target population and problems. The research outcomes help in additional information, and practicing social work with cultural sensitivity. The research tools of case study, observation, family visits and group discussion are vital in relation to strengths based practice as it substantiate the strengths of the client system. The tenets of strengths based method and the value of competence urges the social work professionals to generate evidence based field researches, publications and presentations in the area of social work and dispenses the knowledge to the entire social work fraternity. The M.Phil. and doctoral thesis are also to be linked to the social work research method and practice which will strengthen the profession. This will result in strengthening the social work practice across the globe through filling the gaps in social work practice.

One of the core values of social work profession is competence. If the profession has to address the emerging issues in present scenario of fast changing socio-economic and technological context, research occupies prime position among the methods of social work. Although several schools of social work are engaged in generating knowledge through research in the form of M.Phil./PhD dissertations and projects of varying nature, there is hardly any visibility of their outcome. In fact, many schools also have dissertation in post-graduation programmes. Some of the universities also offer courses on research at not only for PG level programmes but also for the BSW programme. Hence there is clear evidence of the efforts and will on the part of social work academics and curriculum designers in promoting social work research. The strengths based method view the research component in social work curriculum as great opportunity, and portray the need of channelizing these dissertations and thesis to fill the gap of social work literature and practice. What is required is the proper utilization of these opportunities as well as their dissemination for enhancing the knowledge base of the professionals. The hidden or yet to be uncovered talents or strengths of the professionals is much needed in the present day context. Strengths based practice method of social work can enable the profession to re-vitalize itself with a wealth of information and knowledge of various communities spread across the Indian sub-continent. This would also be equally relevant to African and South American continents as well, as the rest of the world yet to fully understand the cultural richness of its people which remain a mystery to the academic and professional world of the social workers.

Therefore the relation between social work research and strengths based practice methods need to be recognized and benefited from by the social work fraternity.

Public Interest Litigation (PIL)

Public interest litigation (PIL) is described as a type of litigation where the interest of the public is given priority over all other interests with an aim to ensure social and collective justice. This helps social workers and other persons with bona fide intentions to approach the court for the interest of the public in general as well as the disadvantaged or under-privileged segment of the society. PIL becomes a necessity when protection of the affected under law is unavailable to the public or a segment of it due to ignorance, poverty, fear or lack of organised endeavour. It has come as strength in the hands of social workers. The strengths based method helps the social workers to identify the strengths of the people and the strengths in the socio- political and judiciary in the form of policies, programmes, schemes and laws to fetch the maximum possible help to the clients. In recent times the civil society movements for ensuring the rights of people took a new approach with the judiciary being increasingly occupied with public interest cases seeking relief against administrative anarchy and ignorance. Social workers seek to gain strengths in their practice with the disadvantaged people and ensuring them their due share by making use of the available opportunities and strengths in the constitutional provisions of the country. PIL has given strengths to the social activists and functionaries in social and welfare sectors to address the issues of the marginalised through judicial system. This is bringing about relief to large sections of the society from various walks of life. The strengths available under PIL includes relief for the petitioners from legal expenses, facilitating justice for the poor and the affected, safety and protection of the clients, to name a few.

The linkage between PIL and strengths based practice method of social work is well established. Some of the initial and famous cases considered by the Supreme Court of India under PIL show the motive, commitment and concerns of certain people with judiciary and among social welfare agencies to address the problems of the under trials and in several cases innocent prison inmates. This alone shows the outcome of some of the core social work values such as service, social justice, dignity and worth of the person, responsibility and commitment, hard work, and loyalty to the profession.

One professional with whom Gracious Thomas worked with in the Supreme Court of India during the early 1980's is Fr. P.D. Mathew, a Jesuit priest who has MSW and LL.B and now an advocate in Supreme Court of India. Fr. Mathew has generated several volumes of information on the what, why and how of PIL and quoting several cases which were considered by the Supreme Court and High Courts in India. A glance at his writings will show the extent of involvement of a professional social worker in PIL and in motivating several professionals to follow suit. In fact Fr. Mathew conducted several legal training programmes which enabled both practitioners and social work teachers to learn, teach and undertake PIL cases.

PIL is enabled by the method of strengths based practice to restore the dignity of the under privileged and the marginalised. It enables the professional to identify the strengths of the affected parties, strengthen them within legal frame work and judicial system of the country and the service providers who are well versed with the environmental and cultural context of the client system. Therefore strengths based method and PIL go hand in hand as contemporary method of social work.

Resource Mobilization

Resource mobilization is a process of raising different types of support for the client. These resources can be manpower, money, material, various forms of expertise or any other thing which can potentially assist in the process of rendering help offered to the client. Resource mobilization is basic to strengths based method as it operates on the resources/ strengths of the client system: whether individual, group or a community. Strengths based method aims to mobilize the internal and external resources available to the client and build on the available strengths. This strengths based method in return help the social workers to identify the available resources in the client system and in the environment. Some of these resources can be client's strengths, competence, talents, family support, government policies, programmes and so on. Resource mobilization method and strengths based method are more relevant to developing countries, and particularly while working with the poorest of the poor and the marginalized. A professional social worker with the imbibed value of service to humanity is the most appropriate person who can facilitate the client system in harnessing the resources within the community through strengths based method of social work.

In most developed countries over eighty percent of the resources are mobilized from the public while in developing countries including, India most funds are from government sources. Public participation and contribution is much limited in India, although traditionally, charity mind set is an inherent virtue of most of Indians and reflected in the teachings of various religions of Indian origin. The incorporation of strengths based method to the resource mobilization will serve as a great force in boosting the public participation/ contribution in resource mobilization.

The recent policy of the government of India to promote Corporate Social Responsibility (CSR) among corporate bodies is a welcoming initiative. This is creating a new trend and voluntary agencies can mobilize resources from within the country. It is estimated that the corporate bodies would currently require over hundred thousand professionals to effectively implement the scheme. Therefore job opportunities for social workers would increase and the need to practice strengths based method along with resource mobilization by the professionals became more relevant in this fast changing global economy and the changes occurring in the market which require qualified professionals. The strengths based method will be of great use in identifying these CSR resources and channelizing these resources for the upliftment/ strengthening of the marginalized and disadvantaged group.

Networking

Networking is a method of creating useful linkages, both within and among social work profession, communities, organizations, and societies, in order to mobilize resources, maintain good will and achieve various goals. The method of networking is operating on the principles of strengths based method. Networking is a process of developing and activating social worker's relationships to enhance their knowledge expand service sphere to the client by using all the available resources. Professional bodies, associations of schools of social work, seminar, forums etc. acts as sources of strengths for the practice of social work profession to the diverse population. Networking occurs at various levels. Strengths based method is a source of support for practicing effective network with government bodies, various institutions, donor agencies, and bilateral agencies and will help the social workers to bring the best outcome for their service in the society. At the level of neighbourhoods and communities, it is a matter of creating reciprocal relationships with other members of society. This requires the social workers to know the strengths of the diverse population and institutions and to build relationships, identify resources, and work together in an organized way for social change. These social connections allow social workers to help individuals, groups, and organizations to find allies, access tools, share practical wisdom, and build collaborative strategies.

Networking method and strengths based method are very much interrelated. In order to practice the method of networking, one needs to enlist the strengths required and available with the individuals, groups and communities for a particular issue or a problem. For example: An agency or an institution interested in organizing a national or international seminar on social work will have to engage in a series of activities from planning to the implementation and evaluation of the seminar. To begin with, a good proposal has to be prepared, find out the resources available within the organization in regard to academic expertise, infrastructure, and amount needed for the same. This exercise alone requires net working within the agency.

In order to get additional funding from external sources, one should have adequate information and access to donor agencies and other sources. To get quality papers, delegates, resource persons, volunteers etc. one needs to have solid networking. The networking will also include reaching out to all stakeholders, getting the paper works done, registration formalities are completed well in advance, arrangements for stay, meals, cultural programmes, local site seeing, management of various session etc. are taken care off. One has to get ready with the seminar venue, programme schedule, refreshments, certificates, transportation, emergency service facilities like health care including first aid and to ensure the availability of couple of physicians in emergency situations on a phone call, disbursement of travel grant etc. Networking is also needed for clearing the abstracts, timely communication as well as editing for all seminar publications. All these can be done if one can get the cooperation of several experts from all these sectors based on their strengths in relevant areas. One has to own shared responsibility and harness the dedicated services from various quarters to have a successful programme. The school of social work at IGNOU organizes an Annual National Seminar ever since 2004 in collaboration with one or another reputed institution which is being appreciated by the professionals from all over India. This alone shows the relevance of strengths based method of social work and the need and importance of networking practice method.

Awareness Campaign

An awareness campaign is a process of awareness creation using media, messaging, and an organized set of communication activities to generate specific outcomes among a large number of individuals and in a specific period of time. Awareness campaign is an effective method of social work practice especially in the developing countries that uses the strengths of available resources like TV, radio, newspapers, street plays and other popular models to reach to a larger population very effectively in a shorter span of time. The awareness campaigns on polio eradication programme, awareness campaign on HIV/AIDS prevention, family planning etc. are some of the recent examples of effectiveness of awareness campaign. The strengths based practice enables the social workers to practice the method of awareness campaign upholding the values of cultural sensitivity and dignity and worth of individual.

Strengths based method and awareness campaign method in social work are inter-related. Take the example of the famous "Narmada Bachavo Andolan" of India spearheaded by Dr. Medha Patkar. Narmada Bachao Andolan is one of the most powerful mass movements, started in 1985, against the construction of huge dam on the Narmada River. The Narmada dam has displaced poor people from scores of villages from some of the north Indian states – particularly from Gujarat and Madhya Pradesh. Medha Patkar is a professionally qualified social worker who was an academic in Tata Institute of Social Sciences, Mumbai. She left the academic field and became a practitioner setting an example to numerous social work students in the country showing how social work values of service before self, dignity and worth of person and more importantly loyalty to the profession matters to a professional.

She had to leave the comfort zone and live with the poor, the marginalized and local population affected by the construction of a mega dam. Medha Patkar through the 'Narmada Bachavo Andolan' has challenged the political establishment, went on hunger strike, was jailed and faced several legal hurdles – all for the legitimate rights of the marginalized. In order to continue on her mission, she used several methods of social work including social group work, community organization, social action, awareness campaign and the strengths based practice method.

In order to create awareness among the affected population, often she had to practice both social action and strengths based approach. She could help the affected group to realize their own hidden strengths, help them to organize themselves and fight the political and judicial system in the country. In the long run she did achieve lot of results to bring relief to the target population and she continuous with awareness campaign, social action and strengths based methods to fight the mighty with total dedication.

Advocacy

Social work advocacy is the exclusive and mutual representation of clients or a cause in a forum attempting to systematically influence decision making in an unjust or unresponsive system (Schneider and Lester 2001). Advocacy has clear links with empowerment and social workers have to address issues of rights and social justice and to support people to obtain services and resources in for community. Strengths based method helps the social workers to empower the individuals, groups and communities through the adoption of practice approaches culturally sensitive to the impacts of difference. The strengths based method helps the professionals to appropriately channelize the strengths of media, government policies and machineries to work for the empowerment of the clients. Advocacy and strengths based method in social work go hand in hand. In a democratic society advocacy helps the professional to highlight the actual situation or plight of the clients whether individual, group or a community to those that matters in the country as well as in the larger world who can influence decision making. In order to practice advocacy effectively some of the methods of social work including research, strengths based practice and social action are essential. Advocacy method of social work needs to be viewed in the larger context of social work practice.

Strengths-based method coupled with the method of advocacy enables the social worker to make use of several policies and programmes in the best interest of the client. Some of the popular areas where advocacy has played significant role include the protection of child rights, empowerment of women, reservation for women as well as other disadvantaged sections of the society in various forums, protection of the rights of the minorities and prison reforms. The professional social workers have a responsibility to continue the fight with using the vital potency of the methods of advocacy and strengths based method. Some of the areas that require a blended approach of advocacy and strengths based method, in the present day context include the need and importance of the use of toilets particularly in the rural sector, health insurance, promotion of education from elementary level to higher education for rural masses, reaching the unreached with various developmental projects etc. Strengths based method would be of great help in effectively undertaking advocacy by professional social workers.

Conclusion

Strengths-based method in brief refers to policies, practice methods, and strategies that identify and draw upon the strengths of individuals, families, groups and communities. The strengths based method guides and influences a social worker to practice as professional. It is associated and practiced along with other social work methods to bring the optimum outcome to the clients. It adds 'strengths' to the practice of social work with individuals, groups, families and communities. The incorporation of strengths based method in the practice of other methods help the social work professional to find strengths even in the most affected, downtrodden, oppressed and subjugated clients and to enhance the process of help by building upon the strengths.

Social work, a dynamic profession, has to adapt to the changing needs and demands of the service seekers. The strengths based method along with other "contemporary" methods are of much importance in the changing global scenario, to address the manifold issues of the clients and it will rejuvenate the practice of social work adding the extra mileage. Professional social workers across the globe can have a hope that the twelve methods and the twelve core values of social work being promoted by the professionals from across the globe would go a long way in ameliorating the plight of the poorest of the poor and the marginalized of the third world countries following the examples set by Mary Richmond over a hundred years ago.

REFERENCES

1. Saleebey, D., (Ed.). (1992). *The Strengths Perspective In Social Work Practice.* White Plains, NY: Longman.
2. Saleebey, D. (1996). The Strengths Perspective in Social Work Practice: Extensions and Cautions. *Social Work,* 41, 296-305.
3. Schneider, R. and Lester, L. (2001). *Social Work Advocacy: A New Framework for Action*, Belmont CA, Brooks Cole.
4. Thomas, Gracious. (Ed: 2010). *Case Work and Counselling: Working with Individuals,* New Delhi: IGNOU.
5. Trecker, Harleigh. (1948). *Social Group Work, Principles and Practices.* New York: Woman's Press.

Contributors

Aara, Rafat (Dr.), MSW, M.Phil & Ph.D in Social Work, School of Social Work, IGNOU, New Delhi.

Joseph, Sheeba (Dr.), MSW, Ph.D in Social Work, Head, Department of Social Work, Bhopal School of Social Sciences, Bhopal.

Kaushik, Archana (Dr.), MSW& Ph.D in Social Work, Associate Professor, Department of Social Work, University of Delhi.

Kumari, Nita (Dr.), MSW, M.Phil & Ph.D in Social Work, School of Social Work, IGNOU, New Delhi.

Kurian, Aneesh, MSW & M.Phil in Social Work, School of Social Work, IGNOU, New Delhi.

Mathew, P.D., MSW & LLB, Advocate, Supreme court of India, New Delhi.

Pradhan, Asutosh (Dr.), MSW, & Ph.D in Social Work, Head, Department of Social Work, Central University of Himachal Pradesh.

Ramya (Dr.), MSW, M.Phil & Ph.D in Social Work, Assistant Professor, School of Social Work, IGNOU, New Delhi.

Thomas, Gracious (Prof.), B.A, M.A., Ph.D and D.Litt in Social Work, Director, School of Social Work, IGNOU, New Delhi.

Index

Abuse drugs, 78
Abused children, 17
Academic resources, 6
Accreditation bodies, 1
Acid attacks, 134
Action System for Intervention, 30
Adivasi Bhils, 122
Administrative
  arbitrariness, 119
  mechanisms, 50
Adult learning centres, 61
Adult teaching-learning principles, 56
Advocacy
  actions, 5, 8-13, 17, 19-21, 24-7, 30-1, 34, 37
  actors, 25
  approach, 32
  campaigns, 21, 28, 31-4, 37, 76
  -coalition framework model, 24
  collective, 111
  definition of, 9, 110
  democratic society, 183
  direct, 111
  effective, 33, 36
  electronic, 16
  grassroots, 34
  initiatives, 29, 31-2, 79
  international/transnational, 15
  issue-based, 111
  legal/policy, 16
  legislative, 83
  macro-level, 27
  method, 5, 38, 50, 79, 183
  networks, 16-17, 34, 49
  policy, 9, 17, 24, 29, 81
  political, 15
  programme, 79
  relational, 14
  and resource mobilization, 110
  service provision, 15
  social, 125
  strategies, 26, 32
  trainings, 25
Aggressive media campaign, 35
Aggrieved citizens, 129
AIDS Healthcare Foundation, 146
Akali Dal, 120
Alumni associations, 142
Alzheimer, 74
American Bill of Rights, 118
Anarchy, administrative, 179
Ancillary powers, 124
Anti-smoking campaigns, 80
Artificial limbs, 158
Asiad projects, 121
Assertiveness, 114
Associations of Fundraising Professionals (AFP), 86
Atrocities, 23, 49, 121, 129
Audio-visual
  materials, 56
  advertisements, 53
  resources, 60
Auxiliary Nurse Midwife (ANMs), 77
Awareness campaigns, 4-5, 7, 46, 52-8, 62, 64-84, 92, 98, 109, 111, 128, 133-4, 148, 156-7, 182-3
  and advocacy, 46
  altered, 78
  and awareness raising, 52
  influence, 61
  initiatives, 54

long-term, 58
model of, 73, 83
strategies, 56
Awareness-Raising, 62

Bandhua Mukti Morcha, 117, 122
Baseline research, 80
Behaviour change communication (BCC), 63-4, 72-4, 83
Behavioural
changes, 52, 55, 57, 70
pattern, 156
sciences, 2, 55
Belief systems, 24, 41, 67
Bilateral agencies, 96, 181
Black Law Dictionary, 110
Blood donation, 83
Bonded labourers, 11, 43, 73, 122, 126-8, 134
Bridging networks, 48
BSW programme, 178
Budgetary allocations, 63, 87
Bureaucracy and Judiciary advocacy, 62
Bureaucracy-advocacy approaches, 62

Campaign
coalitions, 28
leaders, 36
materials, 34, 47
planners, 59
strategies, 53
tools, 33
Capacity building, 35
Care-givers, 74, 165
Case work method, 128-9
Caste panchayat, 14
Causal assumptions, 24
Cause-advocacy work, 50
Cause-effect relationships, 69
Central Pollution Board, 133
Centre for Tibetan Studies, 146
Chartered Institute of Public Relations, 61
Chief Executive Officer (CEO), 3
Child
abuse, 14, 62
health services, 75
labourers, 11, 43, 121
marriage, 68
protection, 28
rights, 82, 183
Sexual Abuse (CSA), 56, 72, 79
welfare, 145
Cinema halls, 81
Citizenry rights, 81
Civic
engagements, 16
responsibilities, 83
rights, 109
Civil society groups, 159
society organisations, 24, 62
war crimes, 15
Class barriers, 3
Client
advocacy, 10, 42
-centric Approach, 67
Climate change, 15
Coalition building, 20, 25, 34, 41, 47
Co-curricular activities, 61
Code of ethics, 1-2, 4, 146, 177
of social work obligates, 20
Collaborative
initiatives, 19
litigation, 110
relationships, 6, 20, 138, 159
strategies, 152, 181
Collective action problems, 24
Collective rights, 119, 127
Common advocacy agendas, 156
Communal harmony, 74
Communication
barriers, 58
channels, 54, 56, 70
dynamics, 59
infrastructure, 58
mix, 62
network, 57
patterns, 56, 144
skill, 166, 176
behavior change, 78, 83
effective, 140
mass media, 72
personal, 59-60
two-way, 68
Communities
backward, 105
deprived, 76, 81
excluded, 15
horizontal, 108
knit, 19
larger, 175

local, 88, 90, 92, 94, 99, 104
marginalized, 94
neighbouring, 146
rural, 74
slum, 146
urban, 8, 75
village, 8, 75
Community Based Organisations (CBOs), 144
Compressed Natural Gas (CNG), 131
Conscientization, 76
Constitutional
court, 126, 158
rights, 22
safeguards, 11
Consumer research, 65
Cooperative body specialists, 150
Corporate Social Responsibility (CSR), 180
Corruption-free administration, 128
Cost-benefit analysis, 65
Counseling services, 62
Court of law, 6, 34, 81, 110, 114-15, 119, 129, 131-4, 158
Courts of justice, 114, 117, 126
Cultural inequality, 1-2
Cultural sensitivity, 18, 55-6, 58, 66-7, 83, 141, 146, 162, 165, 168, 178, 182

Damaged reputations, 17
Decision-making mechanisms, 17
Deficit approaches, 133, 173
Delivery welfare, 33
Democratic approaches, 165
Domestic Violence Act, 47, 73
Dowry Prohibition Act, 115
Drug abuses, 64, 73, 159

Economic resources, 79, 156
Elderly abuses, 62
Erroneous actions, 20
Extension
activities, 145-6
services, 146
Face-to-face representation, 36
Financial risks, 87

Girl child, 60, 72
Governmental agencies, 131

Healthcare agencies, 102
HIV/AIDS, 3, 5, 26, 62-4, 72, 74, 109, 138, 145-6, 151, 154-5, 157-8
Holistic analysis, 68
Human behavior, 52, 55, 65, 127
Human resource development, 35
Human Service Organisations (HSOs), 90-2, 95

Ideal schools, 138
Identifying Potential Sources, 95
Ill-effects, 46
Illegal
confinement, 49
detention, 121, 126
felling, 8
Ill-treatment, 11-12, 39, 46, 122
Immoral Traffic Act, 115
Inbuilt mechanism, 37
Indigenous resources, 75, 175
Indira Gandhi National Open University (IGNOU), 1, 57, 63, 128, 145, 182
Information Education Communication (IEC), 64, 83
Injured citizens, 130
Institutional
arrangements, 48
barriers, 19
Integrated Child Development Services (ICDS), 43
Intellectual
class, 44
services, 91
Inter-governmental agencies, 177
International Rivers Network (IRN), 156
Inter-personal relationships, 27, 35, 104, 166
Intrinsic capabilities, 73

Judicial
actions, 123
activism, 135
relief, 118
Justice delivery mechanism, 24
Justice dispensation mechanisms, 46
Juvenile Justice Act, 115

Koodankulam Nuclear Power Project (KNPP), 132

Legal aid services, 33

Legal rights, 6, 28, 62, 81, 110, 114-16, 120, 126, 133, 158
Lethal chemicals, 130
Liberalisation of law, 118
Like-minded individuals, 79, 157
Lokpal Act, 53
Longitudinal research, 46

Mahatma Gandhi National Rural Development Guarantee Act, 77
Maintenance of law, 121
Mass betterment, 76, 105
Mass-media channels, 64
Media-oriented advocacy awareness campaigns, 47

Narmada Bachao Andolan (NBA), 53, 110, 130, 154, 182
National AIDS Control Organizations (NACO), 63, 146
National AIDS Control Programmes (NACP), 73-4
National Crime Records Bureau (NCRB), 46
National Family Health Survey (NFHS), 46
National Sample Survey Organisation (NSSO) 1, 46
Networks information, 79, 157
No smoking zones, 80
Non-conducive environment, 1-3
Non-governmental agencies, 142
Non-Governmental Organisation (NGOs), 8, 24, 31, 45, 47, 49-50, 53, 60, 62, 75-6, 79, 82, 89-93, 108-9, 144
Non-governmental sectors, 27
Non-state actors, 14, 40

Old age pension, 9
One stop crisis centres, 79
One-to-one relationships, 40

Participatory approaches, 19, 157
Paternalism, 164
Patriotism, 67, 146, 169
People's Union for Democratic Rights (PUDR1), 121
Performance appraisal, 98
Personal Digital Assistants (PDAs), 60
Philanthropic activities, 86
Policy research, 24
Political representatives, 16
Post-Traumatic Stress Disorder (PTSD), 40
Powerlessness, 8, 22, 165
Practitioner-client relationships, 112
Prevention of Domestic Violence Act, 73
Prevention of Immoral Traffic Act, 115
Primary Health Centers (PHC), 43, 121
Prioritisation of action, 17
Prisoner's rights, 121
Problem
  -centred approaches, 47
  resolution, 14, 44
  solving, 111, 127, 139, 154
Professional activity, 11, 91
Public cynicism, 59
Public interest action, 117
Public Interest Law Service Society (PILSS), 123
Public interest law, 116
Public Interest Litigation (PIL), 4, 6-7, 17, 49-50, 62, 72, 80-1, 84, 109-10, 114-18, 120-35, 143, 158, 176, 179-80

Qualitative analysis, 131
Quality of relationships, 6, 140
Quality of services, 43, 156
Quasi-personal relationships, 19

Reciprocal relationships, 142, 181
Redressal mechanisms, 129
Referral services, 31, 141-2, 149, 153, 173
Reform, 6, 115
  jail, 121
  political, 106
  social, 9
Refugees, 3, 8, 17, 44-5, 150
Regional imbalances, 45
Regulatory bodies, 29
Rehabilitation of displaced persons, 121
Rehabilitation services, 103
Rehabilitative approaches, 109
Relief workers, 104
Religious
  background, 173
  beliefs, 151, 167
  charities, 152
  commitment, 166
  denomination, 13
  groups, 63, 159
Remedial measures, 134, 143

Renewal process, 175
Research
  and assessment phase, 27
  occupies, 178
  skills, 155
  tools, 178
Resource mobilization, 4-7, 33-4, 48, 50, 58-9, 62, 81-2, 86-8, 90, 92-9, 101, 103-12, 132, 158, 180
Resource Mobilization Approach (RMA), 93
Resource-assessment, 69
Resources
  intangible, 50
  local, 88-90, 176
  material, 3, 87, 145
  minimal, 78, 96
  misusing, 97
  mobilising, 87, 99, 175
  physical, 158
  pool, 177
  prioritize, 97
  saving, 96
  -starved clients, 50
  utilizable, 163
Responsive citizens, 79
Restoration, 8, 103
Rig Veda, 86
Right to Education Act, 131
Right to Information Act, 16, 33, 43, 62, 176
Ring the doorbell (*bell bajao*) campaign, 79
Risk
  analysis, 35
  assessment, 35
Rockwell International, 109
Role reconciliation, 40
RSS, 60
Rule of laws, 128, 133
Rural women, 75

Sarva Shiksha Abhiyan, 77
Schematic Representation of Resource Mobilization, 107
School of Social Welfare, 162
School of Social Work (SOSW), 1, 63, 145
Security risks, 35
Self-
  actualisation, 102
  advocacy, 12, 32, 48
  awareness, 166
  belief, 8, 40
  care abilities, 159
  confidence, 10, 159
  determination, 162
  esteem, 149, 159
  help groups, 74, 150
  interest, 167
  sustainability, 86
Service
  delivery, 21, 45, 76, 149
  mentality, 165, 177
  networks, 5, 86
  providers, 110, 180
Sex trade, 45
Sex workers, 63-4, 74, 134, 174
Sexual abuses, 79
Sexual harassment, 128-9
Shared confidentiality, 140-1
Shriram Foods and Fertilizer Industries, 124, 130-1
Simple Syndication, 60
Situational analysis, 55, 68, 96
Skill-development, 54
Sloganeering, 48
Social action
  method, 4, 176
  movements, 89, 176
Social
  activists, 5, 49, 52, 62, 106, 110, 126, 176, 179
  adjustment, 73
  agencies, 152
  audit, 89
  backwardness, 119
  capital parlance, 49
  capital, 48, 90
  change, 10, 24, 30, 46, 53, 65, 111, 127, 129, 134, 151-2, 176, 181
  development, 11, 43, 101, 125, 139, 145
  events, 60
  exclusion, 15, 29
  fabric, 78
  hierarchy, 56
  institutions, 6, 10, 14, 41, 76, 115, 176
  justice, 5-6, 9, 14-15, 19, 31, 40-2, 44, 50, 55, 79, 97-8, 106, 110-11, 114-17, 167

legislation, 73, 76-7, 105-6, 130-1, 152-3, 177
Marketing (SM), 62, 65-6, 72-3, 78, 83
marketing, 62, 65, 72-3, 78, 83
media, 33, 36, 49, 154
movements, 43, 76, 87, 93, 106, 132
research, 128
wellbeing, 65
Social security
schemes, 73
services, 9
Social work Act, 17
Social-Cognitive Model/Approach, 25
Spiritual beliefs, 166
Stakeholder/actor interventions, 98
State Forest Act, 122
Strategic representation, 28
Strengths based practices (SBPs), 82-3, 112, 159, 161-3, 169
approaches, 111-12, 167, 169
interventions, 169
methods, 47-8, 133, 162, 167, 169
Subjugated clients, 184
Suo motto actions, 14, 39
Sustainable relationships, 139

Theory of reasoned action, 55, 73
Tobacco product, 81
Transnational
activism, 23
coalitions, 15
Transportation services, 103

Unborn child, 81